THE BOY

THE BOY

A Holocaust Story

Dan Porat

HILL AND WANG
A division of Farrar, Straus and Giroux
New York

HILL AND WANG
A division of Farrar, Straus and Giroux
18 West 18th Street, New York 10011

Published in 2010 by Hill and Wang
First paperback edition, 2011

The Library of Congress has cataloged the hardcover edition as follows:
Porat, Dan, 1964–
    The boy : a Holocaust story / Dan Porat. — 1st ed.
        p. cm.
    Includes bibliographical references and index.
    ISBN 978-0-8090-3071-2 (hardcover)
        1. Stroop, Jürgen, 1895–1952. 2. Jews—Persecutions—Poland—
Warsaw—History—20th century—Pictorials works. 3. Jewish
ghettos—Poland—Warsaw—History—20th century—Pictorials
works. 4. Jews—Poland—Warsaw—Biography—Pictorials works.
5. Holocaust, Jewish (1939–1945)—Poland—Warsaw—Pictorials
works. 6. Jews—Persecutions—Poland—Warsaw—History—
20th century. 7. Jewish ghettos—Poland—Warsaw—History—
20th century. 8. Jews—Poland—Warsaw—Biography. 9. Holocaust
survivors—Biography. 10. Nazis—Biography. I. Title.

DS134.64 .P67 2010
940.53'1853841—dc22

                                                        2010005771

Paperback ISBN: 978-0-8090-3072-9

Designed by Cassandra J. Pappas

www.fsgbooks.com

P1

In memory of my mother,
Hannah (Blumenthal) Porat

Contents

Glossary of Terms

Einsatzgruppe	Special operations unit of the SS and SD that operated behind advancing military units to seize state documents and murder political opponents. After occupation of the Soviet Union in the summer of 1941, it took part in mass murders, primarily of Jews.
Einsatzkommando	Subunits of Einsatzgruppe.
Gestapo	Geheime Staatspolizei; Secret State Police. Controlled by Heinrich Himmler and Reinhard Heydrich. Division IV-B4, the Jewish Section, was headed by Adolf Eichmann.
Höherer SS and Polizeiführer	Official with direct authority over every police and SS unit in an area. Answered only to Himmler and Adolf Hitler.

Hilfspolizei	Nazi Party auxiliary police.
Luftwaffe	Air force. Headed by Hermann Göring.
SA	Sturmabteilung; storm troopers, "brownshirts." Paramilitary organization of the Nazi Party.
SD	Sicherheitsdienst; Security Service. A surveillance agency of the SS. In 1939 incorporated into the Reich Security Main Office, Reichssicherheitshauptamt (RSHA), headed by Reinhard Heydrich.
SIPO	Sicherheitspolizei; Security Police. Nazi security police composed of the Gestapo, the criminal police, and the border police. Merged in September 1939 into the Reich Security Main Office (RSHA).
SS	Schutzstaffel; Protection Squad. An elite organization headed by Himmler made up of one million personnel and in control of the police, intelligence, surveillance, and the concentration camps. The SS (and the RSHA) was responsible for carrying out the "Final Solution of the Jewish Question."
Stasi	Staatssicherheit; State Security. The East German (GDR) state security organization. Department IX was the investigation branch. Department XX was responsible for eliminating threats to the Communist Party on the political-ideological front.
Waffen-SS	Combat arm of the SS.
Wehrmacht	Germany's regular armed forces during World War II: army, navy, and air force.

THE BOY

Prologue

On January 12, 2004, I stood in a dark exhibition hall at the Yad Vashem Holocaust Museum in Jerusalem looking at a picture worth one thousand words and six million names: a little Jewish boy, a cap on his head, his arms raised in the air, and a look of deep horror on his face. As I gazed at the photo, a group of men and women in black suits, the entourage of a Slovenian minister, Dr. Pavel Gantar, walked toward me. Like me, the group stopped before the iconic image, an image I had seen so many times that I could no longer recollect when I had seen it first. Their official guide turned to the minister, and in what seemed more like a statement than a question said, "Did you know that this picture tells a good story of the Holocaust?" The surprised men's faces turned toward her. She continued unequivocally: "This boy survived. After the Holocaust, he studied medicine, became a doctor, and settled in New York. A year ago he immigrated to Israel." The men nodded in approval, and the delegation disappeared down the dark museum hall.

This was not the first time I had heard the story of the survival of the little boy. A few years earlier, I had interviewed Shelly, a high school student. Shelly, her father, and I sat in the family's Jerusalem living room to talk about events related to the Warsaw ghetto uprising. At one point, I pulled from my bag a few photographs and placed them on the coffee table. I can still vividly recall the expression on Shelly's face when she saw the photograph of the horrified little boy. A large smile spread over her lips and a burst of laughter rolled out of her throat. She pointed at the boy and proudly declared, "This is our relative." She went on to state that a cousin of the boy was her father's ex-wife, and to my astonishment, her father confirmed every word.

Sometime after my interview with Shelly, I drove to the Yad Vashem library to examine the photograph's origins. A librarian handed me a black, dust-covered book titled *The Stroop Report*, a facsimile of a report produced by the notorious SS general Jürgen Stroop in celebration of his victory over the Jews. On its first page, inscribed in carefully designed calligraphic gothic letters, was the report's title: *The Jewish Quarter of Warsaw Is No More!*[1]

Near the front was a list of the sixteen German servicemen killed in the battle over the Warsaw ghetto; atop the list the inscription read, "For the Führer and for their fatherland. . . . They gave their utmost, their lives. We shall never forget them."

Next came Stroop's daily communiqué to his SS superiors in Krakow, reporting the progress of his spring of 1943 operation to destroy the ghetto: "Progress report of the grand operation on 29 April 1943. Start of Operation: 10:00 hours. . . . Altogether, 36 new bunkers were located; 2,359 Jews were apprehended from these and other hideouts and from burning buildings. . . . Our losses: none. End of operation at 21:00 hours. The grand operation will be continued on 30 April 1943 at 09:00 hours." In his final communiqué of May 16, Stroop wrote, "The total number of Jews apprehended and destroyed, according to the record, is 56,065."

Turning over the last communiqué, I came to a "Pictorial Report," an album of fifty-two black-and-white photographs placed origi-

nally on sheets of off-white heavyweight paper. Here I hoped I
would find a hint about the fate of the little boy. A photo titled
"Pulled from the bunkers by force" depicts a group of women, children, and elderly people walking, flanked by two rows of SS guards.
The guards, dressed in high black leather boots and with rifles at
hand, stalk along a burning ghetto street darkened by pitch-black
smoke. In the first row of Jews walks a little girl in a checkered dress,
her hair done up as if she were off not to Treblinka or Majdanek
but to her first day of school.[2]

Another photo, most likely taken nearby, was captioned "These
bandits offered armed resistance." It shows two Jewish women and
a Jewish man standing in the midst of wreckage and smoke as an SS
man aims his gun directly at them. The man and one of the women
raise their hands in the air. The other woman holds her arms to her
sides, as if in defiance.

In another photo from this album, two Jews stand naked, an ax
between them, their backs to the camera. One of the men's spines is
severely deformed by scoliosis. The other has what seems like a
deformed foot. It was captioned "Dregs of humanity."

Then, as I turned to the thirteenth page of the album, facing me was the photograph of the little boy. The line beneath it reads, "Pulled from the bunkers by force." I stared at this photo in disbelief: What had brought the Nazis to place a photograph of such innocence in an album celebrating their triumph over the Jews of Warsaw? How could this photograph symbolize their victory?

Sitting in the Yad Vashem library on that wintry day, overlooking the majestic Jerusalem hills, I found that my visit had not resolved my questions but rather had inspired new ones, questions that multiplied with time: Did the little boy indeed survive the Holocaust? What was his story? Who was the woman standing on the left? Was she his mother? Who was the little girl? The SS man with his machine gun, who was he? How could he make a little boy raise his hands like this? Who took the photographs? What brought them there? What, I asked myself, had happened to these people before and after being captured by the camera?

In my travels and investigation, I identified five people whose lives intersected in the photograph of the boy and in other photo-

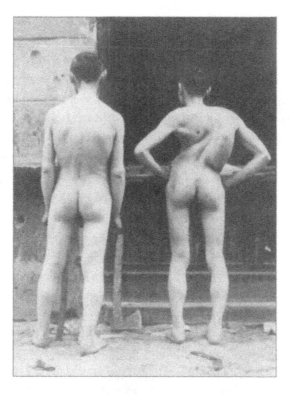

graphs from *The Stroop Report*. Slowly, the maddeningly elusive pieces of the story of how these men, women, and children came together on that Warsaw street in the spring of 1943 fell into place, and I felt compelled to try to tell it.

Only some of my questions, however, found answers. One in particular eluded me: the book does not identify the boy in the photograph. In my opinion, such an identification is impossible. It is also beside the point. Is the lost life of the little boy more important than that of the little girl at the left-hand side of the photograph? Are the lives of this little boy and girl in the photograph more significant than those of children or adults outside the photo frame? The answer is simple and absolute: no.

A far more pressing question, however, is how one set of men saw in that photograph heroic soldiers combating humanity's dregs while the vast majority of mankind sees here the gross inhumanity of man. I have come to believe the answer lies in part in the persistence with which the question is asked, the answer sought.

In the years that followed, the mission of uncovering the story of the little boy became for me no less than an obsession. Wherever I went I saw him: I saw him in the Memorial for the Murdered Jews of Europe in Berlin, I saw him on billboards in Jerusalem; I saw him in books, in movies, in works of art, in poems; you name it, I saw him there. My obsession was such that my three children, having heard me describe the project dozens of times to every guest who passed our doorstep, easily recited the story's basic outline.

Searching for the story of the boy got me in touch with people whose lives would otherwise never have intersected with my own: a Washington-based Polish-American woman who took it as a personal mission to help me and went out of her way to cut red tape in Warsaw; a German archivist who searched the archives for me in Stroop's hometown of Detmold; a Boston gallery owner who represented an artist and Holocaust survivor who had produced seventy-five paintings of the little boy; an Australian archivist who thought she might have identified the little boy in Sydney; the son of an American soldier who had freed a train with a few thousand Jews, including one of the protagonists of this book; a New York Holocaust survivor who believes himself to be the little boy.

Pursuing the little boy's story also brought about some unpleasant and puzzling encounters: a nasty exchange with a journalist who felt I was stepping on his toes; encounters with an evasive academic who did not want to share information; a telephone conversation with a New York–based literary agent who, upon hearing that the little boy had most likely perished, rejected my book proposal, adding that "if the little boy had grown up to be the mayor of Cleveland we would have a story here; otherwise, no chance."

In uncovering this story I also had to reveal unpleasant truths to some people: to several people, lay and educated, who believed that the boy survived, that in fact he had not; to some of those who incorrectly thought they ór one of their relatives were the little boy, that they were not. To the son of a woman protagonist, I had to show a photograph of his deceased mother with her very serious boyfriend, possibly even husband, who was killed in the Holocaust and about whom the son knew nothing.

At moments in this journey, I felt time halt. It was just before noon on Thursday, December 18, 2008, in the reading room of the National Archives in Washington, D.C., when a cart with an archive box on it was rolled toward me. In the box lay the original *Stroop Report*. Finally, after years of investigation, I had the opportunity to observe the real document. It would be, I felt, the closest I would ever come to seeing the little boy with my own eyes. I touched the leather covers, the delicate paper telexes, and the thick album pages that contained so much evil. Carefully turning the pages, I saw the original photos that Stroop himself had selected for this victory report. To my disappointment, however, the little-boy photo had been replaced with a reproduction. Still, my heart literally pounded as I, a Jew, held one of the three original copies of the report that Himmler had taken with him on a visit to Hitler's secret headquarters at Wolf's Lair so the Führer himself could review it, a report that Adolf Eichmann had also held between his hands.[3]

Seeing me in the office or on the street, friends and colleagues would call out to me: "I saw your little boy in the newspaper this morning." One colleague e-mailed me that "on Monday" she had seen "your little boy" in Auschwitz. "*Your* little boy," I thought, and was taken aback. He was never "*my* little boy," nor will he ever be. He is his own little boy, a painful and sorrowful mark on humanity's conscience, a boy whose story I believe can't and shouldn't be forgotten, for the sake of children suffering like him today.

My pursuit of this story was also very personal. In writing this book I came closer to my own familial roots, exploring my parents' past as a boy and girl born in Germany on the eve of World War II (both, rightly, would *never* identify themselves as Holocaust survivors). As a child and teenager, I had drawn a line in the sand: never visit Germany. While only one distant cousin of my mother's perished in Europe, growing up in Israel in the 1970s shaped my thoughts and feelings about Germans and Germany: the children in school who came from survivors' homes; those who had no grandparents to attend the class parties; the survivor who on Friday night at the youth movement told us his story of German cruelty; my many family members who would not buy German products; my high school math teacher who had a number tattooed on his arm. Probably the most vivid memory I have is that of a ragged-clothed middle-aged man, a camp survivor, who every now and then would appear for the Saturday-morning services at synagogue, his head bowed down. Then, suddenly, halfway through the services, he would raise his head high and scream full-throatedly at God—the rabbi and other congregates rushing to shush him up.

So as a youngster I had determined that I was never going to travel to Germany. But researching this book required that I go; I put aside my reservations, promising myself that I would also look into my familial roots. I traveled to the town of Detmold, the birthplace of Jürgen Stroop. The station platform, the loudspeaker, the train, all took on a historical eeriness, a feeling that became even greater when in Detmold I knocked on Stroop's door, entering and looking out a bedroom window at a thin creek and down at floor tiles upon which he had quite likely walked. It was eerie, but frankly, it was also very normal, just a simple home. I found it puzzling.

From Detmold I traveled a couple of hours south to visit my late mother's hometown of Frankfurt, a city where her family resided for many generations. Little was left of their large home, where they had once had a cook, a washing maid, and a driver. Their synagogue—now a furniture store—still stood, near the zoo. Late one night after the 1938 Kristallnacht, when her synagogue and others around Germany were shattered, Gestapo men knocked on the door of my mother's home in search of my grandfather, who was on a business trip abroad. Shortly thereafter the family escaped to Holland, where my mother lived in a boarding school for a year. In 1940 they traveled across the U-boat-stricken Atlantic Ocean, arriving in Boston and finally settling in Washington Heights, in New York City. My grandfather, a successful businessman, found a job as a bookkeeper for a friend's company. What he didn't know was that the friend didn't need a bookkeeper, especially not a lousy one like my grandfather, and was paying him not from his own pocket but from money handed to him by my uncle. My mother, fourteen years old when she arrived in the States, shed much of her German past and adopted American culture, enrolling in a doctoral program at Columbia's Teachers College. After she met my father in 1954, they moved to Israel, where they raised my twin sisters and me.

That visit to Frankfurt ended, and two years later, in 2008, came my next trip to Germany, this time to Berlin with my eighty-two-year-old father (my sisters refused to join). We visited the headquarters of the Stasi (the notorious East German security service), where the photo of the little boy hung on the wall. Later I would go to the Stasi prison at Hohenschönhausen, where in the 1960s the SS soldier Josef Blösche, who had aimed his rifle at the boy, was incarcerated and interrogated. There I peeked into the rows of cells and interrogation rooms still standing in their original setting.

This was not my father's first visit to Germany. My father, who was born in Hamburg and moved to Berlin at the age of three, visited Germany frequently. In fact, as a child I had wondered why he, unlike my mother, so often traveled there. Business was the excuse, but knowing my father—more an intellectual than a businessman— it just did not make much sense.

Arriving with him in Berlin, I understood: he was revitalized. We visited his first home, in a rundown part of East Berlin, Oberschöneweide—located close to the spot where, decades later, the Stasi headquarters and prison would stand. With clear satisfaction he showed me on the following day the location of the next home to which, thanks to my grandfather's growing financial success, his family moved: an apartment on Albert Achilles Street in the up-scale Charlottenburg neighborhood in West Berlin. Walking along the fashionable Kurfürstendamm Avenue with its shops and cine-mas, sitting in one of West Berlin's famous coffee shops and enjoy-ing a black forest cake, my father was glowing. Here he returned to his childhood life, the one he had before fleeing Germany, before moving to Tel Aviv's broiling hot summers.

It was in 1936 that a group of Nazis spotted his father sitting in one of Berlin's public parks, a park forbidden to Jews. He was put on trial and, fortunately, given "only" a suspended sentence. Upon hearing the verdict, my grandfather's attorney advised him to escape Germany at once. My father was pulled out of his Jewish school on Fasanen Street and sent with his brother to friends on the Baltic Sea, as his parents sold all their belongings.

A week later my father and his brother would return to Berlin and board a train out of Germany. He never again saw his home or any of his classmates. All he would have to remember them by in years to come would be memories and one photograph. As they awaited passport check on the train near Salzburg, the little boy who was to become my father asked if it was yet permissible to curse the Germans. "In ten minutes," my grandfather responded.

But despite his cursing the Germans, I now understood why my father returned to Germany so frequently. It was not only for busi-ness. It was also a way to reconnect with a childhood so abruptly interrupted and a culture so ingrained in his blood.*

---

*For an explanation of the choices I made in selecting my style of writing, which includes elements of imagination, see "On Photographs, History, and Narrative Style" on p. 217.

Part I

1913-1938

1

Rising to Power

On a fall afternoon in 1913, eighteen-year-old Josef Stroop stood on the eighty-foot-high observation deck of the Hermann Monument in the Teutoburg Forest gazing up at the larger-than-life sculpture of the first-century leader of Germanic tribes, who, according to legend, had defeated the Romans in a decisive battle. Bright turquoise from the oxidation of the copper sheath, Hermann stood with his chest puffed out, a winged metal helmet covering his head and high leather boots adorning his feet. His fully extended right arm firmly gripped the hilt of a twenty-foot-long sword, the sharp blade pointing high into the blue sky.[1]

A breeze rustled the green treetops in the thick forest. Stroop, enjoying the light wind ruffling his thick dark blond hair, stared into the distance. From this panoramic height he was able to make out a sprinkling of dots on the horizon's green hills. Those were the buildings of his hometown, Detmold—a town of fifteen thousand residents, the capital of the independent principality of Lippe.

As the sun descended, Stroop entered a small opening directly beneath the statue's feet. As on each of his frequent visits, he found it difficult to leave this inspiring shrine to the hero of Germany's glorious past.[2] But it was late and he had to depart. His hand on the rail, he walked down the dark spiral staircase, careful not to stumble. Emerging at the foot of the monument, he soon was walking in the shade cast by the tall trees on either side of the forest trail that led to Detmold. It was an hour's walk, and before he reached home owls hooted overhead.

At dusk, Stroop passed the first houses on the outskirts of Detmold and then reached Neustadt Street. Across the canal that ran along Neustadt Street, over the high walls, he could see the red roof tiles of the royal family's massive summer palace. A bit farther on, he could see the tops of the beech, walnut, and cedar trees, part of royal gardens accessible only to members of the royal family. He had heard of their large, oval pools with fountains and water cascades, but as an ordinary citizen he had, of course, never seen them.

Stroop followed the canal, its banks covered with shrubs, as it veered left onto Wallgraben Street. Across the strip of dark water towered St. Bonifatius Church. With his devout Catholic mother, Käthe Stroop, and his brothers, Conrad Jr. and Ferdinand, he passed through the church's wide arched doors each and every Sunday. And on each and every weekday in the adjacent brown brick building, he had attended the parish school. In 1909, at the age of fourteen, after completing eight years of schooling, he, like most of his friends, had to quit school and find work.

Looking at the school's shut door, he recalled his old aspiration to become a teacher. It was not that he had been a remarkable student possessed by intellectual zeal, or that he held a fondness for children. No, it was the thought of long straight rows of students looking up at him that inspired him. Dressed in a suit, he would tap a foot-long springy wooden cane on his fist as he marched back and forth before the blackboard, dozens of small eyes following his every move. As had been the case in his day, any student whose gaze wandered would be rewarded with a lash on the palm. Naughtiness would result in a more thorough caning. But Stroop's parents had vetoed this aspiration; they couldn't afford tuition for continuing his education.[3]

After church, his father, dressed in his carefully ironed police uniform, took him to stand by the canal and watch the parade of the uniformed and sword-bearing honor guard pass to the music of local marching bands. Following them would roll a horse-drawn carriage carrying the royal family, citizens bowing as they passed by. Then Stroop's father, a former coachman to the royal family, would solemnly remind his son that he must obey the prince.[4]

It was dark when Stroop entered his parents' modest two-story home at 7 Mühlen Street, which his father rented from the municipality of Detmold for reduced rent. The father, now a policeman, oversaw a nearby municipal shelter for the homeless and unemployed. He was frequently called out at night to break up a brawl or resolve a dispute.[5]

Like his father, Stroop was now employed by the local government. He worked in the Land Registry, located in the government building on Kaiser-Wilhelm-Platz, as an apprentice in the tax collector's office. For the past four years he had sat for hours glued to his wooden chair alongside a few other low-ranking clerks, laboriously registering in his stiff calligraphic handwriting the land tax on a farm sale, or hitting the typewriter keys to fill out a building license.

In the summer of 1914, with the clouds of war hovering over Europe, nineteen-year-old Stroop took a leave of absence from his job and volunteered for the 55th Prussian Infantry Regiment. The

lanky six-foot-tall Stroop fit perfectly into the gray military uniform with its shiny buttons. Following a short ceremony under fluttering flags on Detmold's train station platform, Stroop and his comrades, with long guns resting over their shoulders and spiked silver helmets on their heads, boarded a train. Over the sound of a brass band, crying crowds bid farewell to husbands, fathers, and sons destined for the Rhine River.[6]

Within weeks, Stroop's regiment was battling French forces. And near La Bassée, on October 22, a French bullet struck him in the shoulder. This injury took Stroop away from the battlefield, away from his comrades, and away from his service to the fatherland. He traveled back to Detmold to recuperate, where he impatiently awaited his return to the front. Finally, after a few months he was employed in the 256th Reserve Infantry Regiment (RIR) and fought along the eastern front in Poland, Lithuania, White Russia, Galicia, Romania, and Hungary. Bullets and shells hit comrades to the left and right of him, and Stroop suffered light wounds in battles in Hungary and Romania. Not once, however, did he request to be sent back home. Military service agreed with him.[7]

The army recognized Stroop's dedication, ability, and courage. His superiors awarded him three medals: the Lippische Principality Cross for Loyal Service, the Lippische Military Merit Medal with crossed swords, and the Iron Cross Second Class. And Stroop was promoted to vice sergeant, which gave him power to oversee other soldiers. He dreamed of higher ranks, but given his family's modest social status and his limited education, this was an impossibility.[8]

The signing of the armistice on November 11, 1918, ending the Great War caught Stroop and his fellow soldiers occupying Hungarian soil. To them it was self-evident that Germany had not been defeated, and they could not fathom the reason for what seemed an unwarranted, even shameful, surrender. In late December, after a farewell ceremony in Hungary and a speech from the revered German general August von Mackensen about the need to restore national unity at home, the units of the 256th RIR meekly boarded a train. On Christmas Eve, after four years on the battlefield, Stroop stepped out onto Detmold's almost empty train station platform. Only a few family members were there to greet the returning soldiers. No local dignitaries awaited them, no admiring schoolchildren, no town band, not a flag or banner.[9]

Days after Christmas, he returned to his tedious job at the Land Registry. While stationed in Bucharest, Stroop had taken a four-month topography course. He presented his new credentials to his superiors at the registry and requested a promotion. They rebuffed his requests time and again. In the small and poor principality rendered poorer by the war, he could anticipate staying in his current post for the rest of his life.[10]

Frustrated, Stroop took to wandering the corridors during office hours. These outings led him down to the ground floor, where he chatted with the young women at the telephone switchboard. Upstairs, the supervisor noticed Stroop's empty chair. He called him into his office and reproached him for going missing during working hours. Still, Stroop continued to roam. One day, the cleaner's son spotted him with a woman from a local Jewish boardinghouse in the bicycle storage room. He reported the incident to the supervisor, who again called Stroop in. He emphatically denied improper behavior. And any time he had spent in the bicycle storage room during regular work hours, he claimed, he had made up by working late. The supervisor remained unconvinced. A letter on November 23, 1920, warned Stroop:

> You have not only acted contrary to proper conduct, which prohibits you from this kind of intimacy with young foreign women in the office building, but you have also harmed your service duties. . . . We therefore see ourselves obliged to reprimand you for the events in question and at the same time draw your attention

to the fact that the repetition of similar offenses against the service order or justified complaints concerning your service behavior will cause your dismissal from the Land Registry office.[11]

On April 1, 1921, fifteen-year-old Franz Konrad and his handicapped father, Florian, climbed up a narrow road in the small village of Aschbach near Mariazell in the Austrian Alps. The six-and-a-half-foot-tall blue-eyed and light-haired Franz had long dreamed of becoming a musician playing in one of Vienna's coffee-houses or concert halls. This dream had unraveled, however, when his father, a coal miner, had lost his left arm and the sight in one eye in a work accident. The small pension that supported the Konrad family of several brothers and sisters dictated this move, from their hometown of Liezen to Aschbach, where Franz would serve as an apprentice to a merchant and learn the profession of tradesman.[12]

For the first two years of his apprenticeship, the shop owner, Josef Niederauer, taught Konrad nothing about commerce. Konrad pulled weeds out of the merchant's garden, plowed vegetable rows, and washed Niederauer's new car. Only in the third year did Niederauer allow Konrad to assist him with clients in the shop. After work, Konrad took night classes at a local professional school, where he learned about pricing, tax payments, and financial forms, all in preparation for the certifying exam as a commercial assistant. Despite his limited experience, he passed the exam.

On his little time off, Konrad traveled to a nearby city to sing in a men's choir, play in a chess club, and learn Esperanto, a language recently invented with the aim of allowing people everywhere to communicate in a common tongue. Once when he attended an open-air concert, two British women, who spotted on his shirt a green-and-white Esperanto badge, befriended him, going so far as to invite him to join them on a trip to Budapest. But Konrad had to turn the offer down; he could not take time off from work.

After three years of apprenticeship, Niederauer refused to hire Konrad as a permanent employee. Konrad's family faced an immediate financial crisis. Fortunately, within five months, in October 1924, Konrad found a job as a salesman in a food and spice wholesale business in Rottenmann. Two and a half years later, he quit this position and took a job as a substitute salesman in a local cooperative food chain. He rotated among the chain's twelve branches, replacing absent workers. Shortly thereafter, the cooperative's board offered him a permanent position as the head of the warehouse. Working for the cooperative required that he join the left-wing Social Democratic Workers' Party (SDAP) and its trade union, where he served as the local party's treasurer.[13]

At the end of a tedious workday at the Land Registry, Stroop frequented the Hermann Monument in search of solace. Here, beneath Hermann's sword inscribed with the words "Germany's unity, my strength—my strength, Germany's might," he joined other World War I veterans reminiscing about the comradeship and bravery of war. They lamented Germany's disgraceful defeat, encapsulated in the humiliating Versailles Treaty, sang patriotic songs, and, to the sound of drums, marched with blazing torches held aloft.[14]

The veterans gossiped, commiserated, and held strongly to the opinion that German unity was under threat. Alien forces on the home front had betrayed the fatherland. Otherwise, how could one explain the German army's defeat in the war? Backstabbing by liberals, Socialists, Communists, and Jews explained it. Under Hermann's extended sword and the light and shadow of torches, the veterans swore an oath of true loyalty to the German nation and pledged themselves to protect it from the forces threatening to destroy it from within. In 1926, the charismatic leader of the Nationalsozialistische Deutsche Arbeiterpartei (NSDAP, or the Nazi Party), Adolf Hitler, visited the Hermann Monument and in the guest book wrote: "I believe in the people, and in the power of the person, and in the necessity of fighting."[15]

One weekend when he was not at the monument, Stroop strolled down Paulinen Street and ran into Max, a childhood friend who like Stroop was wounded in the war and was now a decorated veteran. But Stroop did not greet Max; he snubbed him. Max was Jewish. And Jews, Marxists, intellectuals, scientists, artists, and journalists, Stroop knew, were all enemies of the German nation. From his like-minded comrades, Stroop concealed that as a child he had played after school with Jewish friends, the children of neighborhood families Herzfeld and Examus.[16]

His comrades in the 256th RIR Veterans Association chose Stroop as editor of the veterans' news bulletin, a position that, despite his nonofficer rank, put him in close contact with some of the regiment's officers.[17] On November 20, 1927, at the regiment's memorial ceremony, Stroop delivered the keynote address in honor of Germany's fallen soldiers. Standing by the monument in the regiment's courtyard, Stroop spoke to the crowd of veterans, bereaved parents, widows, and orphans. The fallen, he lamented, fought and suffered,

> hour by hour, day and night, in pain and sorrow, and suddenly, they were torn from your side, because they gave the highest sacrifice for their fatherland, because they found the glory of dying in battle. All over German lands, where memorials for these heroes were built, today come together war veterans to show they have not forgotten their dead comrades. Likewise, we turn up by the memorial of our regiment's comrades, who as members of the 256 gave their lives for the beloved fatherland. The stone in front of us marks 1,255 dead! . . . Loyalty, as it was in the field, must keep us survivors united! The spirit of 1914, which especially in the first postwar years lay dormant, is slowly gaining momentum. We must allow it again to completely ignite us! We must believe in the fu-

ture of our fatherland! With this belief our comrades stayed behind in foreign lands, and when we hold on to this belief then the death of our comrades is not in vain![18]

With soldiers standing at attention, Stroop marched to the monument, saluted, and placed a wreath before it.

At 7:30 p.m. on October 9, 1931, the Austrian police arrived at the home of twenty-five-year-old Franz Konrad in Liezen, where he now lived with his wife, Agnes, and their newborn son, Franz Josef. The cooperative store had reported that 900 schillings were missing from the store safe. The policemen arrested Konrad as a suspect.

Konrad denied the accusations. A coworker who wanted his managerial job at the cooperative was the culprit. He provided an alibi. On the eve of the theft, the local Social Democratic Party heads had asked him to help in an operation to retrieve weapons stored in a police building, arms that the police had confiscated six months earlier. Such requests were nothing new for Konrad, who had agreed in the past to spy on the meetings of the local branch of the Nazi Party, a rising force on the Austrian political scene. So on that rainy night, Konrad and a few party comrades had quietly sneaked through a window into the cellar of the building. They found no weapons. Disappointed, they returned home. It was during this escapade, Konrad stated, that his coworker took advantage of his absence to break into the store's safe and take the 900 schillings with the goal of having Konrad sacked and himself promoted.

The district attorney did not believe him and pressed charges. At the trial, which took place in the Leoben District Court, Konrad pleaded not guilty. At the end of the hearings, Konrad stood in the dock and awaited the judge's reading of the verdict. Guilty. Konrad was sentenced to three months in jail.

Upon his release in early 1932, Konrad joined the many thousands of unemployed Austrians. What was more, he felt betrayed by the Social Democratic Party, which had not confirmed his alibi or supported his family during his imprisonment. The local Nazi Party, into which his attorney had recruited him, however, did come to Konrad's assistance, despite his having spied on them for the SDAP; they paid his legal fees and helped his family financially while he was behind bars. In April 1932, Konrad joined the Nazi Party, and a few months later he enrolled in the SS, the Nazi Party's elite paramilitary unit.

On July 25, 1934, a group of eight Nazis entered the Chancellery in Vienna. The group made its way to the office of Chancellor Engelbert Dollfuss. Otto Planetta, one of the eight, pulled out a pistol and shot Dollfuss twice. The chancellor bled to death. This was the first move in a coup. Nazis quickly thereafter overtook the Chancellery and the radio station in Vienna. Across Austria, Nazi supporters took to the streets.

That night, Konrad, now working in road construction, marched with a group of approximately one hundred armed farmers and lumbermen from Liezen to the Pyhrnpass, a serene alpine pass on the border between the Austrian provinces of Upper Austria and Styria. These Nazi supporters rolled large boulders onto the one-lane road that crossed the hilly terrain, an obstacle aimed to block Austrian armed forces from coming to the support of the government in Styria. At sunrise, Austrian troops reached the pass and halted by the boulders. From treetops and from behind rocks, the Nazis shot at them. Soon a unit of Alpine soldiers joined the pinned-down troops; the shooting went on for hours. Leaving several casualties dead on the mountain slopes as well as on the road, the military forces eventually broke through the pass and entered Liezen that evening.[19]

In Liezen and elsewhere, Austrian armed forces successfully suppressed the Nazi revolt. Those who took part in the attempted coup went into hiding. On August 11, the police again knocked on the door of Konrad's home. Again he was arrested. The court convicted him of betraying the state and sentenced him to four months in jail and the revocation of his Austrian citizenship. Together with hundreds of other Nazis, Konrad served his sentence in the detention camp of Wöllersdorf.

Released in December, Konrad took charge of an illegal SS volunteer unit in the Austrian town of Schladming. Soon the authorities were after him again on charges of illegal activity. Unwilling to be jailed a third time, he escaped with his family in July 1935 to the Waischenfeld SS camp in Germany, where many other Austrian expatriates had gathered. Here he worked in the administrative offices and, with Agnes, their son, Franz, and daughter, Gertrude, born in October 1936, awaited their uncertain future.[20]

On July 17, 1932, Stroop, who had a month earlier joined the Nazi Party, stood in a party assembly at the Hermann Monument and listened to the widely admired General Karl von Litzmann speak. Afterward, the tall, commanding members of the SS in their dark uniforms marched along. At the assembly's end, a party official approached Stroop and asked if he would help establish a local SS unit in Detmold. Stroop agreed. He enrolled in the SS as member number 44611.[21]

Soon thereafter, Stroop, dressed in a black SS uniform, began patrolling the streets of Detmold with two large, fierce dogs and a whip at hand. Spying him in the distance, those residents targeted by the Nazis would quickly duck down alleys; many other residents, however, approached him with reverence and gifts. At times Stroop rode through the town on a horse, a gift from one of the residents.[22]

On January 4, 1933, Stroop entered a large tent erected in Kronenplatz just across from the Detmold train station, where a local band was rehearsing marches and the buzz of an excited crowd of five thousand filled the tent decorated with red flags sporting white circles and black swastikas. Stroop approached a group of Aryan-

looking boys and girls, some dressed in their best clothes, others in Nazi uniforms, holding bouquets of colorful flowers. Stroop examined the red and white flowers not for their quality but to make sure that no weapon or bomb was hidden among them. After hours of waiting, near midnight, a couple of cars drove up, and the audience's excitement grew. As the cars rolled in, the band struck up patriotic marches. To the cheering of the crowds and the upheld bouquets, Hitler disembarked. He had come to Detmold to campaign in the local elections. Over nine days, he delivered to enthusiastic audiences all around the Lippe principality sixteen long speeches rife with attacks on the Social Democrats, the Jews, the Communists, and others.[23]

Ever since the July 1932 parliamentary elections, the Nazi Party had faced a serious crisis. Several members had distanced themselves and even denounced the party. Some opposed the Nazis' increasingly

violent acts, and still others thought Hitler's public influence had peaked and that he stood no chance of seizing the reins of power. In the November 1932 election, Nazi representation in the Reichstag shrank by 34 seats to 196 out of 584 delegates. As one means of reestablishing their dominance in German politics, the Nazis believed they must win a victory in the January 15, 1933, election for the parliament in the tiny Lippe principality. "Lippe must be a success. We have done everything for that," Joseph Goebbels wrote in his diary.[24]

Stroop and his men from the local SS eagerly played their part. They worked to "convince" those citizens of Lippe who did not already intend to vote for the Nazis to do so and caused others to avoid the elections. With his black leather riding boots fitted with steel heels, Stroop beat up Jews and Social Democrats, smashed the store windows of opponents, and set their homes on fire. His tactics proved effective. When the election was held, the Nazis "won" in Detmold. And it was during the Nazis' push to win that Heinrich Himmler, the leader of the SS, who joined Hitler on his visit, took note of Stroop. For his part, Stroop already looked up to the soft-spoken Himmler and the great authority he wielded.

On January 30, 1933, Hitler became Germany's chancellor. In March, Stroop took a leave of absence from his clerical position at the Land Registry. Leaving his desk in the clerks' room behind, he moved up into a private office just beside the wide stairwell that led to the ministers' floor in the Lippe government building. In addition to heading the SS II/72 unit, he had been named commander of the newly established party auxiliary police (Hilfspolizei). Now at his disposal was a force of 229 men, 30 in Detmold alone, 15 of them full-time employees, the rest volunteers. He frequently marched across the canal and over the moat and into the royal residence. There, over a glass of red wine and beneath the sixteenth-century tapestries in the castle where Johannes Brahms had been employed some seventy years earlier as the court's theater director, the prince held personal consultations with Stroop, the leading SS man in town.[25]

Within weeks of the Nazis' rise to power, Jews in Detmold, as in all Germany, lost their jobs and livelihood. In Lippe, Stroop made sure this was seen to. Three weeks before the April 1 national boycott of Jewish businesses, Stroop ordered a local boycott throughout the principality.

He also took personal interest in ridding the government of Jews. Summoning his former superior, inspector Hermann Brand, to his new office, Stroop demanded to know why he was still employing the shorthand typist Erna Hamlet, the last Jew working in the Lippe government. Ten minutes later, Hamlet walked out of the building.[26]

The Detmold Hilfspolizei arrested Felix Fechenbach, the thirty-nine-year-old editor of the local Social Democratic newspaper, *Volksblatt*. For years, the Jewish editor had ridiculed the local Nazi Party. Now he numbered among the 120 Social Democrats, Communists, and other political opponents arrested and harassed in the weeks following the Nazis' assumption of power. Like the others whom the Nazis arrested, Fechenbach was delivered to Stroop's office in the government building and then placed under "protective custody."[27]

For five months, Fechenbach sat in his prison cell waiting for a decision about his fate. Believing he might be transported to a

concentration camp, he wrote his wife, Irma, "Maybe the transport will take place in the coming days. Maybe it will take place in a week. I do not know. . . . I think of the time when my protective imprisonment will be annulled and I bless and kiss you and the children from [my] heart. Yours, Felix." Below his signature he added: "Just now I have learned that today, August 7[, 1933], I will be transported."[28]

Stroop ordered that Fechenbach, the father of three young children, be driven to Dachau, accompanied by four SS and SA men (storm troopers). In Kleinenberger forest, between Detmold and Warburg, the car stopped. The Nazis pulled Fechenbach out. They beat him, then one of the men pulled out a pistol and shot Fechenbach in his forehead. The SS later laconically informed Irma that her husband had been shot attempting to escape. Family members who came to pick up the body did not recognize the disfigured face. Only a birthmark allowed them to identify him.[29]

The sun had already set when Josef Blösche stood in the kitchen of his father's inn and with his rough-skinned hands scrubbed dishes. Short and slender, with large ears, high cheekbones, and narrow lips, he looked much like his father, Gustav. That morning, Blösche had harvested his family's hay field. After harvesting, he had gone to the barn to take the livestock out to graze in the low hills of Sudetenland in Czechoslovakia. Only in the early evening did he arrive at the family inn. Like every other day of the week, his father gave him a set of tasks: clean the dishes, wash down the tables, tidy up the floor, and prepare food.[30]

Starting at the age of ten, when he had attended the local German-speaking elementary school, he had worked before and after school at the family farm and inn. Four years later, at the age of fourteen, his father had pulled him out of school to work full-time. Even on weekends, Blösche cleaned, washed, and served in his father's busy guesthouse.[31]

Blösche's broad-shouldered brother, Gustav, fifteen months his senior, was taller than he was, and neighbors named the two brothers "the big and the little Blösche."[32] As the older son, Gustav was to inherit the family farm and inn, but he had fought with his father and left home during the recession of the early 1930s. After Gustav left, Blösche's father decided that the little Blösche would one day inherit his inn, the field, the stock, and a small brickyard. He enrolled him in a professional school twelve miles away in the city of Liberec, where Blösche traveled twice a week to learn the profession of waiter.[33]

As night fell and the food cooked, small groups of villagers and miners gathered in the inn. Blösche poured pints of beer and served platters of sausages. In the dimly lit, smoke-filled room, guests chatted and laughed. The guests that evening were members of the Sudeten German Party, headed by Konrad Henlein, of which both Blösche and his father had been members for many years. They

spoke about their discrimination by the Czechoslovakian government, the German minority's inability to become civil servants, and
the lack of government assistance to German-owned businesses.[34]

The platters lay empty when Blösche's father shushed the noisy
patrons. He raised the volume on the radio. All awaited a broadcast
from Germany to the Sudeten-Germans. Here, for years, Blösche and
his fellow Sudeten-Germans had heard passionate denunciations
of their discrimination at the hands of Czechoslovakia. Long convinced of the party's arguments, on his limited time off he volunteered for it. He gathered party taxes, posted election banners, and
informed members of upcoming assemblies. In a white shirt and
black tie, the uniform of the party's paramilitary organization, the
Freiwillige Selbstschutz, Blösche secured the assemblies, frequently
getting into brawls with political opponents.[35]

He also read in the Nazi newspapers *Der Stürmer* and *Der Völk-
ische Beobachter* how the Jews came to Germany with rucksacks on
their backs and, like vampires, further drained the already weak-
ened German economy, and in so doing made millions within months.
He saw the sketched images of Jews with their crooked noses, slanted
eyes, wrinkled faces, black bristles, and beards. Fat beasts seated
atop the globe, they conspired against the Aryans and lured into
their beds innocent, young, smooth-skinned, blond German girls.
The Jews had gained control over the German nation, Blösche
thought. How else could one explain the fact that Jews arrived pen-
niless in Germany only to amass vast wealth within a year? It was
almost midnight when the broadcast ended and Blösche completed
his workday. He would get a couple hours of sleep before having to
begin another.[36]

On the morning of November 14, 1933, Stroop left his one-story
house at Am Eicheneke 3, where he lived with Käthe, his wife of
ten years, and their five-year-old daughter, Renate. With three of
his SS subordinates—the unit doctor, Dr. Kopsch, and two other

men, Wolfgang Bothe and Hunke—he set off in a car to a forest near
the Lopshorn hunting lodge. The four SS men worked all day ham-
mering poles and arranging sanitary facilities for the upcoming fall
maneuvers of the unit under Stroop's command. When they had
finished, Stroop led the tired men to the local Kuhlmann pub for a
cool beer. A young innkeeper greeted them, serving them steins of
beer and glasses of schnapps.[37]

Several pints into the evening, Stroop stepped outside into the
night to get some fresh air. He had been standing in the pub's courtyard for a couple of minutes when he noticed a shadow along the
ground. On the other side of the courtyard he spied the profile of a
woman in a lit window. Stroop trotted over and saw the young innkeeper ironing. He stuck his face through the window. "You should
stop mending socks and entertain dashing SS men. Have you already given your heart to an SS man?" he asked. The young woman
did not respond. Stroop pulled on the handle of the door, but it was
locked. He pushed it, but it did not budge. Then he broke in. The
innkeeper, crying for help, ran to the upper floor. Stroop ran after
her. He trapped her in the corner of one of the rooms. At that moment, Dr. Kopsch and Bothe, who had been searching for Stroop,
came running up the stairs. Stroop turned to Bothe and said in a
commanding tone, "Bothe, you really are a jolly good fellow. Go
ahead, give the girl a kiss." Bothe followed orders. The screaming
girl twisted her head back and forth, her body pushing and shoving,
attempting unsuccessfully to evade Bothe's embrace.

A few minutes later, Stroop returned to the pub. Seeing him, the
Nazis gathered around the table burst into laughter. Stroop's face
turned red as Dr. Kopsch, who had also returned to the pub, came
to his aid. He leaned forward in his seat and took a woman's hairpin
out from under Stroop's SS armband. "Ah, now I have the grounds
for your divorce from your wife," he said to the sound of giggling
men. Dr. Kopsch put the hairpin away, and they turned to other
topics.

During the conversation, Bothe ran back into the pub. Stroop turned to him and commanded, "Bothe, did you leave 'the Thing' in order?" Bothe left the pub. Hearing this cryptic exchange, Hunke gave a loud giggle. Stroop turned to him and barked, "Do not laugh like that. Soon it will be your turn, and then comes Castellan!" Castellan, an SS man who had joined the group a few minutes earlier, responded, "This is not an option for me." Stroop, livid with anger, shouted, "When an SS man receives it [a command], he must carry it out! [Even] when he knows that an hour later he is going to be shot dead!" Kuhlmann, the pub owner, tried to leave and rescue his innkeeper, but Stroop spotted him. "Stay here! The fire is still burning!" Just then, Bothe opened the door, stood at attention, and announced, " 'The Thing' is in order."

Later that evening, the men drove back from Lopshorn to their homes in Detmold. In town, rumors of what had happened to the young innkeeper swept like wildfire through the pubs and coffeehouses, eventually reaching city hall. The town's mayor, SS member Hans Keller, was shaken. He questioned a few of the Nazis present at Kuhlmann's pub and then ordered Assessor Hagemeister to investigate the case. Hagemeister collected testimony from the Nazis but not from either the innkeeper or the pub owner. Stroop gave Hagemeister his word of honor that "as far as I can remember . . . I did not get closer to the young girl than to hug and kiss her." Stroop's word of honor was enough for Hagemeister. "It is true," he wrote in his report, "that Stroop flirted intimately with the girl, as the people say, and that he hugged and kissed her . . . but there is nothing serious enough to require a disciplinary investigation." The matter was dropped.

Only a few weeks after Stroop was cleared of any wrongdoing, he was promoted to the chief of staff of SS-Abschnitt XVII in the city of Münster. There he learned that Käthe was pregnant with their second child. On October 3, 1934, a son was born, filling his father with pride. Stroop chose a true Nordic name, Jürgen, partly compensating for having named his eldest daughter Renate, which he considered a Franco-Mediterranean-sounding name.

But the happiness and pride that filled the Stroop household ended five days later when Jürgen died. In years to come, Stroop would change his own name from Josef—which he thought had Jewish overtones—to Jürgen, in memory of his lost son. For years he would berate Käthe for having been "unable to give birth to our first son correctly."[38] (A little over a year later, in February 1936, Käthe gave birth "correctly" to Olaf.)

In June 1935, the SS promoted Stroop again, this time to the commander of the 28 SS-Standarte unit in Hamburg. Among other things, this meant that when Hitler attended a ship-launching ceremony at the Blohm & Voss shipyard, Stroop oversaw the Führer's visit.[39]

In January 1938, Stroop was summoned to the third course for SS-Führers at the SS leadership school in Dachau. There he read and reread, among other books, Hitler's Mein Kampf, Alfred Rosenberg's The Myth of the Twentieth Century, and Oswald Spengler's The Decline of the West. At the culmination of the course, he was drilled on history, SS structure, leadership, and military law. In his final exam, he wrote, in his distinctive cursive script, "By releasing the Jews from the ghetto and by granting them civil rights, the state structure and authority were undermined." He also repeated the key values of the SS: "total obedience, unwavering discipline, fate, honor, strong character, and unconditional willingness to sacrifice one's life for the fatherland."[40]

Later that year, Himmler chose Stroop to join him in leading the SS men marching in the Nazi Party rally in Nuremberg. Just behind Himmler and his staff, the stiff-necked Stroop stumped in his black leather riding boots, a helmet on his head, and his hands firmly holding the hilt of the SS sword that Himmler had given him as a present. As he marched by the Führer, he raised high into the sky the shining sword upon whose blade was inscribed, "My honor is named loyalty."[41]

Part II

1939–1945

2

The Road to Warsaw

On a cloudy day in March 1939, sixteen-year-old Rivkah Trapko-vits', a suitcase in her hand, walked up a street bordered on both sides by factory buildings with tall chimneys billowing black plumes into the sky of Lodz. Trucks loaded with textiles rolled up and down the street, and groups of rough Polish men rushed home as Rivkah struggled onward. She was exhausted from her long jour-ney and could hardly wait to reach her destination.[1]

A few minutes later, Rivkah stood at the rusty gate of a five-story redbrick factory building at 41 Leszno Street. She rang the bell. A young man walked out of the building, crossed the enclosed court-yard, and pulled open the squeaky gate. Rivkah was welcomed to Kibbutz Lodz-Borochov. Inside, in the secretariat room, she put down her suitcase and told her story. A few days earlier, Rivkah had left Lomza, where her family lived. Rivkah was seven years old when her mother, Devorah, passed away. Less than a year later, her fa-ther married Sheindal, who soon thereafter gave birth to a daughter,

Zeldah, and a son, Efraim. Sheindal demanded that Rivkah quit her studies at the Polish school for Jewish children, take care of her newborn children, and maintain her house. For years Rivkah did so. Her father became aloof, her two older brothers unavailable; the only person she confided in was her elder sister, Dina. In the past months, she had learned that Dina, eight years her senior, planned to immigrate to the Land of Israel, sometimes known simply as the Land, to fulfill the dream of life on a kibbutz. Determined to follow her beloved sibling, Rivkah packed up her belongings and came to Lodz to join the kibbutz in preparation for her own immigration.[2]

This was a familiar story to the members of the kibbutz secretariat. Many of the four hundred kibbutz members had left against the wishes of their parents and planned to build new homes and lives in the Land of Israel. The socialist-Zionist youth movement Dror He-Halutz had planted in many of them the first seeds of collective life. For Rivkah, the promise of close friendships with comrades, and the warmth and caring they would offer, inspired her to join the kibbutz.

Rivkah opened her suitcase. She pulled out a few shirts and dresses, some of them self-embroidered, some books, a few coins, and all of her other belongings and handed everything over to the secretariat member. He dispersed them among the joint clothing storage room, culture room, and kibbutz treasury. From now on Rivkah would have no private possessions. She needed none; as it did for every other member, the kibbutz would provide her clothing, books, linens, and anything else she needed.[3]

She climbed four floors to the women's dormitory. The long white-walled room with its two straight rows of beds covered with white linens reminded Rivkah of a hospital ward.[4]

That night, because the kibbutz was so crowded, Rivkah shared a bed. Under her blanket, she longed for her childhood home and deceased mother. She recalled Sabbath, when her mother lit the candles, her sister and two brothers gathered around the table, and their father raised a large cup, filled to its brim with red wine, chanted the

Kiddush blessing, and broke challah. Together they ate the Sabbath foods, whose memorable aromas came back to her as she awaited sleep in the unfamiliar room.

Rivkah woke up to the daily kibbutz bustle. Members rushed downstairs to the dining room. She ate a slice of bread and some vegetables. A list on a bulletin board assigned members to their jobs, and Rivkah was assigned to the sewing shop. She joined eighty other women who sat on long wooden benches, one group marking lines on cloth, another cutting sleeves, and still another sewing a pocket to manufacture a worker's shirt. As she ironed and packed finished shirts for export to Great Britain, Rivkah met her new sisters like comrades.[5]

On Friday night, the kibbutz members assembled in the dining room decorated with pictures of the movement's leaders and a sign reading WORKERS OF THE WORLD UNITE! All dressed up to welcome the upcoming day of rest, the Sabbath, they sat at tables covered with white tablecloths.

Halfway through the meal, a bald man of medium height and thick eyebrows entered the noisy room. A hush fell as the poet Itzhak Katzenelson, followed by his wife and three young boys, joined the celebration. To the hundreds of attentive listeners, he prophesied that the socialist comradeship of the kibbutz would truly revolutionize the Jewish nation. They would fulfill this revolution in the Land of Israel, where they would create a new productive and equal society. He recited one of his poems: "Beautiful are the nights in Canaan / cool and bright they are . . ."[6]

The kibbutzniks united their voices in chorus as they imagined their future homeland and the pleasures of joint labor. As on every Friday at midnight, Katzenelson called out: "Hand on shoulder / this way brothers / exult / this way, this way / together all the assembly!"[7] All rose to their feet, placing their arms over the shoulders of the comrades by them until a large circle was formed. Bound together, they hopped in unison, as if animated by one pulse, and danced into the night.

On weekdays after work, Rivkah sat in the kibbutz culture room to read. The radio broadcast the latest news. Hitler constantly demanded that Poland cede the corridor of territory that separated the free city of Danzig (Gdansk) from Germany. Rivkah paid little attention. Within weeks she would immigrate to the sunny shores of the Middle East, far away from conflict-ridden Europe.

On August 23, 1939, a radio broadcast announced the signing of the Molotov-Ribbentrop Pact, a nonaggression treaty between the Soviet Union and Germany, which everyone knew signaled an imminent German invasion of Poland. The kibbutz secretariat called an urgent assembly, at which members deliberated what to do. One group wanted to relocate immediately eastward; others countered that they should not abandon their life's work in Lodz. "We lived together in normal times; we will continue to live together in danger." A vote was called, and a majority raised their hands in favor of staying put. Only a few left, under pressure from parents who wrote long letters begging their children to return home. Rivkah remained in Lodz with her comrades.[8]

In preparation for war, the kibbutz stocked food, medical equipment, and gas masks. Members joined other citizens of Lodz to dig air shelter trenches. On the night of September 1, the howling of air-raid sirens awakened Rivkah and her friends; the buzz of planes came next, followed by loud explosions. Their building was located between a Polish army barrack and a train station, both primary German targets. The kibbutz members huddled for hours in the basement until all was clear. In coming days, refugees from other kibbutzim in western Poland streamed in. They described the helplessness of the Polish armed forces in the face of the German attacks and artillery.

On the night of September 6, Colonel Roman Umiastowski issued an order over the radio, calling on all draft-age Polish men to escape east and prepare a new line of defense on the Bug River. Thousands fled Lodz. The kibbutz secretariat called an assembly. In a broken voice, one member of the secretariat told her comrades, "There is no point in our death here under the ruins. Better we should equip ourselves with food and go to border towns. Possibly from there we can get to the shores of the Land." A decision had been made. The kibbutz was to abandon Lodz and head east.[9]

All that night, Rivkah and her friends assembled equipment for the journey ahead. They filled backpacks with food, water, and clothes. With first light they completed their preparations and gathered in the building's courtyard. On the central notice board, a list designated groups of twenty men and women. Each group, headed by a kibbutz veteran, would independently advance to Warsaw. Just before they embarked on their journey, every member was handed a note with the address 34 Dzielna Street, the location of a sister kibbutz in Warsaw. Rivkah placed it in her shirt pocket.

The front gate was thrown wide open and they rolled out. Rivkah looked back at the shrinking factory building; for six months it had been a source of friendship, comradeship, and unity. But the home she had found there wasn't defined by the rapidly vanishing building; home was the men and women who now accompanied her.[10]

Her group marched through the streets of Lodz, already filled with evidence of war's destruction. The group left the city heading northeast. They passed cabbage fields and apple orchards, and joined long columns of Polish refugees and soldiers escaping the German Wehrmacht. Advancing along the road, suddenly they heard the whine of Luftwaffe plane engines. Within seconds, the earth under Rivkah shuddered and the air burst. Heat radiated all over her body. The group scattered, some seeking shelter in the field, others in the shallow trenches beside the road. Clods of earth were sent into the air and landed on Rivkah. When the sky finally cleared, the group scrambled to reunite and continue their treacherous journey to Warsaw, eighty miles away. The sound of every plane buzz sent them to shelter.[11]

On the eve of the second day, after advancing only thirty miles, the group entered the major train junction of Lowicz. They walked along the city streets and neared a bridge that crossed the Bug and led to the city center. Just then, German artillery and airplanes blanketed Lowicz with bombs and shells. Orange flames leaped from trees. Electricity poles fell across the road. Roofs collapsed. A few bombs hit the bridge and it caught fire. Rivkah tossed aside her bag and scuttled for shelter.

A lull in the bombing was followed by a deadly silence and cries for help. From under the debris, wives called the names of their husbands, children cried for their mothers. All around lay mangled dead and groaning wounded. Rivkah bumped into her friend Tsipora. Neither knew what had happened to the other group members. Retreating Polish soldiers ran passed them. Tsipora followed them. "Tsipora, where are you running?!" cried Rivkah. Tsipora neither paused nor answered, just disappeared. In the midst of all the devastation, Rivkah was alone.[12]

Desperate, she searched the stream of shocked faces all around her for someone familiar. For a moment each face reminded her of a kibbutz member. But none responded to the names she called out. Frightened, distressed, and above all exhausted, she moved on. Her shoes rubbed her feet raw, so Rivkah threw them away and continued barefoot, walking through the night. The next morning, outside the city, she entered a farm's courtyard and lay down on the ground. She fell asleep. Minutes or hours later—she had lost track of time— she woke up to see the barn engulfed in flames and smoke rising high into the sky. A hen ran between mutilated human corpses and flapped its wings. She arose to continue her journey.[13]

Rivkah numbly followed wrinkle-faced Polish men and women, an occasional small child embraced by arms and clinging to a parent's chest. The stream of people moved with slow purposefulness between devastated villages and burning haystacks. In the light of the fires, Rivkah navigated around horse cadavers, human corpses, and twisted carriages. In the ruins of a house she noticed charred family furniture, torn clothes, and what seemed like a bent child's toy. Amid this destruction she worried about the health and safety of her family back in Lomza: her father, Shmuel, her two teenage brothers, Nissan and Baruch, her young half siblings, Zeldah and Efraim, and her aunt Liba with her four teenage children.[14]

She also thought of her comrades of Kibbutz Lodz. Every few minutes she slid her hand into her shirt pocket and with the tips of her fingers touched the crumpled piece of paper with the address of the kibbutz in Warsaw. Though she had memorized the address, feeling the paper offered a sense of security. Her bare feet were covered with blisters and wounds, her throat was dry from thirst, and her stomach grumbled. Still, despite the anguish, Rivkah continued her journey into the night along the route to Warsaw.[15]

On Saturday morning, September 9, Rivkah reached the outskirts of the Polish capital. Starting that day, German artillery relentlessly pounded the city. At a hastily built barricade constructed of scraps of metal, pieces of furniture, and piles of boxes, Polish guards stopped each person who wanted to enter Warsaw. They searched for German infiltrators, presumed saboteurs. While Rivkah stood there, the guards stopped a German Jew who had lived in the kibbutz in Lodz and asked for his identity. He spoke only German. Suspecting he was a German spy, they arrested him. Rivkah watched, her heart torn, all but certain that if she came to his aid, she too would be arrested.

Hearing Rivkah's perfect Polish dialect, the guards allowed her to cross the barricade. About her thronged the thousands of young men who, under orders from Polish authorities, had rushed eastward. She moved along the streets, scrambling to avoid exploding shells, blazing buildings, and water flowing from burst pipes. The smell of rotting corpses filled the air, and in parks volunteers buried the bodies of the many thousands killed by the German bombing. On one charred street sign after another Rivkah searched for Dzielna Street.[16]

Hours later she finally located it in a cramped Jewish neighborhood in the northern part of town. She hastened along the side-

walk. Many unfamiliar faces stood in front of the locked door of 34
Dzielna, a few dozen members of other Dror He-Halutz kibbutzim
from western Poland. More than two hundred members of her kibbutz had turned back en route. Some had been killed. Only a few
dozen of them had reached Warsaw.[17]

They crouched on the staircase and waited for someone to fetch
the keys. After a few minutes, Fischel Farber, a former member of
the Lodz Kibbutz who now lived in Warsaw, brought them. Rivkah
and Fischel had overlapped for a few weeks in Lodz; Fischel also
had listened to radio broadcasts in the kibbutz culture room. Later
they took the same Hebrew class and sang together in the kibbutz
choir.[18]

The group entered a courtyard walled by four buildings. They
walked into the stairwell of one building and climbed to the third
floor. Fischel unlocked the door marked number 8. Inside they
found a clean and tidy apartment. The kitchen cupboard contained
rice, cocoa, and sugar. Rivkah set a pot on the stove and prepared
hot rice pudding. For many, it was the first warm meal they had
eaten in days.[19]

A constant stream of refugees flowed into 34 Dzielna. The apartment quickly overflowed. Some moved to another apartment at
14 Gesia Street. One evening, as a group of kibbutzniks neared that
apartment, a German bomb fell and destroyed the building. Luckily,
no one was hurt. The group returned to Dzielna Street. Electricity
and gas supplies had ceased. Water no longer ran from the taps. The
rooms filled, as more young men and women sought refuge. Forag-
ing for supplies was imperative, and always German bombs fell on
the city streets.

On the eve of Yom Kippur, a couple of the refugees ran to draw
water from the Vistula River. During heavy bombing, one of them,
Itzhak Engelsberg, was struck in the head by shrapnel. He died
that night. Later, two women who had gone for water from a well
in the Gesia Cemetery were found dead. Others stood for hours

risking their lives on queues for bread, flour, rice, and water. Men used large knives to carve meat from horse cadavers. When word spread that a pickle factory on Stawki Street had been bombed, Rivkah and a handful of others rushed to collect the cans of pickles scattered on the shattered factory floor.[20]

After four weeks of siege, Nazi forces conquered Warsaw on September 28. Shortly thereafter, they entered the city and immediately began to harass Jews. From food lines, they pulled out bearded and sidelocked Orthodox men. Some Polish citizens pointed their fingers at the Jews whose appearance did not immediately identify them, saying in their heavy Polish accents, *"Ein Jude!"* In predominately Jewish neighborhoods, German units blocked off streets and kidnapped dozens of men for slave labor. They broke into Jewish businesses and looted them, arrested well-dressed Jewish women and forced them to clean their offices with their shirts or underwear. After the Jews completed the cleaning job, the grinning Nazis demanded they dress back in their soiled clothes.[21]

Within weeks, the German authorities announced several decrees: Jews above ten years old must wear a four-inch-wide white armband with a blue Star of David on the sleeve of their right arm; Jews must take off their hats in deference to Germans; Jews were limited to specific trams; Jews who owned businesses must mark them as Jewish owned; Jews couldn't sell their businesses without special permission; Jews were not permitted in public parks; on certain streets they were not permitted on a given sidewalk; on still other streets they were not permitted at all. Approximately 95,000 of the 175,000 Jewish wage earners in Warsaw lost their jobs.[22]

The apartment at 34 Dzielna stood a short distance from the Pawiak Prison, located at 24–26 Dzielna. A small balcony in the apartment overlooked the street facing the jail. One day while lying on the balcony, Rivkah and her friends spotted a Nazi soldier stop an elderly Orthodox Jew. The soldier grabbed a fistful of the Jew's beard and yanked. Blood trickled down the old man's face and onto the street's cobblestones. Then the Nazi ordered the Jew to stand with his arms high up against the jail wall; the Jew followed orders. Rivkah could hear the metal click as the soldier cocked his gun. The Jew mumbled a prayer. The Nazi aimed his rifle and pulled the trigger. A second before firing, the Nazi slightly diverted the gun. The Jew's life was saved. At the sight of the terrified old man who still prayed, not believing he was alive, the Nazi burst into laughter.[23]

At 34 Dzielna, the refugees elected a kibbutz secretariat. To ease living conditions, the secretariat requested some members to leave and smuggle themselves across Nazi-controlled lines east, in this time not yet a very risky task. Others left of their own accord. One day an elderly Polish peasant knocked on the kibbutz apartment door. He had come for Rivkah. The peasant told Rivkah he had been sent for her. She learned that her home, with all its belongings, had been destroyed in a fire. All her family members in Lomza—a town over-taken by the Germans and handed a few weeks later to Soviet forces—were safe. Rivkah's father had sent the peasant to smuggle Rivkah across the border into Soviet-occupied territory.[24]

Rivkah requested permission to go to Lomza, promising to re-turn in a couple of weeks. The secretariat rejected the request. Rivkah now managed the kibbutz kitchen and household and was consid-ered essential. Unlike other kibbutzniks who had ignored such or-ders, Rivkah sent the Polish peasant back alone.[25]

In the early mornings, the kibbutzniks left for work, many of them to forced labor. Rivkah stayed in the apartment. She and her companion worker, Peshka Harman, rinsed dishes, cleaned rooms, washed laundry, and cooked meals. At night, Rivkah would burst into tears at the sight of her friends: weary, soiled, hungry, and at times wounded. During a winter marked by fierce snowstorms and temperatures far below freezing, all she could offer them were a few soothing words and a dish of warm soup.[26]

The household duties slowly became routine. With the support of the Judenrat—a council the Nazis required the Jews to form in order to manage their own administrative needs—the kibbutz established a soup kitchen for needy Jews. The kibbutz also rented additional apartments to house members and their clandestine schools.

On their journey to Warsaw, many kibbutz members like Rivkah had lost clothes and other basic items. In a storage house in Warsaw were suitcases of Dror He-Halutz members who had immigrated before the war to the Land of Israel. After receiving approval from the movement's headquarters, each kibbutznik was permitted to take one suitcase.

When Rivkah opened her suitcase, she found a neatly folded dress and shirt, which she placed on her bed. At the bottom lay two photo albums. She flipped through the pages. At the sight of the first photos, she almost fainted. Looking up at her were her brothers, sisters, father, and late mother. The suitcase was her sister Dina's. From that day on she kept the clothes and photos near to her wherever she went.[27]

On Monday, December 4, 1939, a special messenger knocked on the door of the Blösche home in Frydlant and delivered an envelope to Josef Blösche. It was a draft order. Blösche, who with the annexation of the Sudetenland by Nazi Germany had volunteered for the local SS, was to report the next day to the border police school in Pretzsch, near the town of Torgau, 125 miles to the north, where he would go through basic training for SS personnel. Blösche's plans to run the family businesses, to sell produce in the market, to serve beer and sausages in the guesthouse, had abruptly ended. Instead of serving his fellow townspeople, Blösche would now serve his fatherland.[28]

On the following day, for the first time in his life, twenty-seven-year-old Blösche traveled out of the landscape of his childhood and into new and unfamiliar scenery. Looking out the train window at the monumental buildings of Dresden, at the wide Elbe River with its large ships, he knew he would one day return to his small and familiar hometown, to its well-walked alleys and familiar faces.

Blösche arrived later that day at the border police school located in a castle, where he and sixty or seventy other recruits enrolled in a basic training program. Each received a Walther 7.65-mm pistol and a Karabiner 98k rifle, which they would be required to carry from that day forward. In the castle's courtyard, the recruits marched in straight lines for hours on end; they stood at attention exactly at arm's length from each other; they grasped the rifle butt and tilted it forward at the same exact angle. Any deviation, whether in the distance between men or the tilt of the rifle, resulted in immediate reproach. Life in the SS demanded total obedience. An order, no matter what, was to be followed to the letter. "A command is a command."

In between one drill and the next, Blösche studied the job of border control. He learned how to fill out forms, respond to correspondence, and write up incident reports. Also, he learned to recognize passports of different countries and to identify falsified papers. Looking at a passport photo, Blösche analyzed the two-dimensional image—how far apart the eyes were, the size of the forehead, the shape of the eyebrows, the angle of the nose, the thickness of the lips, the outline of the chin. Any difference between image and subject, he was instructed, must arouse suspicion. Even if a passport was not falsified, one must search for its owner's name in the multivolume suspect book before granting permission to cross the border.

Blösche also internalized the fact that despite the Jews' physical build, which seemed similar to that of other humans, they were in truth dreadful creatures. Blösche had already learned at home that Jews were loathsome, but in Pretzsch he was instructed even further in racial theory. He read parts of the key Nazi ideologist Alfred Rosenberg's *The Myth of the Twentieth Century*. He did not understand much of it, but certain sentences were clear: "World Jewry was the irreconcilable enemy of all Aryan civilization and culture, and especially of Germany." The Jew was responsible for the German nation's failures in the past, causing it real damage in the present, and posing a threat to its very existence in the future.

For Blösche, recent history confirmed the truth of these claims. After all, since Germany had begun its battle against the Jews in 1933, its economic situation had improved and unemployment rates had dropped. The lesson seemed clear enough: Only battling the Jews could save the German nation and the cultured world from total devastation.[29]

On March 14, 1940, Blösche completed his basic training and was ready to begin his service in the office of the commander of security police and security services of the Warsaw District, or the KdS. During his first couple of weeks in Warsaw, he hauled furniture from the KdS headquarters to eastern outposts. Then he was posted to Platerow, seventy miles east, on the newly formed border between the Soviet Union and Nazi Germany. Here at the border crossing, under the command of Edmund Lange, Blösche, his Pretzsch comrades Karl Beer and Friedrich Moritz, and others inspected freight trains before permitting them to continue their journey. Blösche also patrolled a six-mile stretch along the Bug River in search of border infiltrators, his Walther pistol and his Karabiner rifle always at hand.[30]

In the spring of 1940, the kibbutz assembly selected Rivkah and sixteen other members to relocate to a farm in the town of Grochow on the outskirts of Warsaw. Prior to the war, this seventy-five-acre farm owned by the Jewish community had served as an agricultural training site for those immigrating to the Land of Israel. Now the group of seventeen intended to work the land and provide food for the kibbutz. On April 23, Rivkah and her friends celebrated their upcoming departure from Warsaw.[31]

The following morning at six o'clock, the group left Dzielna Street and traveled by tram to Grochow. They discovered the farm's kitchen and dormitory in ruins, the result of German bombings. Local Poles had looted the little that was left. As the kibbutz members walked over the rubble, a group of Polish children surrounded them. Cursing the Jews, they tossed stones, one hitting Shmuel Greenberg in the head.[32]

Undeterred, over the coming days the group placed brick upon brick, plank beside plank, and tile next to tile, to rebuild the kitchen, dormitory, and cowshed. In the fields, they planted rhubarb, onions, cabbage, asparagus, beans, red beets, and sugar beets. In the summer, the plants sprouted, flowers blossomed, and rich vegetables ripened. They shipped the crop to 34 Dzielna, where members sold the produce to other Jews. The proceeds helped finance the kibbutz kitchen that every day served soup, porridge, and dough crumbs to six hundred needy Jews.[33]

Every night, the group at Grochow, which now numbered thirty-five—augmented from other kibbutz movements—sat together in the dining room to read, debate ideology, and discuss the distribu-

tion of their farm produce among the various kibbutz movements. On Friday nights, they welcomed the Sabbath and sat shoulder to shoulder as they sang solemn Hebrew songs of yearning for the Land of Israel.[34]

During this time, seventeen-year-old Rivkah formed a connection with Shmuel Greenberg. Shmuel had black hair like Rivkah and eyes almost as dark as hers. They dreamed about their common future on a kibbutz in the Land of Israel.

On November 15, Rivkah, as she did every day, woke up early to prepare breakfast for the farmworkers. On this day her thoughts turned to her friends on Dzielna Street. A few weeks earlier, on Yom Kippur, the Nazi authorities had decreed that all Jewish fami-

lies in Warsaw who lived outside a designated area had to abandon
their homes and relocate to a new Jewish ghetto surrounded by a
wooden fence and barbed wire. Dzielna Street was located within
the borders of the new ghetto, so none living there would need to
move. Today was the day the Nazis had threatened to seal the ghetto
gates. What precisely this would mean for the future of her kibbutz
friends and for Warsaw's Jews was unknown.

An hour later, a group of Polish policemen arrived at the farm's
gate. Though the Nazis had assured the head of the Warsaw Judenrat that the Jews at the farm need not relocate to the ghetto, the
policemen would hear nothing of it. They gave everyone fifteen
minutes to board horse wagons for transfer to the ghetto. The kibbutz members resisted. The argument dragged out. Finally, the policemen agreed that the farm manager, Moshe Rubenchik, would
remain behind and guard the facilities. The wagons rolled out of
Grochow and along the streets of Aryan Warsaw.[35]

From the back of the wagon, Rivkah and her friends watched
Poles looting evacuated Jewish homes. Other Poles, some who had
been forced by the Nazis to abandon homes in the area of the newly
enclosed ghetto, prepared to move into homes evacuated by Jews.

Rivkah, sitting next to Shmuel, felt his arm move. She noticed
he had pulled the white armband with its blue Star of David off his
sleeve. He pushed it into her hands. As the carriage turned a corner,
Shmuel leaped out of the wagon in a split second. The last Rivkah
saw of him, he was ducking low near a courtyard entrance.[36]

The wagon continued on and crossed the Vistula, nearing the
ghetto. Hundreds of Jews lined the fence, hoping to cross over to
the Aryan part of town; Nazi guards turned them back. At the
ghetto gate, the kibbutz members disembarked and walked to 34
Dzielna, now overpopulated like every building in the ghetto. Dzielna
Street, only a few hundred yards long, was now home to some eigh-
teen thousand residents. As Rivkah walked on the sidewalk, she
was struck by the press of people. The ghetto comprised just one

and a quarter square miles. Here resided more than 380,000 Jews, with an average of more than seven people per room. Unlike green Grochow, the ghetto had no parks or gardens, only gray buildings.

At 34 Dzielna, the Grochow group was greeted by old friends; Rivkah's thoughts, however, remained focused on Shmuel. She yearned to escape the ghetto and return to Grochow. Two days later, she trotted nervously back and forth along the tram tracks, which still ran through the ghetto. At the squeak of the tram's wheels signaling its approach, Rivkah rushed to the barbed-wire fence that encircled the ghetto. She scrambled over the coils to reach the tram station, suffering only minor scratches. Some Polish boys pointed at her and shouted, "Zyd." Rivkah held her breath, climbed up the tram stairs, and with a stern face sat in a seat marked "for German citizens only." The tram rolled off. After a forty-five-minute journey, it arrived at Grochow. Rivkah stepped off the tram and back into Shmuel's arms.[37]

With the approval of the Nazi authorities, in the coming weeks other members also returned to Grochow. Now they were no longer owners of the farm nor of the produce they grew. The Nazis had given the fields to an ethnic German from Poznan. Overnight, the kibbutz members had become employees of an anti-Semite who paid them no wages. All they received for their labor was a limited daily ration—some potatoes, coarse-meal bread, milk, and beans.

Every morning before dawn, while the rest of the commune members still slept, Rivkah drew two buckets of water and stealthily plucked fresh carrots, cucumbers, and tomatoes for breakfast. During the day, while her friends tended the fields, Rivkah cleaned the dining room and dormitories. On the wall of the dormitory she hung a small tapestry of a wooden house standing on the bank of a creek. She sewed white lace curtains and placed a vase of colorful flowers atop a cloth that covered a small table at the center of the room.

In January 1941, a small group of kibbutz members, which included Shmuel, left Warsaw in an attempt to sneak across the bor-

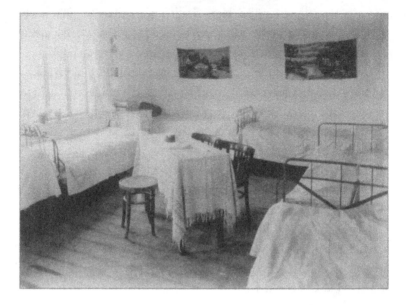

der into Slovakia, and from there find a route to the Land of Israel. The risk was great; Nazi law prohibited Jews from traveling by train. Secretly the group boarded one heading south via Krakow to the border. In Nowy Sacz they disembarked. As they walked on the train platform, a local man identified Shmuel and his friend Tsvi Kutzer as Jews and pointed them out to the police. They were arrested on the spot and remained imprisoned while the rest of the group crossed into Slovakia, one even reaching Palestine. After months of interrogation and incarceration by the Gestapo, Shmuel and Tsvi were released and returned to Grochow. Black bruises encircled Shmuel's eyes and his front teeth were missing. He was a shattered man.[38]

n late June 1941, two days before the launch of Operation Barbarossa—Germany's fateful invasion of the Soviet Union—Blösche watched Wehrmacht trucks, tanks, and artillery roll through Siedlce, the town to which the KdS Warsaw had posted him a few months earlier.[39] Blösche's job was to guard an investigation facility of the Gestapo. Day in and day out, he took detainees from their jail cells up to the investigation rooms, from which piercing cries echoed down the halls. A few hours later, Blösche gathered the bruised and wounded inmates and led them back down to their cells. When he was not ushering inmates around the Gestapo facility, Blösche patrolled the quiet town streets.[40]

Within days of the launch of Operation Barbarossa, the KdS Warsaw summoned Blösche back to headquarters. Along with twenty-five to thirty Warsaw Gestapo men, he was posted to Einsatzkommando 8, a subunit of Einsatzgruppe B (and part of a fifth Einsatzgruppe of SS men and policemen assisting other murder units). In early July, Blösche and his squad traveled in three personnel carriers past the city of Bialystok and into the area of Baranovichi, a territory newly captured from the Soviet Union.[41]

With the other members of his Einsatzkommando, Blösche scouted villages north of Baranovichi to locate "unwanted elements"—Jews, Gypsies, and Soviet sympathizers. They led those arrested out of town, where Blösche guarded the prisoners on a side road as other squad members led them into the forest, from where shots were heard.[42]

Toward the end of August, Einsatzkommando 8 was assigned to a small town between Novogrudok and Lida, north of Baranovichi. The Nazi soldiers combed the hamlet's homes in search of members and activists in the local Communist Party. They located a dozen or so middle-aged men and returned with them to camp. The men were to be killed, and for the first time Blösche was part of such a mission. In one of the unit's trucks, they traveled a mile west of town to the edge of a forest. As the Einsatzkommando members unloaded the Soviets, each man took control of one prisoner. Blösche gripped his man firmly, joined the column headed by the unit's commander, and pushed his prisoner down the dirt path into the thick forest.

They walked for a few minutes to a clearing punctured by three bomb craters. The Soviets were forced to dig a ditch in one of the craters. When they finished, the Nazis ordered them to stand side by side in the ditch, facing one wall. Blösche and his group stood in a row on the ditch edge. His hand gripped the wooden stock of his rifle. He raised the butt to his shoulder and through the rifle's scope focused on the backs of the heads of the men standing a few yards below him. The gun fit comfortably on his shoulder. His fingers rested on the trigger. The commander called out the order to shoot. All the guns thundered in unison. Beyond the small cloud of smoke that emerged from his gun's barrel, Blösche saw his man collapse. The others also fell to the bottom of the soggy ditch.

Blösche lowered his gun. His breath was short, his mouth dry, his legs shaking. The squad members grabbed shovels and hurled dirt over the bodies of those who had just a moment ago tossed the earth up. Blösche's arms were heavy. Between one toss and another, he stared at the corpses below, a bullet hole in the back of each of their heads. To his horror, in the mix of excrement, blood, dirt, and water, he noticed a movement. One of the corpses jerked and his eyes twitched. The man gasped for air. A fellow Nazi noticed Blösche's fixed look and followed it to the jolting body. He pulled out his pistol, aimed, and gave a "mercy shot."[43]

Blösche was horrified. On the way back to the truck along the forest path, each of his footsteps echoed that fatal shot, each rustle of leaves brought to mind the man's final gasps for air. Despite the alcohol he drank that night—bottles handed out by the unit commanders—he could not overcome the sight of the man's rolling eyes in the ditch. A command is a command, he constantly reminded himself. The commander has a justification for all his acts, he repeated in his head. It had been correct, worthy behavior he had learned in his basic training, he reiterated. It was wrong for a simple soldier like him to question his superiors' commands. Nevertheless, the victim's face flashed back at him.

A few days later, Blösche's commanders called on him again to join a shooting squad. Ten Soviet citizens were to be taken to the same forest clearing and killed. As he walked along the path behind his prisoner, Blösche's heart pounded, and sweat ran down his back. The men entered the forest clearing. Blösche searched for the place where he had seen the dying man, his eyes twitching, his mouth gasping for air. All he saw was dark brown earth and green foliage.

The Soviets dug a ditch in another bomb crater. The job completed, they lined up inside the ditch. Blösche stood on its edge in line with the rest of his squad. The commander shouted the order to aim, and all raised rifles to their shoulders. Then came the order to shoot. The rifles to Blösche's right and left blasted in unison. One second later, Blösche pressed his trigger. His man collapsed. Blösche lay down his gun, shaken but relieved. He had fulfilled the command; his qualms had not overcome his senses. After the shooting, squad members filled the ditch with earth; it looked almost identical to the other ditch. Within days this piece of upturned earth, he told himself, would also become an unnoticed forest patch with a few fresh grass sprouts.

In 1942, the Nazis put an end to the enclave of Jews who toiled under open skies in the fields of Grochow. Rivkah returned to the ghetto. Chaim Kaplan wrote in his diary that "it is now three years since we have seen grass growing and flowers in bloom. . . . We have been robbed of every tree and every flower."[44]

Rivkah joined kibbutz members who worked as maids in the few remaining comfortable ghetto homes, many of which belonged to Gestapo collaborators or professional smugglers. After work, she had to fight her way back to Dzielna, maneuvering her way between ghetto masses and skeletal children with dry skin and sunken cheeks, their thin fingers spread forward as they begged in hoarse voices for "A piece of bread! A piece of bread!" The wailing of the even less fortunate children, youngsters covered with flies and fleas lying beside the corpses of their parents, was lost in the constantly roaring noise that filled the crowded ghetto streets.

At first Rivkah was horrified by the sights, but with time she grew accustomed to them. The little food she was able to procure from her employers she hid under her jacket, fearing that if those starving Jews saw the bread, they would grab it and gobble it down their throats before anyone could retrieve it.[45]

In his diary, the historian Emmanuel Ringelblum—who in Warsaw gathered documents for a secret archive about the ghetto— wrote that "the first frosts have already appeared, and the populace is trembling at the prospect of cold weather. The most fearful sight is that of freezing children. Little children with bare feet, bare knees, and torn clothing, stand dumbly in the street weeping. Tonight . . . I heard a tot of three or four yammering. The child will probably be found frozen to death tomorrow morning, a few hours off. Early October [of 1941], when the first snows fell, some seventy children were found frozen to death on the steps of ruined houses."[46]

In the morning, corpses lay on the sidewalks. Judenrat workers "use horse-drawn wagons," wrote Ringelblum, "pull handcarts, rubber wheeled carriages, litters, etc. The horse-drawn wagons are loaded with bodies. The coffins of the poor are piled on top of one another. In some of the houses . . . whole families die out. There are cases where the body of the last family to die lies untended for days until neighbors smell the odor of death. . . . There have been cases . . . of rats gnawing at corpses that have been allowed to lie untended for several days. . . . This death of entire families in the course of one or two days is a very common occurrence."[47]

"Life in the ghetto," wrote Chaim Kaplan, "does not flow, but is stagnant and frozen. Around us—walls. We have no space; we have no freedom to move and act. . . . We are not allowed even to live. . . . Sixty out of one hundred are hungry in the full sense of the

word. . . . 'Our life'—if it can be called life—has become shapeless, boring, and dusty, and no kind of change occurs. The only ones who insert a little bit of movement in the moldy and fouled ghetto life are the murderer and his friend, death."[48]

A few months into his employment with the Einsatzkommando, Blösche was posted from the eastern front back to KdS headquarters in Warsaw. Dressed in his gray-green uniform, every day he crossed Szucha Street—known also as *Strasse der Polizei*—on his way from the police barracks to KdS headquarters. Here he reported to Walter Stamm or his deputy, Gottlieb Höhmann, at the KdS department IV-A, the Gestapo's unit responsible for rooting out sabotage activity.[49]

Blösche gathered information about suspected sympathizers with the Polish underground. At night he helped arrest suspects. One such night in September 1941 as Warsaw lay under curfew, Blösche sat in a car speeding through the city's emptied boulevards. He and his associates searched for sixteen-year-old Helena Kusmierczyk, who had escaped from a forced labor camp in the village of Stary Borek near the Baltic Sea. The car halted in front of an apartment building at 54 Kordeckiego Street in Grochow. Blösche, his gun drawn, and a Gestapo agent in civilian clothes climbed the building's stairs and knocked on the Kusmierczyks' door. The door opened and the two stormed in. They located Helena in her hiding place. When both Helena and her mother tried to resist arrest, the Nazis pushed the two women down the stairs and into the car. Back at Gestapo headquarters, they shoved the two down to the cellar and locked them behind iron bars.

The following day, Blösche dragged the women to the interrogation room. He seated them on small wooden stools. Blösche, together with two other Gestapo men, questioned them. Helena crouched down and kissed the black leather boot of one of the Germans, begging him to spare her ailing mother. A powerful kick hit her jaw. Teeth flew out of her mouth and blood streamed from her nose. The Gestapo men beat Helena's shrieking mother. At the end of the interrogation, the Gestapo shipped Helena and her mother to the notorious Pawiak Prison, where they seperated the two and harassed them for half a year, after which Helena was sent back to Stary Borek for forced labor till the war's end. [50]

On April 18, 1942, the Gestapo commanders assigned Blösche to a special mission with division IV-B4 (the division headed by Eichmann and responsible for the arrest and deportation of Jews). Occasionally, Blösche's commanders had ordered him to accompany this division as it patrolled the ghetto streets. On this night, a Gestapo unit guided by Jewish policemen drove into the ghetto in search of specific suspects. The truck halted at the gate of 34 Dzielna.

The kibbutz guard on duty in the courtyard entrance rang the alarm bell inside the building. Gestapo soldiers and officers broke in through the gate and rushed up the stairs. They were searching for Antek (Itzhak) Zuckerman and Lunka Kozibrodzka, leaders of the Jewish youth movement. In the course of their search, the Nazis shot a kibbutz member in his foot. Another kibbutz member told the Gestapo men that Antek and Lunka no longer lived there. Antek, she claimed, had already been taken to a labor camp (in truth, the two were hiding in another ghetto apartment at the time).

When the Nazis failed to locate Antek and Lunka, they broke into another apartment. In the kitchen, Aron Schultz and his ten-year-old son, Jozio, sat at a table poring over the boy's homework. The Nazis arbitrarily arrested father and son and dragged them down the staircase. Rivkah heard the two screaming as the Germans pulled them out onto the street. Then two sharp shots echoed throughout the building. Lying on the balcony, she peeked over the ledge. A group of Germans stood around Schultz and his son, who lay on the ground.[51]

On that moonless night, during which fifty-two Jews were murdered in the ghetto's first mass execution, Blösche stood on Dzielna Street with a warm pistol in his hands. Behind him stood his Gestapo commander; before him towered the spires of St. Augustine's Church; a short distance away rose the Pawiak Prison wall. Underneath him, just by the wall, within a hand's touch of each other, lay the motionless bodies of a man and a boy, facedown on the cold sidewalk. Blood had pooled around them and into the gutter. One of the Germans forcefully kicked the bodies. Neither reacted.[52]

In the summer of 1942, Chana and Yosef Nussbaum and their seven-year-old son, Tsvi, were living in the town of Sandomierz, 125 miles southeast of Warsaw. Almost half the residents of this scenic town, with its castle and old wall situated at the meeting point of the

Vistula and the San rivers, were Jewish. Before the Nazi occupation
of Poland, Jews had lived and flourished here for hundreds of years,
and famous rabbis and authors had developed a vibrant culture. Some
Jews traded in wood, crops, and eggs, and others owned small shops.
Yosef owned a small electrical goods shop. Tsvi's grandfather Jacob
was the chairman of the town's Revisionist Zionist youth movement
(Beitar).[53]

Eight years earlier, in the summer of 1934, Chana and Yosef
had married in Sandomierz. Shortly thereafter, the couple boarded
a ship to Tel Aviv. Here they settled and built their new home. On
August 31, 1935, Chana gave birth to Tsvi. Eight months later, in
April 1936, mass protests by Arabs took place in reaction to Jewish
immigration to Palestine. In Tel Aviv as elsewhere, the protests developed into a violent revolt. Back in Poland, Yosef's worried parents, Ziporah and Jacob, wrote long letters urging the young couple
to return to Poland. Chana and Yosef conceded. They secured a
British Mandate passport for Tsvi and sailed back to Europe, and
eventually to Sandomierz.

A few months after their return, in September 1939, Nazi planes
flew overhead and tanks rumbled through the streets. On the first
day of their occupation, the Germans herded all adult Jews to the
marketplace. Here the Jews stood for hours with their hands raised
in the air. Then the Nazis forced them to a nearby farm, where they
were stripped of their watches and valuables. In the following weeks,
the Nazis ordered the Jews to wear a band with the letter *J* on their
upper arms. They established a Judenrat, of which Yosef Nussbaum
was a member. The Nazis then demanded that the Judenrat pay a
480,000-zloty ransom (about $70,000). Together with the chair of
the Judenrat, attorney Henrik Goldberg, Yosef collected the money
and delivered it to the Germans.[54]

In the summer of 1942, a few prominent Sandomierz Jews were
taken hostage by the Nazis. Thirty-six-year-old Chana, now a mother
of two, went to the Gestapo headquarters to beseech their release.

In her fluent German, she appealed to a Gestapo agent. He ignored her. As she turned to walk out of the office, he pulled out his pistol and shot her. Chana stumbled down the stairs, dead. Around the same time, the Germans also murdered Yosef, as well as grandparents Ziporah and Jacob Nussbaum. Seven-year-old Tsvi and his two-year-old brother, Ilan, were orphaned.[55]

The two young orphans' aunt and uncle, Chana and Shulim—Chana, the sister of the children's father, and Shulim, the brother of their mother, who had married each other during the war—took charge of their nephews. They placed them in the hands of a local Polish photographer and traveled to Warsaw. Within days of their arrival, Chana and Shulim arranged a hideout and sent Miriam Szydlowski, an Aryan-looking Jew, to fetch the boys. Miriam traveled to Sandomierz but feared taking both young black-haired and dark-eyed children back on the same train. On this journey she decided to take only Tsvi.

Miriam delivered Tsvi to Chana and Shulim in their clandestine apartment on the Aryan side of Warsaw that they shared with Tsvi's aunt Regina and his two cousins, Marek and Aron. Miriam returned to Sandomierz to fetch Ilan. But he was no longer there. While she had been traveling with Tsvi, Ilan and his great-grandmother had been forced into the local ghetto. After a fruitless search, Miriam returned empty-handed to Warsaw. On October 29, 1942, the Germans conducted a two-week *Aktion* in the Sandomierz ghetto. They shot dozens of Jews and loaded others on trains headed to the extermination camp of Belzec, where hundreds of thousands of Jews were murdered. Nothing would be heard of the two-year-old Ilan and his eighty-six-year-old great-grandmother Genendel ever again.

In Warsaw, Tsvi and other family members hid in their apartment. Tsvi's aunt Frumcia, who had a Polish look, supplied them with food. They walked barefoot so neighbors wouldn't hear them; they relieved themselves in buckets so as not to encounter anyone in the building's common bathroom. The sound of a car brake in front of their apartment building, or a knock on their front door, caused mortal fear; either might signal that the Gestapo had uncovered their hiding place.

One day a knock came at the door. A Pole had discovered them and demanded blackmail. If they paid him, he promised not to reveal their hideout. Shulim extracted from his shoe heel a gold coin and handed it over. Still, the Nussbaums had to locate a new hiding place. Blackmailers, they knew, soon returned either to extort more money or as guides for Gestapo agents.

I n early summer 1942, the Gestapo commanders transferred Blösche permanently to division IV-B4. Every day between 8:00 and 9:00 a.m., Blösche, together with Carl Brandt, Heinrich Klaustermeyer, Fritz Rührenschopf, and a few other Nazis, boarded a truck that drove north from Gestapo headquarters along Warsaw's Aryan streets. After a couple of minutes, they turned onto Nowolipie Street. The truck slowed as it neared the ghetto entrance, where two German, two Polish, and two Jewish policemen stood. A large sign warned of an EPIDEMIC AREA. The gate—one of nine remaining entrances into the ghetto—opened and the truck drove inside. A mass of men and women in ragged clothes and barefoot children selling trinkets assailed Blösche's eyes. As they drove into the ghetto alleys, between rickshaws and crowds of people, Jews pulled off their hats at the sight of the SS men. Spying the Gestapo car, others who were looking out their apartment windows retreated into their rooms. The car eventually arrived at a three-story building at 103 Zelazna Street, the Gestapo ghetto command post inside the ghetto.[56]

On the ground floor of the Zelazna Street outpost, occupied between 8:00 a.m. and 5:00 p.m., sat Brandt, its commander.[57] Blösche loathed the arrogant Brandt, who never chatted with him, never sat at his table during dinner in the Szucha Street canteen. He spoke fast and swallowed his words. If Blösche asked for clarifications, Brandt reproached him. Blösche followed orders to the last detail, but Brandt never expressed gratitude. To Blösche, it seemed that Brandt had a greater appreciation for the Jewish officer who served as liaison between him and the Judenrat than for the Aryan-bred Blösche. That the Jew had long discussions with Brandt was troubling; far more humiliating, Brandt asked the Jewish officer to report whether Blösche did his job.[58]

At times, Brandt called Blösche and Klaustermeyer to his office: "Too few Jews have reported for work. Off you go and make a bit of a racket."[59] Blösche sat on the rickshaw's wooden passenger seat and Klaustermeyer pedaled through the ghetto streets. Seeing the speeding rickshaw, ghetto inhabitants, who had nicknamed Klaustermeyer and Blösche the two Frankensteins, fled into courtyards or ducked down alleyways. As Klaustermeyer pedaled, Blösche felt the wind across his face and watched the shrieking Jews scatter. He raised his gun and aimed at his favorite prey, pregnant women and young children. By the time Klaustermeyer and Blösche completed their mission, several Jews lay dead on the streets.[60]

Beginning in July 1942, and for the next two months, SS men, German police, Blue Polish police (local Polish policemen who took part in policing the Jewish ghettos), Jewish police, and Latvian and Ukrainian gendarmes executed the first mass deportation of Jews from Warsaw for "resettlement" in the east. At first they swept up beggars and children from the streets. Over the following days, they blocked off courtyard exits, shouted *"Raus!"* and stormed the buildings. Trapped, Jews ran to the windows and jumped out; Jewish policemen rounded up those who survived. Up in the apartments, the soldiers and police yanked Jews out of their hiding places, pushing them down and out into the courtyard. Jews pleaded with the Jewish police or the Ukrainian collaborators, waving work permits or other papers in an attempt to save themselves. Only a few succeeded. A worthy bribe or a special connection could, at times, keep a Jew from deportation. Eventually, a mass of shrieking Jews, with their bags or suitcases, assembled near the courtyard gate.[61]

Blösche, Klaustermeyer, and the other Gestapo men stood and watched the operation's progress. At times, Blösche entered through the gateway and stood in the courtyard. He raised his gun, firing a shot or two into the air. The deafening sound echoed among the surrounding walls. Then he shot out a window near the building's top. Glass rained down on the courtyard. Blösche then entered the building stairwell. Like a cat, he stealthily climbed to the top floor. Silently, he entered the empty rooms, where the smell of cooking still filled the air. He listened for any sound or movement. A child whispering to his father in a cupboard, a mother sighing from relief, a slight motion in the ceiling wallpaper—all signaled hidden Jews. Once he found a two- or three-month-old baby lying on a bed. He shot it in the head.[62]

Back on the street, Blösche saw the massed Jews in groups or crammed in wagons and trucks waiting to be delivered to the Umschlagplatz, where trains departed for the east. Blösche, like the others, examined their faces. When he spotted an elderly person, a crippled man, or a pregnant woman, he approached and, following Brandt's instructions, shot them dead.[63] On September 12, 1942, the first phase of the "Great Deportation" ended (with a few shipments lasting until September 21, Yom Kippur), an *Aktion* that sent 265,000 Jews from the Warsaw ghetto to be gassed at Treblinka. Only several tens of thousands of Jews were left still breathing within the ghetto's borders.

Franz Konrad leaned over his office desk in the ghetto and with a magnifying glass closely examined a stamp held in his tongs. Stamp catalogs lay open on the desk, as did a stamp album, the initials F.K. imprinted in gold on its cover. On the office shelves lay more than forty such thick stamp albums bursting at their seams, a collection that included stamps from many of the lands now within the borders of the Third Reich. Every time he opened one, Konrad was awestruck by these pieces of fine art: their colors, their beauty, their perfection, their intricacy. But above all it was the monetary value of his collection that pleased him: his collection of Austrian stamps alone was worth more than 300,000 RM (about $70,000). He had also collected paintings and delicately woven tapestries.[64]

Careful not to harm the stamp, he mounted it on a hinge and glued it to the heavy black paper. Satisfied with the new addition to his massive collection, he limped on his sore foot—a result of an accident he suffered in 1939—to the corner window of his office on Niska Street. Snow covered the windy ghetto streets and reminded him of the previous winter of 1942, when he served as supplies officer of the 1st SS-Totenkopf Reiterregiment headed by Hermann Fegelein. Konrad had been stationed in the vicinity of Minsk when a Soviet offensive cut the lines to his unit's front forces. Faced with the mission to deliver a convoy of ten three-ton trucks loaded with supplies for the regiment, Konrad embarked on a week-long six-hundred-mile roundabout journey in the freezing Russian winter. He successfully delivered the supplies to the front-line forces, an act that earned him the Iron Cross Second Class.[65]

In late spring of 1942, Himmler recalled Konrad's commander, Fegelein, to Berlin to head the newly established SS cavalry and transportation unit and help prepare its upcoming invasion of the Caucasus. From this powerful position, Fegelein did not forget Konrad's bravery and dedication and arranged with Dr. Ferdinand von Sammern-Frankenegg, the SS and Police chief for the Warsaw district, for Konrad to be removed from the eastern front and allowed to serve in the more comfortable position of administrator in the Warsaw ghetto. In his first months in Warsaw, Konrad was in charge of the Jewish transportation firm of Kohn and Heller, agents for the Gestapo. Konrad also arranged for ghetto production of toilet articles and other personal necessities to be sent to the front lines.

Fegelein continued to pull strings in Berlin in favor of Konrad.
Beginning in September 1942, he arranged for Konrad to replace
Ernst Geipel as the head of the ghetto's confiscation division (Werterfassung), the unit in charge of all items left behind by Warsaw's
Jews transported to Treblinka. Konrad's crew, which totaled four
thousand Jewish forced laborers, entered the homes of the deported,
loaded up each and every remaining good—toothpaste containers,
women's dresses, clocks, sewing machines, silverware, flytraps, arm-
chairs, mattresses, food containers, children's toys—for delivery to
a central warehouse. After hearing from one of his Jews, Schoen-
berg, about an uncle who in 1938 traveled to the United States with
a trunk full of old Jewish manuscripts that he sold for no less than
$1 million, Konrad ordered the collection of Jewish manuscripts,
some eight hundred years old.

Every hour of the day, wooden carts rolled in and out of Konrad's warehouses. There, Jews, who viewed joining the Werterfassung as a safeguard against deportation, sorted, cleaned, registered,
and stocked the goods. Finally, Konrad either sold the confiscated
objects in Warsaw or shipped them to the fatherland and, of course,
took a cut for Fegelein and for himself. The rumor among Jews was
that Konrad, whom they nicknamed "the ghetto king," had accu-
mulated more gold than the Reichsführer-SS, Himmler himself.[66]

On January 9, 1943, Himmler, along with a small staff, arrived
in four armored vehicles to tour the storage houses.[67] After greeting
him, Konrad showed him around. On floor-to-ceiling shelves were
stacked carefully marked boxes and cases. Konrad opened the door
to one room, where Himmler saw two hundred upright and grand
pianos, each as if ready to be played in a concert hall. In another
room, Konrad boasted of artworks by Vermeer and a collection of
buttons worth 100,000 RM.[68] Konrad pointed to more than fifty
thousand toys confiscated from the homes of Jewish children, which
he intended to ship to German children in Ukraine.[69]

Himmler was impressed. He tapped Konrad fondly on his shoulder and said, "Konrad, if one of my SS men acquires even only a pin

of Jewish property, I shall ruthlessly punish the accused with death."[70]
As he nodded approvingly, Konrad's heart contracted. The stamp
albums piled on his office desk, the tapestries and the panoramic
paintings in his bedroom, all swung like the sword of Damocles in
his mind.

A week later, on January 17, Konrad led a group of his forced
labor Jews to the Lejzerowicz brothers' tannery on Gesia Street, a
business that supplied SS officers with quality leather goods. They
entered a large room heavy with the odors of rotting animal skin
and shaved animal hair. Between dry pelts and in barrels of chemi-
cals, Konrad was convinced, lay piles of cash. The Lejzerowiczes
had had a bustling business with the SS, and before the last brother
was murdered, he must have hid a treasure there.

Over the next several hours, the Jews sifted through the skins
and barrels until the tannery stood empty. At the end of the day,
Konrad lined up the Jews. Hand over everything, he commanded.
A couple of Jews produced a few coins and some pieces of jewelry.
You have no more? Konrad asked. All the Jews shook their heads.
Konrad approached the first Jew. He pushed his hands into his
pants pockets. He demanded another to open his mouth. He found
some jewelry and a couple of coins. One Jew had taken a few sugar
cubes. Konrad pulled out his pistol and shot two of the Jews dead.
Shoot the rest, he ordered his subordinates, and walked off as five
more shots echoed behind him.[71]

3

Inside the Ghetto

It was April 18, 1943. With no warning, the door to the office of SS-Oberführer Dr. von Sammern-Frankenegg swung open. Von Sammern-Frankenegg, Franz Konrad, and the other officers seated around the table turned their heads. In the doorway stood an SS officer. He wore dark leather gloves. A leather belt was tightened around his waist, its silver buckle engraved with a swastika and the words "My honor is named loyalty." On his chest was pinned an Iron Cross Second Class, driving goggles dangled from his neck, and a Tyrolean cap covered his narrow head. Glancing at the officer's collar, the assembled officers noticed a silver-colored oak-leaf cluster, and the gold-colored shoulder board of an SS Brigadeführer und Generalmajor der Polizei. Von Sammern-Frankenegg and his officers jumped to their feet and saluted.[1]

The SS Brigadeführer informed the officers that the Reichsführer-SS, Himmler, had personally ordered him to Warsaw to supervise preparation of the ghetto liquidation. He entered the room, ignored the officers, and stood face-to-face with von Sammern-Frankenegg. He introduced himself: SS Brigadeführer Jürgen Stroop. Continue plans for ghetto liquidation, he ordered. Von Sammern-Frankenegg, Konrad, and the other officers stood speechless as Stroop turned and walked out of the room.

His pants tucked into black cavalry boots, Stroop tapped down the marble staircase from von Sammern-Frankenegg's office, his gloved hands sliding smoothly along the carved wooden handrail. He stepped out of the SS and Police commander's headquarters into a bright morning. Sheltered between the backs of his Gestapo bodyguards, Stroop crossed the sidewalk, entered the open door of his car, and settled into the car's black leather seat. A bodyguard shut the door behind him. The driver ignited the four-cylinder engine of the Mercedes 170 and shifted gears.

Behind Stroop's Mercedes stood two other Gestapo cars. Bodyguards in full military regalia ran to the escorting cars. One of these bodyguards was Blösche. Two of his friends, agents Klaustermeyer and Rührenschopf, jumped into an escorting car. Beginning with Stroop's early morning visit to Dr. Hahn, the head of the Warsaw KdS, the three had been assigned to accompany Stroop wherever he went in Warsaw and secure him at any cost.[2]

Stroop's Mercedes, marked with two oak leaves on the finely curved wheel protectors, cruised down the lime-tree-lined Ujazdowskie Boulevard for a short visit with Dr. Ludwig Fischer, the Warsaw governor. Only a few days earlier, in Lvov in southeastern Poland, where Stroop had been stationed as the SS and Police commander for only a couple of months, his phone had rung. He instantly recognized the voice of the Reichsführer-SS from Berlin. Himmler ordered him to leave at once for Warsaw and supervise the upcoming ghetto liquidation. The incompetent Austrian intellectual von Sammern-Frankenegg, he told him, was to begin the liquidation on Monday, April 19. Himmler wanted Stroop to supervise his work.

Stroop embarked immediately on the 250-mile journey to Warsaw. He made a short stopover in Krakow to meet with Höherer

SS- und Polizeiführer of the Generalgouvernement Friedrich Wilhelm Krüger, to whom he would report. Himmler, Stroop was convinced, had selected him deliberately to fight the Reich's implacable enemy—the Jews. He knew that Stroop would act without mercy. Many times before he had proved his willingness to use any measures necessary against the Reich's enemies, such as when units of ethnic Germans that he had trained butchered hundreds of Polish citizens in Poznan or when his forces battled partisans along a road construction route from southeast Poland to eastern Ukraine. Stroop drove into Warsaw on Saturday night, April 17, confident that he would justify the trust Himmler had placed in him and that he would quickly deal with the subhuman Jews locked inside the infested ghetto walls.[3]

A cross the ghetto's redbrick wall topped with barbed wire, on a wooden floor at 44 Muranowska, Rivkah, wearing a kitchen apron, crouched on her knees and brushed feathers into a dustpan. She remembered her shock at the sight of the ghetto street after she returned there with other kibbutz members at the end of her summer labor in the fields of a local Polish landlord in Czerniakow. She had looked out the window to a street that once bustled with Jews. The street was empty. Even beggars did not sit there anymore; only feathers lay on the sidewalks and cobblestones. White down feathers floated out of shattered windows and over balcony ledges. The remaining ghetto Jews emptied their winter comforters and tightly rolled the remaining pieces of textile so children could smuggle them out and trade them for some meager food.[4]

Rivkah brushed dirt out of a kitchen cupboard. She was readying the house for the Passover holiday, which was to begin the next day, Monday, April 19. Ever since the summer *Aktion*, the Dzielna kibbutz had, for safety reasons, split into smaller groups, each located in a different ghetto apartment. At 44 Muranowska, where some top Judenrat members and Jewish policemen lived, a few kibbutz couples, including Shmuel and Rivkah, shared one roof. Also Tsvi Kutzer, Shmuel's friend with whom he had attempted to cross the border to Slovakia, lived here with his girlfriend. Rivkah had asked Kutzer's girlfriend to help her clean for Passover. The girlfriend refused. Rivkah, angry, toiled alone.[5]

Rivkah picked up a bucket and splashed water into the cupboard. She had not wanted to serve anymore as the kibbutz *baleboste* (traditional housewife). What she really wanted was for her and Shmuel to join a "fighting group," a small unit of five or six trained to resist the Germans when they attempted again to deport Jews out of the ghetto. She and Shmuel were young and athletic, devoted to the movement's ideals, and determined to fight to their very last breath. To Rivkah's deep disappointment, the heads of the resistance movement had selected others to join the underground Jewish Fighting Organization (ZOB)—a mix of different youth movements that had united to fight the Germans. Occasionally these fighting groups dropped by the Muranowska apartment. Rivkah hated it when they boasted of their military training and showed off the handful of weapons in their possession. She saw nothing that could explain why the kibbutz and resistance leaders selected these youngsters over her and Shmuel, why she was always selected as *baleboste*.

Rivkah walked to the large window overlooking the Muranowska and Zamenhof street corner. She had cleaned this window many times, but a stubborn stain stuck to the windowsill. With a knife gripped firmly in her hand, Rivkah scraped the stain. She recalled the day three months earlier when Tsivyah Lubetkin and Antek Zuckerman, two leaders in the underground movement, had stormed into the apartment at the head of a breathless group of fighters. They had been stationed at a kibbutz apartment at 58 Zamenhof when the news had come that a new *Aktion* had just begun. The poet Itzhak Katzenelson, who had lost his wife and two of his boys in the Great Deportation of 1942, called out in his prophetic voice, "The

Germans have killed millions of Jews, but they will not stand up to us—the Jewish nation will live on." In the apartment, the fighters quickly planned an ambush.[6]

Then the Nazis stomped up the stairwell. From other apartments they pulled out shrieking Jews. Two Nazi soldiers busted down the Zamenhof apartment's door. The armed men ran past Zacharia Artstein, who sat reading a book in the apartment corridor. They rushed to one of the rooms, searching for hidden Jews. Zacharia approached them from behind and shot both at point-blank range.[7]

The Jewish fighters escaped the apartment, and after a treacherous journey over the snow-covered roofs, they arrived at 44 Muranowska and proudly presented the inhabitants with weapons they had just plundered from the SS soldiers. But there was no time to celebrate. They broke up into small units and dispersed among other apartments. With their limited stock of weapons—a couple of pistols, a rifle, knives, and containers of acid—they took up positions. In one apartment they heard Nazis kicking down apartment doors below to screams of "*Schnell! Raus!*" Shortly thereafter, a soldier rushed into the apartment. One of the rebels shot at the German. Another soldier ran in, and two fighters grabbed him and dragged him to the stairwell, where they pushed him over the rail. He dropped all four floors, landing with a thud. Hearing the shots and seeing their comrade's smashed body, the remaining Nazis escaped down the stairs and out into the building courtyard. A Jew, standing on the building's roof, hurled a homemade hand grenade at them.[8]

Instead of being a part of such acts of resistance, Rivkah cleaned the kitchen. She completed scraping the stain on the windowsill and put down her knife, looking out the apartment window. In the courtyard, children stood in line to kosher dishes for Passover in tubs of boiling water. The home was tidy and clean, ready for the holiday. For supper, Rivkah served the last leaven, a thin slice of bread spread with jam, and a cup of coffee substitute. Next evening, Seder night, Rivkah planned to serve matzo, which just the previous week the Germans had permitted the ghetto bakeries to prepare.[9]

After dinner, the kibbutzniks retired to their bedroom. Rivkah too went to bed. A few of her friends lay awake and read while others played the "wood guessing" game. From a pile by the furnace, one person raised a piece of wood, timber that they had collected from abandoned ghetto homes and from furniture trashed in courtyards. He displayed it to the others gathered around him. The wood veneer was rubbed off on one side, proof, he claimed, that it had been a chair's armrest. With such a perfect round shape it can't be an armrest, argued another; it was a chair leg, he asserted. A third interrupted, claiming it was too thick for a chair leg. Deep nail holes in the upper part of the wood, he pointed out, indicated it must have been a closet strut. They all laughed at their Talmudic argument over a piece of wood, which landed a minute later in the fire. Tossing in a last piece before going to bed, the argument concluded in general agreement that one day all Jews—man or woman, short or tall, black or blond—will turn like all pieces of timber into gray ashes in Treblinka's ovens.[10]

Noise from the courtyard awakened Rivkah and she jumped out of her warm bed. Looking out the window, in the light of the full moon she saw Jewish resistance fighters, armed with guns, axes, or metal rods, knocking on apartment doors and windows. Every twenty-five yards around the ghetto, they reported, stood Askari men—Ukrainian, Latvian, Lithuanian, and other Eastern European collaborators, also known as Trawniki men. The meaning was clear to everyone: a new *Aktion* was planned for April 19, the eve of Passover.

Rivkah and Shmuel grabbed a sack with their belongings and ran out of the apartment. In the stairwell, neighbors ran to shelter in underground bunkers that ghetto residents had built after the January *Aktion* in the hope they might be safe from the Germans until the Red Army liberated Warsaw. Rivkah and Shmuel rushed down the stairs. Rivkah stopped—she had forgotten something. She dashed back to her bedside and grabbed her family photo albums.

With the albums under her arm, Rivkah again rushed down the stairs and entered an apartment. She removed layers of white feathers that camouflaged the opening of a hiding place and crawled in. Dozens of other Jews already sat crowded together, tensely waiting to see what the new day would bring.

Outside the bunkers and hideouts, beyond the ghetto wall in Aryan Warsaw, rays of soft morning sun awakened Stroop in his bed in a suite on the top floor of the luxurious Hotel Bristol, where he had settled in on Saturday night after driving in from Krakow. It was 6:00 a.m., April 19. Stroop rose, stretched his arms, and looked out the window at the grand buildings across the street. This was the day he would prove to Himmler that he was worthy of the trust given him. He looked around in satisfaction at his comfortable room with its walnut armchair and ivory-colored wallpaper. Stroop was convinced that when Himmler had visited Warsaw, he had stayed in this same room.[11]

In the suite's dining room, Stroop ate breakfast. He then went to bathe. Just as he was putting on his bathrobe, there was a loud knock on the suite's door. There stood a red-flushed von Sammern-Frankenegg with his head of staff, SS-Sturmbandführer Max Jesuiter. They entered briskly without waiting for Stroop's invitation. Von Sammern-Frankenegg reported that at 6:00 a.m., SS units had entered the ghetto on Nalewki Street in a two-arrowhead formation. Within half an hour, with Jews pelting the German forces with Molotov cocktails, a Czech-made LT-38 tank had caught fire, twice, and so had a Renault armored car. Armed Jews had shot and thrown hand grenades at the advancing ground forces. In short, the task of deporting the ghetto Jews had failed. Under severe fire, von Sammern-Frankenegg reported, the forces had disengaged, leaving behind their dead and wounded. One must, von Sammern-Frankenegg cried out, phone Krakow immediately and have them rush in Luft-waffe aircraft to bomb the ghetto.[12]

Stroop paused. "Now, don't be so excited," he calmly told von Sammern-Frankenegg. "I will do the job."[13] He strolled to his bed-room, leaving the astounded SS officers to wait in the living room. Stroop dressed in his field uniform, buckled his belt, slipped on dark gloves, and put on his Tyrolean cap. The officers behind him, he walked down the hotel staircase, out the entrance, and into his car. With the cars of his bodyguards and that of von Sammern-Frankenegg trailing, Stroop drove up Krakowskie Przedmiescie Street. He looked out the window at the pedestrians enjoying the early spring day in the Saski Park gardens.

The cars drove past the lifeless ghetto buildings on Gesia Street, emptied out in the previous summer's *Aktion*. A few minutes before eight o'clock, the short convoy arrived at the corner of Zamenhof and Gesia streets by the Judenrat building, where von Sammern-Frankenegg's staff stood in disarray.[14]

Konrad watched the approaching convoy led by a Mercedes 170 until it came to a stop where he stood. Blösche, Klaustermeyer, Rühr-enschopf, and other Gestapo bodyguards jumped out of one of the cars, rifles in hand. The door of the Mercedes opened and Stroop emerged. The scattered officers gathered around a makeshift table with a ghetto map spread over it. A few bullets shrieked by the of-ficers. After introducing his staff, von Sammern-Frankenegg pointed out to Stroop the positions of the various SS units, the Wehrmacht units, and Askaris—1,262 men in total. Konrad and Brandt updated Stroop on possible locations of resistance outposts. Stroop listened and asked questions. He then commanded Konrad, Brandt, and Kaleske to stick by him wherever he went. The briefing over, von Sammern-Frankenegg departed. (In the photograph, Konrad stands at the far left, Stroop fourth from left.)[15]

Stroop picked up the ghetto map, positioning it along Zamen-hof Street. Surrounded by his bodyguards and staff of officers, he looked up the empty ghetto street, where SS forces had minutes ago

encountered Jewish resistance. He saw shabby buildings, broken windows—typical Jewish living quarters, he thought. Within three days at most, he was confident, he would wipe out the Bolshevik Jews. Himmler, who was deeply concerned that Warsaw's Polish population might join the revolt, would reward him for his fast and decisive action. He would show these Jews which was the superior race. This short battle, he was convinced, would be over before Good Friday, April 23.[16]

Three blocks up the road from where Stroop stood, in their hide-out on the third floor of the corner building of Zamenhof and Muranowska, Rivkah and Shmuel lay curled up. Since six o'clock, the ghetto had been filled with the sounds of bullets and shell explosions. Walls shook. Plaster fell over Rivkah's head and tangled in her hair.

Rivkah could hear Shmuel inhale and exhale. Other occupants wept, one whimpered, another whined. They hushed each other and listened closely to hear if Germans were climbing the stairs. Rivkah hugged her family photo album to her chest. All those loved ones in its photographs, she knew, had already been murdered by the Germans. She only wished that her remaining sister, Dina, who lived in the Land of Israel, could know that she had died while resisting the Germans in Warsaw.[17]

There came a lull in the fighting. Rivkah and Shmuel nibbled their last food rations and sipped water from their cups. What little they had to eat and drink was running out. Rivkah and several others crawled out and into the once bustling building's stairwell, and quietly climbed one floor to the kibbutz apartment. As she opened the door, tears filled her eyes. The floors and windows, which Rivkah had labored so hard to clean for Passover, were covered with dust and shattered glass. A day and a half of battle had undone her week of hard cleaning.

They returned to the hideout with a supply of matzo and bottles of water. Sometime later the smell of smoke crept into their shelter. Rivkah looked out the hideout's window: across the street an entire building block was consumed by flames. Smoke and tongues of fire leaped out of smashed windows. A human torch jumped out one of those windows. The blazing body hit the street and lay motionless. In an upper floor, someone tried to extinguish the fire. Wailing and screaming mothers tossed their children down in hopes of saving them. Another person rolled a baby on the street to put out the fire consuming its clothes, hair, and skin. The screaming and crying was overwhelmed only by the collapse of the building's roof. Then Rivkah saw a group of Germans preparing to ignite another building. She pulled herself away from the window.

Half a block away, on 32 Mila, a young woman hid in a bunker. As a building adjacent to her blazed, she wrote in her diary:

> There is a terrible lack of air. People fall down, partly unconscious, on the ground. The enemy bombards [us] with grenades without a break, and sounds of machine-gun fire are heard without end.

Constant, nearly deafening thunder in the air. Despite all the dangers, Jews are running through the streets, in order to save [their] bare life [sic]. Everything is enveloped by fire. It looks as if the end of the world. Save yourselves if you can. It's terrible. Everything [everyone] wants to save [himself]—colossal struggle. Hell has come to earth. Dante's inferno—unbelievable and indescribable. . . . People lay in their corners without food or drink. Burning cemetery.[18]

Stroop stood on a ghetto street beside a burning building and observed the blaze consuming curtains, furniture, and window frames. He had devised this effective means of extracting the Jews from their hiding places on one of the first days of the operation. He was at the Judenrat building when a message came in that Jews had set one of Konrad's warehouses on fire. He hurried there, and seeing Jews rushing out from the flames he had his eureka: fire would drive the Jews out of their bunkers and raze the ghetto to rubble.[19]

Shortly thereafter, Stroop, as always surrounded by his bodyguards, stood at a safe distance from a dwelling on Zamenhof Street as his men started a fire.[20] Observing the smoke billowing up to the sky, Polish firefighters arrived at the scene. They pulled out their hoses, ladders, and axes and prepared to save the people in the burning building. As the firefighters rushed past the group of German officers, Stroop pulled his hand from under his belt and signaled them to halt. He looked up to the building's top floor. A balcony door opened and a mother and child walked out, flames leaping up from behind them. They waved their hands and cried for help. Stroop looked at them with scorn. Those vile creatures, a result of unnatural inbreeding, vermin who had attempted to infest the cultured German people and threatened humanity's well-being, indeed, its very existence, now stood and begged for mercy. He would show them the power of the German nation.

A firefighter raised his hose and aimed it at the walls just behind the mother and child. The water neared the balcony. Stroop
shot an irritated look at the firefighters' commander. Seeing Stroop's
look, Blösche rushed and struck the firefighter. The hose swerved.
Let that crap burn, Blösche shouted at the firefighter. Next time, he
warned, you will end up with a bullet in your head. The water was
turned off. The mother hurled her child over the balcony; seconds
later she too jumped to her death.[21]

A few days into the operation, Stroop and his officers returned
to the Judenrat building. Here, the Nazis assembled more than one
thousand Jews, some whom they had caught as they ran out of the

fire, others whom Konrad had lured from his warehouses with the promise of transfer to work in the east. The Jews sat in the shade of the monumental building and waited as Blösche, Klaustermeyer, and other Gestapo agents, relieved for a couple of hours from their duty to guard Stroop, searched them for valuables. After the search, they shuttled five Jews at a time into the Judenrat's courtyard, from where shots echoed.[22]

The entourage of officers entered the courtyard a couple of hours after the liquidation had begun. On the ground lay scores of corpses, facedown, a bullet hole in the back of the head. The courtyard smelled of sweat, blood, and excrement, an acrid stench that left some officers nauseated. The command group discussed how to get rid of the corpses. One officer suggested hauling them into the cellar. They could then be covered with dirt, he suggested. Bring in a road roller, Stroop suggested; that will smash and compress the bodies to the courtyard surface like asphalt. Several officers pointed out that crushing the bodies would not resolve the problem of decaying corpses. After weighing the options, Stroop and his men decided on the most efficient solution: set them on fire.

The Nazis called in the Jewish Burial Commando unit. The workers stacked the corpses four or five high, sprinkled gasoline over them, and ignited a fire. Within a few hours, the bodies had turned into a smoldering heap. Konrad came with a few of his men to rake through the ashes, picking up a diamond here and a gold tooth there.[23]

Blösche and three or four other Gestapo men left the courtyard to continue the killing. They returned gripping three girls and two boys by their necks. Konrad signaled the Gestapo men, their uniforms splattered with brain and gore, to release their grip for a moment. He raised his camera and looked through the viewfinder for an appropriate frame. Finally, he decided to set the photo so the children stood on the left, and on the right was the pyre, which they would join shortly.[24]

On Holy Saturday, April 24, at 5:00 p.m., Stroop's motorcade drove to the Brauer Company on Nalewki Street in the ghetto. Five days had passed since Stroop had assumed command of the operation, and the deadline he had set himself, to complete the mopping up of the ghetto within three days, had passed. Stroop blamed the delay on the swindler von Sammern-Frankenegg, who in return for money and sexual favors had closed his eyes to the Jews' accumulation of weapons, their building of fortifications, and their construction of bunkers. Besides, he rationalized, von Sammern-Frankenegg's failure on the first day of fighting harmed the troops' morale, and only two or three days into the operation was Stroop able, under *his* powerful leadership, to regain the soldiers' confidence.[25]

Stroop and his command group walked into the courtyard of the Brauer Company, a business that, among other things, restored helmets and produced leather jackets and wool socks for soldiers on the eastern front. It was bordered by several buildings that on "normal" days were home to 4,500 Jewish laborers. Now only thirty men stood in the courtyard with pieces of white fabric attached to their clothing. These had been sold to them for more than 6,000 zloty apiece by the devoted Nazi Herman Brauer, to assure their safety during the battle raging in the ghetto.[26]

Following Stroop was Konrad, his camera hanging around his neck by its strap. Beside them walked armed Gestapo agents, some with rifles resting on their shoulders. One of them aimed his rifle toward the Jews and shouted, "Raise your hands! Do not move from your place!"[27] Konrad, his eye against the camera's viewfinder, took aim. Just as one Nazi, looking for loot, pushed his hand deep down into a Jew's pants pocket, he took a picture.

The Nazis moved on from one Jew to the next in search of valuables. Two empty trucks drove up. Some men rolled carts carrying gasoline canisters into the courtyard. The SS men ordered the thirty Jews to load the helmets onto one truck and then to board the other one. When they finished, the truck holding the men drove off to the Umschlagplatz, from where they would be shipped east. The SS men then searched the Brauer Company for hideouts and bunkers, calling

on the remaining Jews to come out. Very few did. The Nazis poured gasoline on the factory floor and set the building on fire.

Eight hours later, past midnight of Holy Saturday, Stroop left the charred Brauer Company building. The scent of burned flesh still hung in the air. He looked back and in the dim light saw a familar sight: scattered empty gasoline canisters, blankets and mattresses on which Jews had attempted to jump from windows, dozens of charcoaled corpses lying motionless.

Stroop reached his headquarters on Ujazdowskie Boulevard at 2:00 a.m. on Easter Sunday, April 25. As on every day of the operation, he had to report to Krüger in Krakow on his progress. In his office, Stroop paced back and forth as he dictated a telex to Jesuiter, now his chief of staff:

> Today's search operation was . . . especially successful. . . . Our success is also due to the fact that the noncommissioned officers and men have become accustomed to the underhanded fighting and tricks of the Jews and bandits. . . . Today, toward evening . . . a particular block of houses in the northeastern part of the former ghetto was taken on. . . . At 1815 hours, the buildings were sealed off. An assault search party forced its entry and discovered that a large number of Jews were present. Since some of the Jews resisted, I ordered the buildings burned down. Only after the street and courtyard were ablaze did the Jews come out of the housing blocks. Many were on fire, and they tried to save themselves by jumping from windows or balconies into the street below, where they had previously flung beds, blankets, and other articles. Again and again, one could observe that the Jews and bandits, notwithstanding the gigantic conflagration, preferred to go back into the fire rather than fall into our hands. . . .
>
> End of today's operation: 25 April at 0145 hours.
>
> Today, 1,660 Jews were collected for transfer; 1,814 were pulled out of bunkers, circa 330 shot. Countless Jews burned to death. . . .

Altogether, a total of 25,500 Jews who lived in the former Jewish quarter have been apprehended in the current operation. Since there are only vague estimates as to the strength of the Jews, I assume that only very small numbers of Jews and bandits still remain within the Ghetto.[28]

Yearning for a few hours' sleep, Stroop concluded his report on an optimistic note: "As far as can be foreseen, the current grand operation will last until [tomorrow, April 26]."[29] All that was left was to set the remaining ghetto buildings on fire, then sweep the ghetto for one or two more days and Warsaw would be clean of Jews. After all, Jews could not disappear between the street's cobblestones.

Beneath the cobblestones of the courtyard at 44 Muranowska, below a layer of earth, bricks, and metal rods, Rivkah, Shmuel, and others crowded on raised planks and the floor of an underground shelter. Several days ago, she and Shmuel had escaped the fires, abandoned their hideout on the third floor, and descended the stairs into the cellar. Together with their fellow Jews whose bunkers had been exposed, Rivkah and Shmuel groped their way through a dark tunnel until they arrived at a door. They begged the bunker's owners to open up. The door opened a crack. A wave of warm, foul air hit Rivkah's face. The room reeked. Inside, she saw half-dressed people crowded together, sweating profusely in the close, moist room. Her first instinct was to stay out, but Rivkah knew that if she was allowed in, she would have no choice but to enter.

The men who governed the bunker briefly consulted and decided to let the group in. If they refused them, they feared, these Jews would get caught and either for revenge or in desperation betray their location to the Nazis.[30]

Rivkah and Shmuel searched for a place to rest. Men, women, and children huddled on the floor; none wanted to give up an inch of ground. As they stumbled over people's limbs, bodies, and bundles, a small spot opened and they squeezed in. Here they lay for days, moving only occasionally among the dozens of occupants.

Rivkah was surrounded by the heat-radiating brick walls and the wheezing of labored breathing. On makeshift laundry lines, the residents hung moist towels in a fruitless effort to cool the broiling bunker. Shmuel, like everyone else, dozed. In his sleep, he continually scratched his feet with his filthy nails, until they bled. Adding to the fear, crowding, and perspiration, the bunker was infested with fleas.

In the bunker, Rivkah adopted a new way of life. She listened carefully to noises drifting in from the outside to determine if it was day or night. If she heard grenades explode or a building crash, it meant, like the call of a rooster, that it was morning and that scores of German soldiers had returned to their job of destruction. It also meant that greater silence had to be observed than at night, when Germans also searched, but slightly less intensively.

In the morning, Rivkah picked up a container of jam and pushed in a spoon for her daily ration. The bunker's owners, who during the ghetto's "normal" days had run a grocery store, had stacked its cupboards with dry goods. None of it could be used. The smell and smoke of cooking would betray their location. Rivkah cautiously placed the spoon between her tongue and palate, twisting the spoon so that its scoop fit exactly over her tongue. She pulled the spoon handle slowly, swallowing the sweet fruity jelly down her dry throat. She repeated these motions a few times to make certain no jam remained on the spoon.

In the faint light provided by a single bulb hanging from the center of the bunker's ceiling, Rivkah, dressed only in her underwear, examined the world around her. Four walls enclosed a space roughly the size of an average living room. This represented the entire world for the dozens of residents; beyond was only certain death. Her home in this world was the same spot she had occupied

since her first night, a tiny square of floor. Only once or twice a
day could Rivkah leave her "home" and walk across the "world."
With heavy, numb legs she stepped over several bodies to drink
from the water faucet in the corner or go to the toilet to relieve herself. If she tried to get up and walk for any other purpose, she was
scolded.

Suddenly, there were sounds of heavy boots on broken glass
overhead; all the occupants awakened in fright. They kept total silence, choking off coughs, hushing each other, and staring at the
ceiling. The footfalls of three or four soldiers filled the bunker. More
followed.

Everyone listened. After an hour, Rivkah heard one person
stomp from one side of the bunker to the other. These firm steps
were followed by faint ticking and swooshing sounds. Their meaning was clear. The Germans had exposed a neighboring bunker,
and the residents were dragging their bags and suitcases across the
courtyard.

I t was early May when Stroop and his staff climbed the rubble of
a ruined ghetto building near Walowa Street, thirty feet behind a
decrepit Jewish man whom they had pulled out of a bunker a day or
two before. Stroop's commitment to complete the ghetto eradica-
tion within three days was a distant memory; it was the beginning
of the third week of the operation and he was still searching for
Jews. Only subhuman creatures, he thought, could manage to survive the fires he had set. Leaders in Berlin were raising eyebrows
about his progress, and Himmler urged him to complete the job
quickly, before Warsaw's Polish population joined the revolt. With
growing intensity, Stroop's special engineers searched day and night
for Jews in wrecked buildings, underground bunkers, and sewage
tunnels. When they uncovered a bunker or sewage tunnel, the
engineers drilled dynamite into the walls and blew it up. Anyone

trapped inside died from the explosion or under the collapsed debris.[31]

The Jew leading Stroop's staff, whom the Nazis had persuaded to help them by offering food and a promise to spare his life, paused for a moment. He looked around, trying to identify his location without the familiar landmarks. All about him lay wreckage. One of the Nazis urged him on. The Jew walked a few yards and climbed a pile of rubble.

Just as the Jew reached the top of the pile, Stroop heard him exclaim something in Yiddish, which he did not understand: "Girls, you are so fortunate, you are now being transferred to labor camps." What he said was immaterial—Stroop knew that another bunker had been exposed. Reaching the top of the pile, he could not believe his eyes. Three teenage women of the Dror He-Halutz, dressed in pants and wearing men's caps—Malka Hornstein, Bluma Wiszogrodski, and Rukhele Lauschvits—stood by an open bunker door. The Nazis seized them. They found one pistol. In the early days of the operation, Stroop had seen a similar woman jump out of a burning building at the brushmakers' workshop, curse the Germans, fire at them with two pistols, and run back into the fire. Never before had he encountered women such as these. Stroop ran forward, declaring, "Indeed, these are the true partisans!" These women, who had been fighting his forces for weeks, were more demons than human. Catching them, he was convinced, signaled that at last he neared the culmination of the operation.[32]

Noticing Stroop's enthusiasm, Konrad photographed the women. Malka gazed away from the camera with a Mona Lisa kind of look. A moment after the camera snapped, she was hit on her left temple by a rifle butt, and fainted. A powerful kick and a bullet blast woke her up. Her friend Bluma lay beside her in a puddle of blood. With their bayoneted rifles, the Nazis forced Malka and Rukhele to run through the ghetto streets to the Umschlagplatz as the Germans chanted, "We don't want, we don't need, a Jewish Republic."[33]

. . .

Beneath the marching feet of singing SS soldiers, Rivkah sat in almost total darkness and looked around at the exhausted, hungry, and sick who made up this "Jewish Republic." No light had spilled from the lone lightbulb since the electricity had failed a few days earlier. Someone in the middle of the bunker lit a candle. It flickered. In a cracked voice, another resident demanded that it be snuffed out. Candles consumed oxygen. The sound of the singing German soldiers faded in the distance and residents slowly moved about.

The following afternoon, as Rivkah dozed, a woman across the room coughed. People hushed her. Another man coughed. Suddenly, everyone seated near one wall moved away in fear. A heavy smell of smoke penetrated the cracks in the brick wall. All eyes and ears shot open. The building above was on fire.

From outside, the residents could hear German voices call on those hiding in the building to evacuate it. Kutzer, Shmuel's friend from Grochow, ran and poured buckets of water on the walls to stop the penetrating smoke. Still, the heat rose. One person after another fainted. The bunker had turned into a broiling oven. Flames were consuming 44 Muranowska; the shelter had turned into a death trap.

Fire also consumed a bunker at 32 Mila, where another young woman hid. She ran out clutching her diary of graph paper.

I go out into the street, burning! Everything around is on fire. [Whole] streets! Mila, Zamenhof, Kurza, Nalewki, Lubeckiego. Shortly put, all the streets are burning. Apartments are burning, workshops, warehouses, stores and entire buildings. The entire ghetto is a sea of flames. There is a strong wind, which blows out sparks from the burning houses to the ones which do not burn yet. The fire immediately destroys everything. A stunning sight. The fire expands so [fast?] that people don't have time to flee the houses and perish inside in a tragic manner.

The fire causes a huge commotion on the street. People with bundles run from house to house, from street to street, there is no rescue, no one knows where to take shelter. They seek desperately, nothing, no rescue, no protection, death prevails everywhere. The ghetto walls are completely surrounded, no one can enter or leave. Clothes are burning on people's bodies. Screams of pain and crying, houses and bunkers are burning, everything, everything is in flames. Everyone seeks rescue, everyone wants his life.

People are suffocating because of the smoke. All shout for help. Many, almost everyone, call upon God. "God, show your power, have mercy on us." God is silent as a sphinx and does not reply. And you, the nations, why are you silent, don't you see how [they] seek to destroy us? Why are you silent?[34]

These were the final lines in her diary.

Rivkah, Shmuel, and others scrambled to escape. They reached the exit and slipped into the tunnel. Groping along the tunnel walls, they ran into the cellar of a neighboring building.

Rivkah and Shmuel, sweating from the heat and gasping from their escape, hunkered under the staircase leading down to the cellar. Minutes passed. From upstairs they heard steps. Everyone froze. The firm voice of a Jewish policeman called on them in Yiddish and Polish. They would be saved if they came out, the voice promised. The Germans would just take them to work camps. A gruff German voice repeated the promise. No one moved. A round metal object hurled from above bounced on the cellar floor. It was a hand grenade. Rivkah's ears rang in pain. The floor became spotted with puddles of blood. Despite excruciating pain, people kept silent. Only when the footsteps faded in the distance did people cry out for help. Rivkah and Shmuel, who had been among the very few not hit by shrapnel, could do nothing to ease their fellow Jews' suffering.

Shmuel pulled Rivkah out of the cellar and into the night. They ran across Muranowska Street. They climbed over piles of rubble and across the ruins of apartment buildings. The air was heavy with the smell of smoke and burned human flesh. There was no moon. Rivkah stumbled over a deformed body. Rushing through a smoldering courtyard gate, she rolled down a set of stairs and into a cellar.

A group of starving men, women, and children lay there with their rucksacks. The cellar walls, burned out three or four days earlier, still radiated heat. Rivkah and Shmuel sat. Her eyes found a small hole in the cellar's wall, what seemed like a beginning of a tunnel. Noticing her look, a middle-aged man assured her it was a dead end. She sank in despair to the floor.

Early morning sunlight broke the darkness. The familiar sound of Nazi boots came minutes later. A few teenage boys ran down the dead-end tunnel. The voice from outside repeated the words, like an old scratched record: Jews come out. You are going to a labor camp. No harm will come to you. From her pocket, Rivkah pulled a white cloth with a blue Star of David, required of anyone older than ten years, and placed it on her sleeve. Shmuel did the same. Climbing out of the bunker, Rivkah blinked her eyes and was blinded for a moment by the sun's rays. For weeks she had not felt the sun's warmth on her skin. She was disoriented. Within seconds, her sight returned. A Nazi aimed his rifle at her. She raised her hands.

The Nazis hurled smoke bombs into the cellars. Gasping for air, the Jews surfaced. Screaming orders, the Nazis shoved the captives into the courtyard center. Rivkah and Shmuel soon stood with men and women carrying bundles and suitcases, jacketed little girls and cap-headed boys. One boy turned to the Germans and said in Yiddish: "Your end is not far. What you are doing to us will be done to you." His parents hushed the boy: "Don't talk, they will kill us." "Why are you afraid?" Shmuel asked the boy's parents. "We will not remain alive anyhow, so at least let him talk."[35] A stocky Nazi, the letters SD on his uniform sleeve and a helmet on his head, held

a rifle in his rough-skinned hands. He motioned them to march through the gate. Women and men squeezed together. A little boy put his backpack on. A little girl raised her hands.

The column of women and men, girls and boys with their hands in the air, marched out to the cobbled sidewalk where papers from the burned homes were strewn about. In the background one heard shots. The stocky Nazi walked a few steps behind them, his rifle ready. As she emerged from the courtyard, Rivkah saw another group of Nazis. A meticulously dressed narrow-faced officer, medals dangling on his chest, a Tyrolean cap on his head, stood there, his gloved hands on his hips. Just a couple of yards away from him stood a tall, light-haired officer with a camera. As Rivkah passed by him, the tall officer put aside a light meter. Her back to him, she heard a camera shutter snap.[36]

The Nazis led Rivkah and Shmuel in one of many columns of captured Jews destined for the Umschlagplatz. They walked between downed electrical lines, smoldering ruins, walls that in the past housed thousands of Jewish families and now, for thousands, served as their last resting place. Crows landed in between the shattered walls and well-fed cats crossed the ash-covered paths. After weeks in hiding, Rivkah didn't recognize these ruined streets. The ghetto existed only in memory.[37]

On Nalewki Street, another column of Jews lead by SS men headed to the Umschlagplatz. It included Thaddeus Stabholz, a young medical student who had been employed in the ghetto hospital. A group of smirking German officers halted the column beside a four-story building, of which only a façade with balconies and a stairwell were left. "Don't be afraid. You're going to be taken to work. Nothing will happen to you," they told the Jews standing against the wall. "The only thing you have to do is to give up your valuables and money. You won't need them now."[38] Just then, a

shrill cry split the air. The officers looked up. On the top balcony of the building, a young woman stood with a baby in her arms. She walked hesitantly toward the edge of the balcony. Nearing the edge, she swerved back toward the door. A group of SS men rushed up the stairs to fetch her. Hearing them, her back to the street, she quickly walked backward toward the balcony's edge, flipped over, and fell four floors with a terrible shriek, her baby still in her arms. A tall, blond-haired German officer took photos with his Leica. Two more men and a young girl followed the woman, jumping to their deaths, as armed Nazis shot at them like ducks in midair.[39]

The episode was over. The Nazis again demanded the Jews' valuables. A few handed over jewelry and coins. An SS officer ordered the soldiers to search the Jews. They shoved their hands into the Jews' pockets, then they spilled out their luggage. Stacked between rain jackets, underwear, shirts, and shoes, they found a few watches, coins, and bills. The SS ordered all the Jews to undress. Laughing SS men tore off women's dresses and underpants. They examined the

naked Jews like livestock, probing their open mouths, under their armpits, beneath breasts, up rectums, and in genitals. The SS ordered the stripped Jews to run, raising their legs high in the air, and then to sit cross-legged on the street. A metal tinkling sound came from the street. A ring lay beneath a woman. An SS man rushed to pick it up, pulled out his pistol, and shot her in the head. The search over, the Nazis ordered the group to dress and marched them off to the Umschlagplatz.[40]

S troop's command car drove into the Umschlagplatz—a complex of buildings, a yard, and a train station enclosed in barbed wire fence. From here, over the past year, the Nazis had shipped to the death camps hundreds of thousands of Warsaw's Jews. Stroop's entourage entered the Umschlagplatz yard, where tightly packed groups of Jews stood. It looked much like an animal pen, with excrement littered about the ground. Stroop and his staff stood at the yard gate as German soldiers and Askaris herded Jews into the main building, a former school, to await a freight train. Stroop inspected the men and women as they passed by him. Suddenly, he spotted a nineteen- or twenty-year-old girl. Her clothes seemed to hide a generous body. Pull her aside, he ordered. Stroop approached her and ordered her to undress.

Blösche, his rifle gripped in his hands, stood beside Stroop as he interrogated the naked girl. After she had completed her high school degree, she told Stroop in fluent German, she had traveled to Greece. She uttered a few more sentences, but Stroop had had enough. He ordered her to dress. He signaled Blösche to take her out and get rid of her. Blösche walked the girl out onto a ghetto street. The sight of her white skin glittering in the sun in front of all of the Nazi officers lingered in Blösche's mind. Stroop's behavior appalled him—enjoying the sight of a naked girl, humiliating her in front of his entire escort, and then sending her out to be executed. He pondered if he should kill her, as Stroop had ordered, or just let her go. Murdering her felt wrong. He stood there, the girl in front of him, and wondered what might happen if he allowed the girl to escape. But a command was a command. Suddenly, Klaustermeyer leaped from behind, seized the girl by her hair, and shot her.[41]

In one of the Umschlagplatz's rooms, on a floor fouled with clotted blood, feces, and urine, Rivkah, Shmuel, and dozens of others huddled. No water or toilets were available. Their thirst was unbearable; tongues stuck to their palates, lips swelled. They cried for water. No one responded. Anyone who stood up was shot from outside. Graffiti covered the walls, some inscribed in black pencil, others etched with fingernails into the plaster, all describing how in this room people had "died after long and terrible suffering."[42]

In one room, fourteen-year-old Halina Birenbaum hunkered beside her mother. Her older brother, Hilek, sat near them. Every few minutes, SS and Ukrainian men opened the door and cursed them. With their shiny boots they kicked the Jews, demanding that they hand over their gold, silver, and jewelry. The Jews, who had been robbed several times en route to the Umschlagplatz, had nothing left to hand over. Incensed, the guards hit and tortured them. Halina envied the lives of mice and rats.

The door opened again. An armed SS man entered. The Jews must surrender all their gold, silver, and jewelry. The Jews moved closer together. They had nothing, they told him. He was going to throw a bottle, and whoever was hit must rise. Halina covered her face with her hands. Her mother hovered over her. The bottle hit someone, then smashed on the floor. From under the body of her mother, Halina heard footsteps, followed by whiplashes. She stuck her thumbs in her ears, hearing and seeing nothing. Then she felt her mother's chest puff on her back. Her mother held her tears. Halina pulled her thumbs, opened her eyes, and looked out at the person being lashed. It was Hilek.

Several times, the SS man slammed Hilek's head with the butt of his weapon. Hilek stood silently. Another blow broke his glasses. Blood covered his face. Still he did not beg for mercy. Minutes later the Nazi left the room. Hilek crawled back, blood streaming down his face. He lay by Halina as their mother helped him clean his wounds.[43]

In another room, Rivkah and Shmuel sat on the floor. Around them lay several wounded and dead, shot by the guards. They had been there for three days. Then calls of *"Raus! Raus!"* sounded in the hallways. To the desperate Jews trapped in the room, those shouts seemed like liberation calls. The train that was to transport them had arrived.[44]

The door was unlocked, and Rivkah ran down the long corridors. Nazis and their collaborators struck at the rushing Jews with metal clubs. Racing down from the third floor, people slipped and fell. Rivkah stepped over the human pile. She was one of the first to sprint out of the building and into an open space littered with corpses. On the tracks stood freight cars with small guard huts atop. With her dwindling energy, after three days without water or food, Rivkah ran to the boxcar's open door, pulled herself up onto its metal floor and rolled inside.

Rivkah captured a spot beneath a narrow rectangular window and fastened her hands to the window frame. Against the rising human wave that boarded the car, she clung to the frame. Rivkah was squeezed between the press of bodies and the wooden car's wall. She could barely breathe in the tight space. After the last Jew had been forced in, the Nazis slammed the door shut. The odor of chlorinated water with which the Nazis had "sanitized" the boxcar stung her throat and pinched her lungs. Jews begged for water. Outside, a soldier reported to his commander the number of Jews in the car. The commander angrily ordered the door unsealed. German soldiers whipped the Jews by the car's door to make space for more. They pushed back to make room, crushing one another, as the Nazis loaded more onto the train. The door again slammed shut, this time locked and sealed.

Rivkah stood on her toes to escape the crush of bodies. Blood streamed out of the noses and mouths of some. A man vomited. The face of another person turned blue. People cried from pain. Others suffocated. The dead remained erect, held up by the press of human bodies. A small boy fell under the mass and was crushed to death. A frantic mother called out the name of her missing child. Rivkah called out Shmuel's name. She had not seen him since they had rushed out of the Umschlagplatz room. No response came. She tried again. Silence. She asked Kutzer, who stood by her, to search for Shmuel.

From atop the wooden box reverberated heavy footsteps. A thump of a rifle butt hit the roof. The locomotive sounded a toot and the train's wheels squeaked on the metal rails. It was late afternoon as the train shuddered and slowly rolled out of the Umschlagplatz.

Rivkah's heartbeat quickened with the sound of the train's engine. Again she called Shmuel's name. Had he fainted? Was he lying beneath her? She tried to see the boxcar's floor. Slipping down, she felt her face crushed by the bodies all around her. If she went down one inch farther she would not be able to get up again and would die. Pulling herself back up, she thought that possibly he had boarded a different boxcar.

A few minutes after they departed, the sound of the train's wheels suddenly changed. They were crossing the Vistula River bridge. If the train veered right, Rivkah knew, it meant their destiny was Majdanek. If it did not, their destiny was Treblinka. It veered right. Some chanted prayers, others cried out the fearful name of Majdanek. In the Umschlagplatz, Rivkah and Shmuel had agreed that once the train traveled a distance past the Vistula, they would jump out and join the partisans in the forest. Rivkah called out Shmuel's name for the last time.

Looking up at the small window, she saw the black night outside. She wasn't sure if she could squeeze through the narrow opening. Rivkah called Kutzer to join her in jumping out. Kutzer refused. It is an assured death, he called at her over the noise of the train. Even if she survived the jump, he screamed to her, the Poles would turn her in. Better to die jumping off a train than in a German death camp, Rivkah thought. With the support of Jews who stood beside her, she pulled herself up the wooden wall. Reaching the window, she breathed the fresh air that slapped her face and blew her hair. Only a few lit houses stood along the rails. She squeezed herself up, giving a last look at the silhouettes below. Shmuel was gone. Her legs pushed off and propelled her away from the rushing train as she sprang into the abyss.

4

The Road from Warsaw

It was mid-May, and Stroop was relaxing in the office of the SS-und Polizeiführer at 3 Ujazdowskie Boulevard. One task remained in his mission to liquidate the Warsaw ghetto: produce a final report on the grand operation. This report, Stroop intended, would not only summarize the military actions of the past four weeks but also serve as a stirring chronicle of his heroic activities. It was meant to impress the highest echelon of Nazi leaders and, he hoped, would result in his being awarded the Iron Cross First Class.[1]

On his table lay a pack of bristol paper, pencils, glue tubes, and a pile of photographs. How much had changed, he thought as he examined the office equipment, since his days back in the Lippe government building in Detmold. Just ten years ago, he had toiled as a clerk for hours to compose reports for the head of the Land Registry; now he was inspecting the equipment with which *his* staff would prepare *his* report. In Detmold he had described the extraction of one or two more pfennigs in land tax revenue from a reluctant farm owner; now he chronicled *his* impact on world history as forces under *his* command eliminated the eternal enemy of Germany from its stronghold in Warsaw. Back then he had delivered a report to the hands of a local clerk; now *his* report, bearing *his* signature, would be placed in the hands of the Reichsführer-SS, Himmler himself.

A knock at the door, and a staff member and a secretary entered Stroop's office. He signaled them to sit. Like an orchestra conductor performing in front of a full concert hall, Stroop waited until the room was in complete silence. Then he started dictating an overview of the recent history of Jews in Warsaw. Special restrictions had been imposed on the Jews, he began, "with the intention of protecting the Aryan population from the Jews. . . . The need to create a Jewish quarter in the city of Warsaw . . . became more and more pressing in the summer of 1940, when, with the end of the French campaign, even larger numbers of troops assembled in the district of Warsaw. At this point, the Department of Health strongly urged the establishment of a Jewish quarter in order to preserve the health of the German troops as well as that of the civilian population. . . ."[2]

Stroop continued. "It soon became clear that not all dangers had been banished by confining the Jews to one district. Security considerations necessitated that Jews be completely removed from the city of Warsaw," and with that aim in mind an *Aktion* had been conducted in the summer of 1942. The Germans' lack of control over the Jews in the ghetto was such that in "labyrinths of buildings, . . . rich Jews disguised as defense workers had found accommodations for themselves and their families and were leading magnificent lives."

He stood and paced the room, his boots on the floor the only sound. In the spring of 1943, Stroop recommenced, "the SS and Police Leader [Himmler] decided that a forced transfer be carried out by means of a three-day grand operation (*Grossaktion*). . . ." He paused, thinking of the four weeks it had taken him to bring the ghetto under control. Speaking in the first person, he added, "I cannot imagine another place as chaotic as the Warsaw ghetto. The Jews controlled everything." As a result of Jewish trickery, he went on, "while it was possible at the beginning to catch considerable numbers of Jews, who are inherently cowardly, it proved increasingly difficult to capture Jews and bandits in the second half of the grand operation."

Stroop sat down, leaning back in his chair as the secretary continued transcribing his words. "Only the continuous and tireless commitment of all forces made it possible to apprehend and/or destroy 56,065 Jews. To this confirmed number must be added the Jews who lost their lives in explosions, fires, etc., whose number could not be ascertained." He concluded his dictation on a high note. The Waffen-SS, police, and Wehrmacht, he said—also thinking of himself, but not saying so—"tirelessly fulfilled their duties in true comradeship and stood together as exemplary soldiers. . . . They must be given special recognition for their daring, courage, and devotion to duty."

The secretary left to type up the report. Stroop turned to examine the pile of more than one hundred five-by-seven-inch black-and-white photos, each with a quarter-inch white border, which he planned to include in a pictorial appendix. Most of the photos had been taken by Konrad; KdS officers had taken the rest.[3] It had been Krüger's idea to include the photos, and Stroop had wholeheartedly agreed. This appendix, he anticipated, would help elevate the report from simply another technical military memorandum into a historically valuable artifact, a graphic account that would symbolize for generations to come the Third Reich's persistent struggle and final triumph over the Jewish enemy.[4]

He picked up a photo. It showed a group of SS men seated on ghetto ruins with no weapons or helmets, enjoying a lunch break. It was decidedly not appropriate to the spirit of his album. He pushed it aside.[5]

The next photo showed bearded, sidelocked Jews. Here was clear proof of their inhuman nature, Stroop thought. He noticed the long hair of a woman on the left-hand side. He was reminded of when he ordered the shooting of a group of redheaded Jews, the worst racial category, the result of cross-racial intercourse between Aryans and Jews.[6]

Stroop passed the photo on to the staff member, who carefully glued it to the bristol paper. Stroop dictated its title: "Jewish rabbis." The staff member wrote these words in calligraphic letters, adding beside the title a small decorative tilde.

Stroop closely examined another photo. It showed a naked young Jewish woman. He paused. If he included it, he thought, some high-ranking SS officer might infer a fondness for bare bodies of inferior Jewish women. He put it aside.

The next photo swelled Stroop with pride: an image of himself, his arms at his sides, his chest decorated with medals, and his convoy of cars surrounding him; his bodyguards raising their weapons at both of his sides; flames blazing all around him. Here was the im-

Jüdischer Rabiner.~

age of a true German commander, calm and calculating. He named the photo "The leader of the *Grossaktion*."[7]

He flipped through the pile, pulling out a photo of his bodyguard Blösche standing with his machine gun behind a little Jewish boy. He did not remember where or when it was taken. Seeing Blösche and, slightly behind him and to his right, another of his bodyguards, Klaustermeyer, he knew he must have been present at the scene. This photo, he thought, would demonstrate the orderly manner in which Jews were extracted from their underground burrows. It would emphasize his command of the forces under his control. Stroop dictated the title: "Pulled from the bunker by force."

He glanced at the boy for a moment longer. Probably a seven- or eight-year-old. His son, Olaf, was seven years old too, but that was the only similarity. Olaf was bright haired, the Jewish boy was dark haired; Olaf's legs were powerful, the Jewish boy's legs were crooked;

Der Führer der Großaktion —

Olaf's bright-colored eyes radiated vigor and beauty, the Jewish boy's dark eyes showed weakness and fear; Olaf was human, a member of the superior race, the Jewish boy was inhuman, a member of the most inferior race, the race that plotted to eradicate the Aryans.

When Stroop completed sorting the photos, he flipped through them once more and handed his staff member a series of photos of the destroyed ghetto buildings, to be used in the final half of the pictorial appendix. This evidence of the razing of the once Jewish-infested ghetto streets would show the Nazi leadership the ultimate sign of his true and final victory. He gave the first photo the title "Views of the former Jewish quarter after its destruction." The rest of the photos did not need titles. They spoke for themselves.

On the following day, the head of staff, Jesuiter, presented Stroop with three leather-bound copies of the 125-page report, made up of his introduction, paper copies of his daily telex communiqués, and the pictorial appendix with more than fifty photos glued safely

to the thick paper. Stroop felt the reports' smooth leather covers, inhaling their fresh smell: a true work of craftsmanship, he thought. He gently turned the pages, careful not to harm them. The title of the report, taken from his final communiqué of May 16, was beautifully inscribed in calligraphic letters on the cover page: "The Jewish Quarter of Warsaw Is No More!" This report, he was sure, would elevate his status in Berlin.

On May 18, 1943, Stroop presented the report at a conference of SS and Police leaders, where he personally handed two copies to Krüger (he kept one copy for himself). A few days later, Stroop received a telex from Krüger's office requesting clarifications: the number of Jews apprehended in the ghetto; the number of bunkers exposed; the ammunition and money recovered; the condition of buildings. Stroop telexed the answers on May 24. Krüger's staff attached the addendum to his copies of the report and sent one to Himmler's office, where it arrived on June 2.[8]

Days later, Stroop got word that for his actions in Warsaw Himmler had bestowed upon him the coveted Iron Cross First Class. A special ceremony was organized on June 18, 1943, in Warsaw's Lazienki Park, situated between monumental palaces. The chief of the General Staff, Generalfeldmarschall Wilhelm Keitel, and Krüger honored the ceremony with their presence.[9]

Other Nazi leaders sent him congratulatory letters. In response to a letter from SS-Gruppenführer und Generalleutnant der Waffen-SS Maximilian von Herff, the head of the SS personnel office, Stroop wrote: "For the congratulations of the bestowment of the Iron Cross First Class medal, at which I rejoiced, I thank you. This award is for me a reason, even more than up until now, to employ myself for the Reichsführer-SS [and] his mission in our SS."[10]

It was early morning when Rivkah opened her eyes and saw rusty railroad tracks. She could not make out where she was or how she

had gotten there. She raised her head slightly, but a dizziness overtook her and her head dropped back down to the ground. She reached
for her face and felt warm moisture above her eyebrow. Looking at
her fingers, she saw thick red blood.

Rising slowly to her feet, Rivkah staggered for a moment and
finally got her balance. She looked around. In the distance she saw
scattered a few Polish farmhouses and barns. No ghetto buildings,
no storefronts, no densely populated streets. Standing in the morning sun, piece by piece her memory came back to her. She remembered the ghetto battles; she remembered her jump from the moving
train. But where was she?

She walked along the train tracks in what seemed the direction
to Warsaw. After days without food and drink and weeks without
proper sleep, every step was an effort. She halted every few minutes.
Then she spotted a barn and a few farmhouses near the tracks. Heading to the barn, she walked along a picket fence and through an open
wooden gate. A dog barked. In the yard she moved between a few
hogs and hens and opened the barn door. There stood a pile of straw.
She collapsed and fell asleep.

In late afternoon, a heavy stamp of footsteps aroused Rivkah. Her
eyes opened to stare into those of an astounded farmer looking down
at her. He caught his face between his hands, and before she uttered
a word called, "Oh, God, what are you doing here?! Quickly, run
away from here. There are many Germans and policemen around,
they are searching for Jews." Rivkah begged, "I have only one request. Please bring me some water."[11] The farmer rushed out of the
barn and returned a moment later with a full bucket. She devoured
the water, spilling it over her face and down her tattered dress, a wild
cough interrupting her gulping. Rivkah caught her breath, recalling
those Jews in the ghetto who had grabbed a loaf of bread from pedestrians and gobbled it down in seconds.

She put her hand in her jacket pocket in search of a mirror and
comb. She felt an envelope, which contained a few photos, including
one of her beloved mother, that she had salvaged before she escaped

the fire at 44 Muranowska, in which all her other family pictures were reduced to ashes. Her pocket also contained a gold watch and a few coins, which she had found at the Umschlagplatz. Finally, she pulled out the mirror and the comb. Looking at her image in the cracked glass, she saw her face covered in blood. Dry clumps matted her hair. She wet her hands to wash off the blood, combed her hair, and walked out the barn door and onto a gravel road.

Down the road she saw uniformed Polish policemen and Nazis. She quickly turned back, past the few farmhouses and into the fields. Sometime later she came upon a hamlet. A woman stood in a yard hanging laundry. Rivkah neared her. I am en route to Warsaw, she told her, and I can't find my way when it gets dark. Could I stay with you for the night? Seeing the cuts above Rivkah's eyebrow, her black hair and dark eyes, the ragged dress, the woman recoiled. "Do you know what it means to hide a Jew in my house? They will kill us all!" Rivkah beseeched her: "Maybe just for one night? I jumped from the train and I am hurt."[12]

The woman paused. She looked around. Then she motioned Rivkah to her home's back door. Rivkah walked around the house and entered the dining room. The smells of cooking stew filled the room and on the walls hung images of saints. Rivkah could hardly recall when she had last entered a Polish home and seen such images, or inhaled such an odor, let alone eaten such food. It had been years.

The woman placed a bowl of stew on the table and Rivkah took a spoonful. It stuck in her throat. She tried to chew, but after weeks of hunger she could not eat this kind of food. Instead she ate bread and butter. After supper, Rivkah showered her bruised body. The woman washed her ragged clothes and hung them up to dry. She cleaned Rivkah's wound, placed ointment on it, and covered it with a large bandage. She then offered Rivkah a linen-covered bed, the first bed on which Rivkah had slept since she went underground in the ghetto weeks earlier. Lying down, a blanket over her body, Rivkah felt pain in her arm. For the first time she noticed that in jumping from the train she had sprained it. She lay in bed and thought of the few Jews still breathing between the ghetto walls. Was Shmuel alive? Where was he now? What had happened to him? She had no answers. As she fell asleep, the thoughts of her survival, of Shmuel, of her friends in the ghetto tormented her.

After four days of rest, just before dawn, Rivkah readied herself to leave the farmhouse. At the door, she pulled out the gold watch and handed it to the woman who had risked her life to hide her. She walked away into the new morning light, journeying across potato fields and over small wooden bridges toward Warsaw. It had been almost a year since Rivkah had last passed by green bushes or the blue waters of running creeks, but advancing along brown mud roads she almost did not notice the scenery. Progressing through Polish villages, Rivkah did not know whom she could trust and who might rob, rape, murder, or surrender her. The only place she had friends, Rivkah was convinced, was in the ruined ghetto.

Along the road stood whitewashed shrines with icons of the Virgin Mary and Baby Jesus, each adorned with a large black metal cross. Flowers, candles, and other tokens surrounded the shrines. Passing by a village church, a group of children ran after Rivkah crying in German, "*Jude! Jude!*" The boys tossed stones at her. Rivkah reached the village outskirts and the children turned and ran back to their church school.

That night she shared a shed with cows. By day she journeyed along roads marked by wagon wheels, always fearing that a farmer would spot and surrender her. A path veered off the road and into a forest. Rivkah followed it, walking under the canopy of dense leaves that shaded her from the Polish sun. Then a voice from behind called her to stop. She ran, but the man and his friends reached her and grabbed her dress. They rifled Rivkah's pockets; everyone knew that the pockets of a Jew must be loaded with money. They pulled out her remaining coins. "Wait here," one of the men said. "If you want me to help you, I will try to do something." "Fine," Rivkah replied. They disappeared back down the forest path, and Rivkah raced away before the Gestapo could arrive to arrest her.[13]

She walked along a narrow road. Farmers in horse wagons shuttled to and from Warsaw. One, an old man, agreed to give her a ride. As the cart rolled along the twisting road, the aged farmer praised Hitler for ridding Poland of its Jews. Rivkah kept silent, trying her best to ignore his babble. They rolled into Warsaw's Praga district on the eastern side of the Vistula. Pointing at a group of Gestapo men in their olive-colored uniforms, the farmer whispered into Rivkah's ear, "Look, all is 'green.'"[14] These Nazis examined pedestrians' papers in search of the few remaining Jews still hiding in Warsaw and for Poles fit for forced labor in Germany. They pulled down a man's pants to examine if a circumcised penis would give him away as a Jew. Thanking the farmer as she quickly jumped from the wagon, Rivkah squeezed her way past the German patrols and boarded a tram.

Gripping the railing as the tram rolled along Warsaw's Aryan avenues, Rivkah looked out the window. Uniformed men walked along the wide streets. Large swastika flags fluttered in front of fine homes. Grandparents watched their grandchildren in the playground. The tram traveled over the Vistula, and Rivkah heard a whisper in her ear: "*Ladna Jydowska*" (Beautiful Jewess). Reflected in the window, she saw the white teeth of a smiling middle-aged Polish man. She paused for a moment, turned, and screamed in her rolling Polish, "Do you know what it means to say such a thing? Maybe you want to come with me to Szucha Street? Let us go over there and we will see who I am and who you are." At the threat of going to Gestapo headquarters, the man recoiled, his smile evaporating. "No, I did not say you were a Jewess, just that you look like a '*Ladna Jydowska*,' and everyone is looking at you." He pointed at a large rip in her sleeve and at the white bandage over her eyebrow. At the next stop Rivkah got off, swearing never to travel by tram again.[15]

She vaguely knew the area. Continuing by foot, she kept glancing over her shoulder for undercover Gestapo or Polish blackmailers following her. Turning onto a busy boulevard, she neared Muranowska Street. Once life at 44 Muranowska had seemed so difficult, but now, alone, on the Aryan side of Warsaw, Rivkah missed those days. Then she had a roof over her head, a bed, a meager meal, and, above all, friends. She walked hesitantly through the commotion of rushing people, trams, cars, and wagons. People bumped into her. She saw Nazi soldiers standing by the barbed-wire ghetto gate. Behind them black smoke still rose from the ruins. Walking along the redbrick wall, she searched for an opening. No sound of life came from its other side; all she could hear was the occasional collapse of a wall or building.

She passed once more near the ghetto gate and saw German forces patrolling the street. Not a single ghetto Jew was in sight, not even one being led to the Umschlagplatz. To reenter the ghetto, she realized, meant handing herself over to the Nazis. Turning her back on the ghetto wall, she walked off.

Rivkah drifted along the streets. Hours passed and the curfew neared. A handwritten note on a grocery store's window caught her eye. The owner sought a young and able woman as a sales assistant. Rivkah pushed open the door and a bell rang. The elderly store owner examined her. Rivkah presented herself as a hard and loyal worker. She would work for just bed and food. The store owner asked to see her identification papers. The Nazis had abducted her for forced labor in Germany, she told him in fluent Polish, and she had escaped back to Poland without her papers. He seemed to believe her, but despite his empathy, he could not give her the job without identification papers. In other stores, Rivkah repeated her story, and again and again shop owners expressed understanding, but without identification papers they could not employ her or offer her a night's shelter.

The curfew was less than an hour away. At night, Nazis patrolled the streets and arrested or shot pedestrians on sight. She had to locate a safe place to sleep. As she entered a building passageway, the wife of the superintendent spotted her and asked what she was searching for. She had come from a village to find work in nearby Czerniakow, Rivkah told her, and been caught by the curfew. Rivkah begged to be allowed to sleep in the building's stairwell for just one night. In the morning, she promised, she would go to the farm in Czerniakow, where a job awaited her. Did Rivkah have identification papers? No. The woman flatly refused. She told Rivkah she could still catch the last tram to Czerniakow. Rivkah did not move. The woman regarded her with a penetrating look. Rivkah saw in her eyes that she knew she was Jewish. "Maybe you do not have money?" she asked. Rivkah nodded. The superintendent's wife handed her the tram fare and some food. Having no other choice, Rivkah, who had just that morning promised herself that she would never again ride a tram, boarded one and sat by an Aryan-looking woman.[16]

Minutes later Rivkah arrived in Czerniakow. She walked over to the farm where she had worked with her kibbutz friends in the summer of 1942. She followed a stream amid chirping crickets and croaking frogs to the home of Zatwarnicki, the farm's landlord.[17]

Most of the windows were already dark. She decided not to knock on the door but to sleep by the stream.

Early the next morning, she woke up itching all over from mosquito bites. It was Sunday, so she hid in the thick bushes nearby to wait until mass was over before she emerged and knocked on the landlord's door. Moments later, a rattle of dry leaves behind scrambled her thoughts. A few steps away she saw men's boots. Two deep voices greeted each other in German. Rivkah did not move. She was convinced that the men could hear her pounding heart. The minutes seemed to pass like an eternity. Finally, the two bid farewell and turned away.

Rivkah crawled out of her hiding place, walked to the front door, and knocked. The cleaning girl opened. Seeing Rivkah, she rushed to call the landlord from his bedroom. When he saw Rivkah, he cried, "God in heaven, where are you coming from?! How are you still alive?!" He pulled her into the house and shut the door behind her. Rivkah told the elderly gray-haired man about her life in the ghetto, the Umschlagplatz, and her jump from the freight train. He shook his head in disbelief. All those who jump from trains, he said, either die on the spot or are surrendered by farmers and murdered by the Nazis. "As you see," Rivkah said in a bitter voice, "to my regret I am still alive."[18]

Early on a July morning in 1943, a tall, plump-faced young woman, her long eyelashes and thick lips carefully made up, walked briskly along a busy Warsaw street on the Aryan side. Shadowing her steps—so close that his feet almost tripped over hers—was an eight-year-old boy, a cap on his head. The pale-skinned child, whose charcoal hair and dark eyes matched his black shoes, followed the woman as she turned onto Dluga Street. Here the woman, Frumcia Nussbaum, slowed down as her nephew Tsvi remained only a hand clasp behind her.[19]

On the left side of the curving street, above the building at 29 Dluga, a sign read HOTEL POLSKI. In front of the hotel's gate was a group of people. Frumcia avoided eye contact with the milling men and women as she and Tsvi continued past the hotel.

A minute later, Frumcia swerved back, pulling Tsvi after her. Together, they made their way through the crowd and into a curved-ceilinged arcade. The sound of people chatting and laughing in the courtyard reverberated against the walls. As they emerged into the hotel's courtyard, Tsvi saw scores of people, some of them dressed in elegant clothes, cigarettes in their hands, chatting in what seemed at first an unfamiliar language. Then it became clear: they were speaking Yiddish. Tsvi clutched his aunt's hand. A window in the courtyard looked into the hotel's restaurant. The bar was filled to the last seat with customers enjoying light music and drinks. Young Polish waitresses carried trays piled with exotic foods. Here too people spoke Yiddish in full voice. Tsvi was taken aback. After almost a year of living with his family in hideouts, where speaking out loud was deadly dangerous, Tsvi was baffled by these outspoken Jews.[20]

Frumcia placed her arm around Tsvi's shoulder and pulled him through the crowd and into the hotel. She navigated their way through corridors where dozens of other Jews huddled over bags and suitcases. They continued up the staircase, where groups of four or five men and women leaned toward each other, whispering. Here were gathered feeble and unshaved Jews who had emerged hungry and weak either from weeks of hiding in the ghetto's ruins or, like Tsvi, from months of concealment. They had all learned of a German plan to use the few surviving Jews who, like Tsvi, possessed foreign papers, as bargaining chips for German nationals interned abroad. Those with foreign papers who sought a free ticket out of Europe, the rumor went, were to assemble at the Hotel Polski.[21]

Frumcia pulled Tsvi past a large group clamoring in front of a room where, in exchange for hefty sums, two Jewish Gestapo agents,

Lolek Skosowski and Adam Zurawin, offered forged South American passports or *promesas*—promises of citizenship. They continued along the corridors to a closed room where a smaller crowd gathered. In this room sat Engel, who entered people on the "Palestine list," Jews possessing passports, certificates, or promises for certificates, which would permit them to enter British-controlled Palestine. Further rumors had it that, unlike the Nazi-sponsored South American documents that Skosowski and Zurawin offered and promised to honor, the Palestine list was a Gestapo swindle. Tsvi and his aunt stood in line among the other edgy people waiting their turn.[22]

Sometime later, Aunt Chana, Uncle Shulim, and the other family members arrived from their hideout to the hotel and joined the line. For the Nussbaums, hiding on the Aryan side of Warsaw had become too dangerous. Their money was running out. Besides paying an exorbitant amount for rent and services, they had to pay blackmailers who knocked on their door and threatened to surrender them to the Nazi authorities. One day gentile-looking Frumcia, who supplied the Nussbaums with food and news, had told them about the refuge offered at the Hotel Polski. For weeks, they deliberated whether to emerge or stay put. To quit the secretive and perilous Warsaw apartment for the jungles of South America or the sunshine of Palestine sounded like a fantasy. It was too good to be true. Chana and Shulim feared that the Nazis had set a sophisticated trap for Warsaw's few remaining Jews. Their money, however, was nearly gone. Learning that key Gestapo agents Skosowski and Zurawin, as well as one of the heads of the humanitarian assistance organization of the Joint Distribution Committee in Warsaw, David Guzik, had taken their entire families to the hotel seemed to indicate that this was not another Nazi ambush. Perhaps it really was a true route out of German-controlled Europe. The Nussbaums decided to take the risk. Tsvi's authentic Palestine papers, they hoped, would save him and the rest of the family. In his hotel room,

Engel added the names "Nussbaum, Shulim," "Nussbaum, Chana," and the rest of the Nussbaums to the Palestine list.

Two other Jews who emerged from hiding places on the Aryan side of Warsaw were Jan Rolnik and his eleven-year-old son, Artur. From the Hotel Polski courtyard, Jan wrote a letter to his wife, Ella Sendowska, a musician who remained in hiding and who had placed their four-year-old daughter, Danusia, in yet another hiding place:

> I am writing this letter on the top of my knee. I am outside. There are hundreds of familiar people around here. . . . There are many [male] friends here and every other person is familiar. There are people here who are waiting already two to four weeks and not leaving thinking that this is a better refuge.
>
> Tomorrow a group of people is supposed to leave but I am not sure if they will. It all depends if Pani Ewa [the mistress of Gestapo agent Skosowski] is able to take care of everything. . . . There are people here who were discharged three or four days ago from the hospital [code for the ghetto]. There are also those who were in the hospital a week ago. . . . Some say that all this is a big deception and others remain full of optimism. . . .
>
> Artur cried when he found out that you and Danusia are not coming with us, but it just has to be like that for now or fate will dictate that anyway. . . .
>
> Artur says that they are too nice to us and they are trying to fool us. They select groups of people and send them out and these people get caught somewhere else and they are finished off somewhere else. Isn't this just a big shame and a lie?
>
> Pani Helenka [a friend] found me. She has papers and is leaving here on a Palestinian visa. . . .
>
> It is 7:20 p.m. There was Pani Ewa who said that my departure tomorrow is assured, but I have doubts. Those who were supposed to leave tomorrow got some papers. . . .
>
> I started [to] believe that all this is just a big fraud, for god's sake.

Please wait for my letters.

Artur is a great person.

Kisses,

Jan

Artur added a short note to the letter:

Beloved Mini [Mama],

I am letting you know that I am well, healthy, and worried. I
would like to see you so much, Danusia. I am so worried, but you
shouldn't be surprised because everything that happened scared
me so much. I didn't expect this. I am afraid they will [murder]
us all. Mama, I would so much like to see you again.

Loving,

Artur[23]

After writing the note, either Jan or Artur tried to erase the word
"murder," but it remained legible. That night, Jan, Artur, and an
acquaintance, Helena Goldberg, and her daughter left the hotel,
searching the streets for a different hiding place. After fruitless
hours of pursuit, they returned and slept on the stairs at the Hotel
Polski.[24]

At the completion of the ghetto liquidation, Brandt ordered Blösche
and other Gestapo men to the Pawiak Prison courtyard, where
some fifty Jewish policemen who had assisted in the liquidation stood
at attention. Brandt paced back and forth along the lines. When he
was assured that all were accounted for, he signaled to the Gestapo
men with his hand. They raised their rifles and aimed directly at
the Jews. The policemen, well acquainted with the procedure, raised
their hands high in the air. Then Blösche, Rührenschopf, and their
comrades hauled the policemen one by one to the ruins of a nearby

ghetto building. The shots sounded in Pawiak's courtyard, where the remaining Jews awaited their last journey. Blösche grabbed a policeman by his arm and led him to the neighboring building's passageway. Just as they entered, the policeman broke loose from Blösche's grip, swiftly turned, and punched Blösche in the face. Startled, Blösche tottered a few steps back. The policeman ran for his life. Klaustermeyer, who stood on guard, raised his gun and fired. The Jew fell dead.[25]

Brandt ran to Blösche, who was just recovering from the shock. He was infuriated, scolding Blösche for allowing a Jew to escape. Brandt yanked the rifle out of his hands and sent him back to the Pawiak courtyard, prohibiting him from taking further part in the killing. Blösche stood in shame in the center of the courtyard just a short distance from the policemen. Watching the other Gestapo men continue to haul policemen out and hearing their shots, he felt deeply humiliated, angered, and frustrated. He, who was such a dedicated soldier, who had fulfilled every assignment, who had

taken part in several of the ghetto's mass shootings, who had dirtied his clothes with blood and brains, was being publicly and unfairly reproached by Brandt for his one and only minor error.[26]

Just before noon on July 13, Nazi trucks drove up Dluga Street. German forces blocked off the street. The trucks halted in front of the Hotel Polski and Gestapo men armed with rifles and pistols jumped out. Brandt, Gerhard, and Mende oversaw their men who walked down hotel corridors ordering all Jews to exit. Rushing to comply, the Jews ran down the stairwells and out into the courtyard. Hundreds of men carried suitcases, while women and children held handbags and backpacks. In the flow of people, Tsvi stayed close to his aunt and uncle. The Nazis ordered family members to stand together. The Nussbaums clustered near one another. Before Tsvi towered Shulim and Chana; beside him stood his aunt Regina and her sons, Marek and Aron.[27]

Brandt pulled out a list of those who possessed South American documents. He read the names aloud, and men, women, and children with their luggage walked forward and onto a truck. Two Gestapo men placed a stool near the truck platform and assisted those who had difficulty climbing up. Some Jews viewed this as a sign that the Nazis indeed saw them as valuable bargaining chips; others saw it as additional proof of the trap the Nazis had set for them. Brandt called out the name of Frumcia, the only one of the Nussbaums who possessed South American documents. She walked forward and climbed onto the truck. Tsvi remained with the rest of his family.

Brandt had completed the first list. The trucks filled, the gates were closed. An empty truck backed up. Brandt started reading the Palestine list, three hundred names long. As one truck filled, another took its place. Eventually, Brandt called out, "Muller, Regina," "Naftali, Jochwet," "Naftali, Maryla," "Naftali, Michal." Each walked to the waiting truck. "Nussbaum, Shulim." Tsvi's heart pounded. "Nussbaum, Chana." Then Tsvi heard the names of his aunt Regina and his cousins Marek and Aron. Tsvi stood alone. Surely his name would come next, he thought. It never came.[28]

He remained alone, his large dark eyes searching for his aunt and uncle in the truck. Other Jews streamed past him to the truck. He stepped forward, toward his aunt and uncle. A stocky Gestapo man motioned with his rifle for him to stop. Tsvi halted and raised his arms high in the air. As in a photograph, time froze. The boy stood face-to-face with the Nazi. Shulim jumped off the truck and ran to Tsvi. Tsvi felt his uncle's arms embrace him. Kiss me, he whispered. They will think I am your father. Tsvi, his arms in the air, turned his face and pressed his lips to Shulim's cheek. Carefully, Shulim rose and approached the SS man. There must have been an error, Shulim said, this is my son. He must have been mistakenly omitted from the list. The Gestapo man refused to allow Tsvi on the truck. Let him on, said another Gestapo man standing beside them, but the first man did not budge. "What does it matter? Let him get on," the other Gestapo man repeated, "after all, he will be killed!" A second later, the stocky Gestapo man motioned with his rifle for Tsvi and Shulim to climb onto the truck. Tsvi was reunited with his family.[29]

Brandt finished calling out the names from the Palestine list. The soldiers shut the last truck's gate and signaled the driver to speed off. The convoy of Gestapo trucks exited Dluga Street, drove through Krasinskich Square and onto Bonifraterska Street, and motored along the ghetto wall. Looking out at the ruins, the empty streets, the burned walls, some of those standing in the trucks wept.[30]

Later that day, another convoy of trucks drove from the Hotel Polski through Krasinskich Square. Standing there, concealed behind a house gate, was Ella Sendowska, Artur's mother, watching the trucks roll past. On one of them were her husband and son. The truck drove into the ghetto. It halted at the Pawiak Prison. Gestapo men awaited these Jews. In the prison courtyard they shot Jan and Artur dead, together with six hundred other Hotel Polski Jews.[31]

Ella received a final letter from Jan, which he had written the previous night:

My Dear and Beloved Lady,

You asked me my love to leave you a letter. . . .

What can I write and tell you? There are no secrets between the two of us. You know what is in my heart, my thoughts and desires and everything about my entire being.

I want to tell you one thing as I am departing. I loved you, desired you, love and will love you always.

You must be strong and remember that you are the mother of children whom we both adore. Don't give up. Take care of Danka, Krysia, and Marysia. You should be a support for each other.

This awareness will make it easier for you to go on and fight for the rest of your life.

I believe that one day, we will be together and we will start a new life over again.

Kisses and hugs also for Danusia.

Yours forever,

Your,

Jan[32]

The truck carrying the Nussbaums rumbled into the Gdansk train station in the northern part of Warsaw. The Nussbaums got off, Tsvi with his backpack and Chana and Shulim with a suitcase. They climbed up the stairs to the train platform, where members of the Red Cross, Swiss diplomats, and journalists awaited them. They handed out food parcels. The children received candy. The names of the Jews were read. One of the officials pulled out a camera and took photos of the Hotel Polski Jews.[33]

The South American and Palestinian Jews boarded a passenger train. Some relaxed and smiled, feeling slight optimism: after all, they were not standing in a cramped cattle car but sitting on upholstered seats. SS men with whips and dogs hadn't driven them onto the train; Swiss diplomats registered and photographed them. The Nazis did not search their bags for valuables but handed them paint to mark their luggage.

The train slowly rolled out of the station with hundreds of Jews aboard. The locomotive whistled as it passed Warsaw's last buildings and sped into the countryside. Staring out the window, Tsvi and the other children saw orchards laden with fruit, farmers picking vegetables in fields, a woman drawing water at a village well, a group of young Poles refreshing themselves in a creek. Jewish children ran up and down the train's narrow passageway. Mothers called out "Bobush, don't lean out, Bobush, you'll fall out. Will you eat something, my treasure?" To some it seemed like the old days, when they had journeyed out for a summer vacation on the Baltic Sea.[34]

The train arrived late that day in Berlin, where it stood for hours. The passengers received no food or water and had to rely on their own supplies. A few people dozed while others could not fall asleep. One passenger complained that another took up too much space; another was angered by a baby's cry.

The following morning, the train rolled out of the station and continued west. The train shook and banged as it passed trains bound east. Out the window, Tsvi saw rows and rows of rail tracks, some veering right, some veering left. In late afternoon, the train swerved off the main track onto a side route. The passengers peered out, noticing the train was on a single-track route. There was no parallel track back. The faces, which had left Warsaw full of hope, fell.[35]

Outside, in the darkening light, they saw no houses, no fields, no villages or towns, just overgrown shrubs and sandy moors. Some passengers said the train was traveling in the Lüneburg Heath near Hannover. It started raining and nothing was visible through the train's murky windows. The few children still playing between the train seats returned to their places. Some fell asleep on their elders' laps. Others, noticing their parents' anxiety, remained silently awake as they traveled on to an unknown destination.[36]

An hour later the train came to a halt. Outside all was pitch-dark. Then torchlights neared the train, beaming into the windows. The train doors slammed open and the scream *"Aussteigen!"* filled the train's cabins. Frenziedly, mothers awakened their children and pushed them toward the door. They disembarked in the middle of a forest. People whispered to each other: "This is the end . . . gas chambers . . . We are lost . . . It was your idea. Didn't I tell you it would end like this? . . . Why did you drag me here, you fool?" The SS ordered men and women to separate. Tsvi joined Chana, Frumcia, Regina, and her children. Shulim was forced to join the men. One woman swallowed a capsule of cyanide and collapsed dead.[37]

The Jews stood in rows of five in the pouring rain. Passing in between them, SS men aimed flashlights into their faces, counting and recounting. Only when they had an exact inventory of the Jews present did the Nazis command the women and children to board tarpaulin-covered trucks. Tsvi, his cousins, and his aunts climbed up and trampled over the mass piled within. Mothers tried to calm crying infants as the truck bumped up a narrow, pitted road. After a few minutes' drive, the truck stopped. From beneath the tarpaulin on this rainy night, in the light pouring from the truck's headlights, the Jews saw a barbed-wire fence. A gate opened and all the trucks drove in. It was July 15, 1943, and eight-year-old Tsvi, his aunts, cousins, and uncle, and the hundreds of other Hotel Polski Jews had arrived at the concentration camp of Bergen-Belsen.[38]

I t was the fall of 1943 and Rivkah roamed the Polish countryside under skies that grew grayer and grayer by the day. With the nearing of winter, Rivkah could no longer sleep in abandoned ruins or in fields under the dim moon. The landlord Zatwarnicki at the farm in Czerniakow had been able to offer her only some money and food. His other laborers knew her; Rivkah had to move on. Dressed as a Polish farm woman, she had, over the past months, gone from village to village in search of work, food, and a bed. Farmers, hearing that she had escaped forced labor in Germany without identification papers, nodded their heads, handed her a loaf of bread, a few potatoes or carrots, and told her they could not offer her work or shelter. At most, they allowed her to remain with them for a night.

As the days grew shorter, farmers assembled every working hand—women, children, and elders—to gather in the crops. On one harvest day, Rivkah approached the landlord of a large farm. Desperate to have his ripe vegetables picked before winter's first snow, he agreed to employ her—food only, no shelter. Rivkah agreed, hoping that over time the landlord would let her sleep on the farm.

Between the field's long rows, Rivkah bowed down like the local women to pick vegetables. During the morning break she tore bread and chewed loudly just like them. She was careful to talk in simple words and affect an uneducated pronunciation. When the other women sang folk songs, she listened and joined in one beat behind. After hours working in the vegetable fields, Rivkah lagged behind the other women. Her back ached and occasionally blood dripped from her nose. She presented the farmer with her half-full bag of vegetables. He pointed at the other women's bags. "See how they are working and how you are working—it can't continue this way."[39] Rivkah doubled her effort to keep up with the Polish farmworkers and the landlord finally offered her a place to stay.

One weekend, the landlord's only son, who studied at a university in Warsaw, came home with some of his friends. Whenever anyone neared the group of students, they hushed one another up. On Sunday, when the other family members went to church, Rivkah approached the son, who was conspicuously not attending services. Gathering her courage, she asked him if he was associated with the Communist Party. He was reluctant to answer. Then Rivkah told him she was Jewish, that she was a member of the Jewish resistance movement in the Warsaw ghetto, and asked point-blank if he could help her get a Polish identity card. The son answered, "I know you are Jewish and I will help you."[40]

Weeks later, the landlord called her over. "Tomorrow morning," he said, "we will take you to a certain address in Warsaw. There people will come and take you. They will arrange papers for you."[41] That night the son arrived, and the next morning he took her with him into Warsaw. They passed German patrols and arrived safely at his apartment. She must stay there for a week, he told her, until she could go and have her photo taken. After that, he added, it would take two more weeks to prepare her Polish identification papers. Before heading to the photo shop, Rivkah put on a flowery dress and combed her hair in the style of an educated woman.

Two weeks after her photo was taken, Rivkah walked all the way

to the center of town. She turned into an alley where the forger had told her to meet him, making sure that no undercover Gestapo agent or Polish blackmailer was trailing her, raising her eyes to see if anyone was watching from a window. The forger stood at the far end of the alley, waving an envelope at her. When she reached him, he unsealed the envelope and pulled out identification papers with her photo atop. They were first-rate forgeries—the purple stamp seal looked authentic, the paper quality was good, and the height, eye color, and age all seemed to match her perfectly. The forger dipped Rivkah's fingertip in black ink, stamped it on the identification card, and handed her the papers. From now on, her birth name was Sophia and her nickname Zosia.

With the identification papers in her bag, beside a copy of the Catechism, Rivkah, gaining confidence, boarded the tram to the home where she would stay until she found work. When she stepped off the

tram minutes later, Rivkah knew by heart her new date and place
of birth, her parents' names, and her mother's maiden name. She
had memorized the date of her baptism and the names of her childhood friends. In her childhood stories, she replaced "Shabbes" with
"Sunday," "synagogue" with "church," "Passover" with "Easter,"
and "Sarah" with "Maria."

Shortly after 5:00 p.m. on a September evening in 1943, Blösche
traveled to the center of Warsaw with his fiancée, Suzanne Held,
an ethnic German five years his senior. They had met a couple of
months earlier in the Gestapo building, where she was employed as
a translator. Blösche felt slightly inferior to Held. She had passed
the qualifying exam, she tutored the children of a wealthy family
in Poznan, and she knew several languages. Whenever she raised
the topic of their wedding, Blösche grew defensive. He would not,
he declared, get married in a church, as Held wanted. He would
not, he further stated, take out a loan to begin life together.[42]

Held and Blösche joined the stream of pedestrians headed home
after a day's work. As they were walking, Blösche heard from behind him the sharp sound of a metal object hitting the ground. He
halted and turned. On the sidewalk lay a loaded 9-mm handgun
magazine. He picked it up and looked around to see who had dropped
it. Suddenly, from between the flow of pedestrians, a gun barrel
pointed at him. Two loud blasts rang in his ears. He collapsed. There
was a moment of silence. Held shrieked. The pedestrians ran off.
Blösche felt pain radiating out from his belly, and he fell to the sidewalk. An SS officer who just happened to be driving by stopped his
car, loaded the bleeding Blösche into it, and delivered him to German Military Hospital number 9.[43]

In the emergency room, blood streamed from Blösche's wounds,
spreading over the white hospital linens. He groaned from the pain
as doctors and nurses scrambled around him. Blösche had been hit

in the abdominal wall. It was a relatively minor wound and no operation was needed. He was extremely fortunate; he would live. The doctors sterilized the wound, bandaged Blösche, and moved him to a ward.

The next day, Dr. Hahn came to visit. Blösche described the events of the previous day. Hahn informed him that a German officer had run after the assassin, caught up with him at the end of an alley, and shot him dead. He was the son of a Polish professor. In retaliation for his injury, Blösche knew, the life of the assassin would not suffice. The Germans would demand a higher price in the lives of Polish citizens. After any incident in which one of their men was wounded or killed, the Nazis executed randomly selected Polish citizens pulled from Warsaw's streets.[44]

After a couple of weeks at the hospital, Blösche was sent home to Frydlant, and then on to the vacation town of Zakopane in the south, to recover.[45]

. . .

The day after she received her new identification papers, Rivkah, now known as Zosia, searched the newspapers for work. No longer satisfied with just food and a bed, she wanted a paying job. There was an advertisement by a pharmacy seeking a cleaning woman. She traveled to the suburb of Mokotow, where the pharmacy's owner examined her papers. He gave her a penetrating look. Then he and his wife offered her a job caring for the house and looking after their son. Rivkah was delighted, especially since the pharmacy owners' home was relatively isolated. Her risk of exposure was that much less.[46]

She cleaned and cooked, and on clear days after the baby woke up from his morning nap, Rivkah readied to go out. She changed the baby, packed a basket of fruit, and before leaving carefully examined herself in the mirror to make sure that she looked sufficiently Polish. Pushing the carriage up the road, passing other women strolling with baby carriages or sitting by them on benches in the park, she heard them whisper, "She does look like a Jewess" or "She does not look so much like one."[47] One Sunday after mass, Rivkah walked back home with the baby's mother, who told her about the murder of the neighborhood Jews. Rivkah remained silent. The mother then looked deep into Rivkah's black eyes, and Rivkah feared her secret had been uncovered. It was time to move on.

Rivkah traveled from one village to another. In one marketplace, a merchant wrapped his produce with paper ripped from a Hebrew prayer book. At another market stand, a Polish woman bargained over the price of the wool taken from a Jewish prayer shawl. In almost every village stood a burned or ruined synagogue. And on many door frames she noticed small gaps in the wood where once a mezuzah had been affixed.

It was in the final months of 1943, as light snow fell upon wooden roofs and forest trees, that Rivkah spotted an advertisement for a shop assistant hanging in the window of a grocery store in Rembertow, a town northeast of Warsaw. She entered and offered herself for the job. The store owner asked about her experience. She said nothing about her work with the pharmacy owners. Rather, Rivkah told him that she used to trade in cigarettes but had quit that work. She pointed at the deep scar above her eyebrow. On a trip she had made to Lublin, she told the shop owner, a German gendarme stopped her on the street to examine her bag. Seeing the stashed packets of cigarettes, he took them all, slammed his gun's butt over her eye, and walked off. She had fallen down and fainted. Pedestrians helped her up and bandaged her wound. Upon hearing her story and examining her papers, the shop owner offered her the job. It came with lodging and pay as well as one Sunday off per month.

On weekdays, Rivkah handed a batch of eggs or a kilo of flour to locals. After attending Sunday mass, she ran through the wintry streets to the owner's coffeehouse, next to the grocery store, to set tables, put out chairs, and brew drinks for the German soldiers of a local outpost. Inside the warm coffeehouse, the Nazi soldiers sat and smoked over steins of beer, singing German folk songs. Some of the tipsy soldiers attempted to embrace the girl with the cross necklace who stood behind the bar. Rebuffing their advances, Rivkah filled the pints of beer for the merry soldiers.

As the weeks went by, Rivkah, the shop owner, and his wife became friends. The couple invited her to join them in their Sylvester Night party for the upcoming new year of 1944. They also invited some German friends. It was a merry party with vodka, folk songs, hugs and kisses. So no one would suspect her, Rivkah participated enthusiastically in the celebration.

The next day, New Year's Day, she woke up with a hangover. Rivkah could not remember the previous night. Had she given away her Jewish name? Had she uttered a Yiddish word? Had she exposed her deepest fears? The look on the shop owner's face that morning, she thought, indicated that he knew something.

That afternoon she said she was leaving. She explained that her mother was ill and she must go immediately. The shop owner's wife hugged and kissed her and asked her to stay. Rivkah insisted she had to leave. The wife gave her some food and paid her salary above and beyond what she was owed. Before she left, she hugged her once more. "Zosia," she said, "if you ever need help, come to us: we will always help you."[48]

In September 1943, accompanied by eleven staff members, Stroop boarded a Luftwaffe plane in Berlin. The plane climbed over the capital of the "Thousand-Year Reich." Looking out the portholes, Stroop admired the wide avenues, the monumental buildings, and the vast German lands that reached beyond the horizon. As if traveling in an honor parade, two Luftwaffe Messerschmitt warplanes accompanied him as he flew southeast. Just a few weeks earlier, Himmler had summoned Stroop from Warsaw to promote him to the position of Höherer SS- und Polizeiführer of Greece.

En route to Athens, Stroop's plane stopped in Belgrade, where he lunched with the heads of the local German police and army. He learned that the Italians had signed an armistice with the Allies, leaving the Germans to control Greece alone with the support of local collaborators. After a short stopover in Salonika, Stroop landed in Athens later that day and summoned Greek prime minister Ioannis Rallis and minister of the interior Anastasios Tavoularis to his office. He informed them that from now on he would be the sole authority in Greece. They would report directly to him.[49]

A month after antagonizing other Germans stationed in Greece, in early November, Stroop was ordered back to Germany. Himmler had promoted him to Höherer SS- und Polizeiführer of Rhein-Westmark.[50] From his castlelike office at 5 Uhland Street in Wiesbaden, Stroop had at his immediate disposal 10,000 policemen and, in case of an emergency, an additional force of 126,000 armed men.

Within his territory of 20,000 square miles, between Lorraine in the west and Frankfurt in the east, were 90,000 POWs and 300,000 forced laborers. He presided over the Allgemeine SS and oversaw the Higher SS and Police courts.[51]

In Wiesbaden, the Stroop family moved into a seventeen-room home in Nerotal, an upscale neighborhood; its previous owner had been a Jewish banker. On his few days home, when he was not off inspecting one of his far-flung units, Stroop ate dinner prepared by the family cook in a room decorated with paintings of battlefield scenes and of cheering peasants to the background music of a Wagner opera.

In his home office, Stroop was surrounded by pictures of Frederick the Great, Bismarck, Mackensen, Hermann der Cherusker,

Hitler, and Himmler. On a Persian rug stood a glass cabinet. It contained Stroop's SS sword, a dagger, an SS ring engraved with a skull, a *Julleuchter* (porcelain candlestick), and insignia, all presented to him personally by Himmler for his achievements. In Wiesbaden, Stroop also kept his personal copy of "The Jewish Quarter of Warsaw Is No More!"[52]

As the year 1944 progressed, sirens wailed with growing frequency in Rhein-Westmark, as in the rest of Germany, warning residents of imminent bombings. Allied plane squadrons droned above and antiaircraft guns blasted. Behind blackout curtains, lightbulbs flickered and windows shattered. From his car window, Stroop saw mothers run with their children to bomb shelters. He also saw residents frantically dig through ruins to excavate someone buried in the rubble. Others gesticulated, crying in despair before burned homes or cremated children. Schools and cathedrals, entire city centers in Frankfurt, Mainz, and Darmstadt stood like smoking skeletons. Ash filled the air, and Stroop breathed in the familiar scent of burned human flesh.[53]

The "terror fliers" who had caused this havoc, those who set large city neighborhoods on fire, Stroop thought, were uncivilized and without human compassion. Based on a secret directive from Himmler, Stroop ordered his subordinates to allow the locals to unleash their anger against any Allied fliers who parachuted down. Any air crew member turned over to security forces, he emphasized, must be shot dead. Encouraged, crowds lynched some American and British pilots, and the security forces murdered others.[54]

One winter night when Stroop stayed home, 1,252 RAF planes bombed Wiesbaden and Karlsruhe. The bombs screamed and exploded, and the house shook. In the cellar, Olaf was shaking with fright, and Stroop was pained by his son's fear. Still, he was confident that despite all difficulties, despite all terrible hardships, despite the seemingly pointless struggle, the Third Reich under the Führer's leadership would overcome the Jewish conspiracy of world powers and go on to eventually win an ultimate victory.[55]

. . .

In late 1944, Rivkah heard the pounding of Soviet artillery grow louder and louder and saw the battered and disarrayed German soldiers withdraw through Radosc, a suburb of Warsaw, where she now lived and worked under her false identity. When the Red Army's armored vehicles rolled into town, Poles filled the streets, laughing and embracing each other, cheering and celebrating their new freedom. Rivkah stood in her room and watched out the window. She was unable to join the festivities. Over the past five years she had awaited and dreamed about this moment. But now that the liberating troops were finally here, she felt no sense of redemption, no sense of happiness, no jubilation. Instead, for the first time, she felt overwhelming pain and grief for the countless missing friends and family members.

A few days later, she packed her belongings and without taking her wages left the home of the Polish family for whom she had worked. No more did she need to examine her Polish look in the mirror before she went out or watch if someone was following her. She wandered the streets aimlessly. Her feet led her to the suburb of Praga, where dozens of Jewish survivors gathered around a building in which a Jewish aid organization had established an office. On the walls of the building, people posted notices requesting information about the fate of family members. No one searched for her.[56]

Rivkah rented an apartment with another female survivor who had lived undercover. Other Jews joined them to form a small commune. They picked apples and dug up carrots from abandoned orchards and farms. Unable to travel to Warsaw, which was still under German control, they went to Lublin and spread their harvest for sale on sidewalks. Some pedestrians bought their fruits and vegetables; others cursed the Jews for reappearing on Polish streets.[57]

. . .

In mid-1944, in German-controlled Warsaw rumors of an upcoming Polish revolt grew stronger day by day. Life had become more and more dangerous for Germans, and the Nazi authorities decided to evacuate women and children. In anticipation of a Polish revolt, the Nazis had also reinforced their units in Warsaw with every available man, and Blösche, who since his injury less than a year earlier had served in the Gestapo archives, returned to active duty patrolling the streets. On August 1, Blösche was on patrol when sounds of gunshots spread across the city. The Polish Home Army began its revolt. Blösche and his squadron returned to headquarters on Szucha Street.

Over the next days, the headquarters was under constant attack from the Polish rebels. The German commander positioned Blösche on the second floor, where he lay amid the toppled office furniture, shards of broken glass, and scattered paper, his eye glued to his rifle's scope, searching for movement in the window of a building across the street. He struggled to keep his eyes open after several days' fighting. Every few minutes, Blösche's eyelids gave in and he dozed, until his rifle fell sideways and he awoke with a start. He raised the rifle, pulled it up against his cheek stained black by sweat and dirt mixed into his unshaven beard, and placed his eye back against the scope. At any movement in the distant window, he released a shot.[58]

The German forces in Gestapo headquarters were under siege for more than ten days, bullets buzzing by their ears. In mid-August, the Wehrmacht broke its way through to Szucha Street, freeing Blösche and the other Nazis holed up there. In the coming days, Blösche battled rebels in the streets. Nazi forces executed many hundreds of Polish citizens, burned and razed one building after another, flattening large sections of town, including the old city, which was five hundred years old.

Even before the final suppression of the revolt, Blösche was transferred with the Gestapo archive forty miles southwest of Warsaw to the town of Skierniewice. There he had no time to reorganize the files. His commanders sent him on with thirty other Gestapo men to Levoca in Slovakia, to help suppress another revolt against the Germans. The soldiers traveled by train to Krakow, and from there Wehrmacht trucks took them through the West Carpathian Mountains and across the border to Slovakia. By the time they arrived, local forces had already suppressed the revolt; Blösche's unit patrolled the thick forest in search of any remaining partisans.[59]

In late April and early May 1945, after Blösche and the other Gestapo men had relocated one hundred miles west to the town of Zilina, they heard Soviet artillery forces advancing across the mountains. The Nazis fled again, this time into Czechoslovakia. Along with scores of Germans in tattered clothes—Wehrmacht soldiers, SS men, civilians—Blösche traveled west on narrow roads. Escapees sat wherever they could, atop a truck's cabin and on its hood, as the burdened vehicles maneuvered their way between the wrecks of bombed vehicles. The stream of cars, carriages, and carts escaping west clogged the roads, and traffic halted for hours at a time.

The Russians continued to advance; there was no hope of escape. Blösche climbed out of the stalled truck and walked over to a small pond. From his pocket he pulled out his SS identity card and pay book. He unpinned his Hitlerjugend medal and his War Merit Cross Second Class with Swords medal, which he had received for his actions suppressing the Jewish revolt in Warsaw. Tossing it all into the water, he watched the documents and medals sink into the mud. Then he studied his rifle and pistol, which had been like arms and hands for him over the past six years, throwing these too into the pond. He took off his SS uniform and, dressed instead in a Wehrmacht uniform, walked back out to the road, where he joined a group of Wehrmacht soldiers. They walked for almost two miles before encountering Red Army soldiers, to whom they surrendered.[60]

Part III
1945–1982

5

Facing Justice,
Encountering Life

Just days before German capitulation, in late April 1945, two men sat in the front cabin of a black wood-burning truck driving down a narrow curving road out of an SS horse farm at Fischhorn Castle in the Austrian Alps. In these final days of World War II, Fischhorn was a beehive of SS members, some in search of escape routes, others attempting to build resistance to Allied forces. Day and night, vehicles drove in and out of the alpine fortress, the last headquarters of SS units still fighting in the national redoubt zone.[1]

The driver, Johannes Haferkamp, turned the truck toward Taxenbach, navigating between snowcapped mountains, through alpine hamlets, across creeks, and slowly climbing in the direction of Schladming, a small mining town almost forty miles east. Beside Haferkamp sat Franz Konrad, throwing wood chips into the truck's furnace.[2] More than sixteen months had passed since the SS posted

Konrad to Fischhorn in December 1943. Thanks to the efforts of Konrad's benefactor, Hermann Fegelein, who had joined Hitler's personal staff and in June 1944 had married Eva Braun's sister, Gretel, Konrad had been transferred away from the deadly battle-fields on the eastern front to handle horse fodder in the Alps.[3]

In the back of the truck lay radio sets, food containers, several wrapped tin chests, and three locked leather suitcases. On the name tag of one of the suitcases was scribbled "Eva Braun." Konrad had carefully wrapped and packed every item in these chests and suit-cases to ensure they would not be damaged en route. Now he was delivering them for safekeeping to the home of his brother-in-law, Willy Pichler, in Schladming. In a few months or years, he planned to sell their contents and with the money buy himself a large estate in Peru. If all went according to plan, at the age of thirty-nine he could retire and return to his hobbies of chess, Esperanto, and choir singing.[4]

It was past 10:00 p.m. when the truck arrived in Schladming and halted in front of Pichler's house. Konrad jumped out just as Pichler, who had been expecting him, opened the front door. They exchanged a few words and then Pichler ran downstairs to open a cellar window. Standing on top of the back of the truck, Haferkamp tossed the food containers and radio sets to Konrad, who passed them down to Pichler. When it came to the leather suitcases, Kon-rad warned Haferkamp to handle them with special care. When they finished unloading the truck, Konrad joined Pichler in the cel-lar, pulling out from one of the suitcases a pair of long, dark trousers and a field jacket with the Spread Eagle insignia, both badly torn. These, he told the astounded Pichler, were the clothes the Führer had worn on July 20, 1944, when a group of Nazi officers had at-tempted to take his life.[5]

The next morning, after Haferkamp loaded the truck with wood, he and Konrad drove back to Fischhorn. A few days later, Hafer-kamp returned to Schladming with another delivery from Konrad. He unloaded part of the shipment at Pichler's home and the rest at the home of Konrad's brother, Fritz. Konrad would use this plunder, too, to help cushion his future.

In early May 1945, the armored vehicles of the 7th U.S. Army arrived at the SS headquarters at Fischhorn and liberated eight Jewish and forty-four Polish forced laborers. These prisoners told the Americans that just days before, Konrad had urged the commander of the farm, Erwin Haufler, to kill them, but Haufler had refused. The 7th Army took Konrad into custody in the nearby town of Zell am See.[6]

Konrad did not remain behind bars for long. One night a few weeks later, he escaped from his cell. In driving rain and wind, he climbed a hill path west to Aufhausen, arriving at the home of former SS nurse Ursula von Bieler. Konrad was soaked to his skin and covered in mud. Von Bieler gave him dry clothes and offered him a warm supper. She had a friend deliver to him a pair of dry shoes. Within hours, Konrad moved on to a different hideout.

There, Konrad sent a messenger to pick up a package he had left with his secretary, Martha von Broskowitz, before his imprisonment. Konrad had told von Broskowitz that the carefully tied package, wrapped in map paper, contained a collection of his personal letters and documents. For a payment of 5,000 RM, the messenger returned two days later with the package.[7]

With the package in hand, Konrad journeyed forty miles west to the home of his nephew, Rudolf Meier, in Kirchberg in Tirol, in the French-occupied zone of Austria. He ordered his nephew to hide the package. He then admitted himself to the hospital in nearby St. Johann complaining of heart problems. Upon discharge, he stayed at the hospital as an attendant, traveling on his days off to nearby Innsbruck, in an effort to obtain papers that would enable him to flee to Peru.[8]

On April 5, 1945, the SS took a few hundred Hotel Polski Jews on an hour-long march out of the Bergen-Belsen concentration camp, where they had been incarcerated behind electrified fences for 632 days. They arrived at the local train station, from which a year and a half earlier, in October 1943, the Germans had shipped those of the Hotel Polski Jews who possessed South American papers, including Tsvi's aunt Frumcia, to Auschwitz to be gassed. Now the SS squeezed the Nussbaums together with seventy other Jews into one of the train's cars. For nine hours the Jews waited. Finally, at five o'clock in the afternoon, the locomotive pulled the thirty passenger and cattle cars containing, in addition to the Hotel Polski Jews, Dutch, Greek, Slovak, and Hungarian Jews—a total of 2,500 people—out of the station.[9]

The train, with fifty armed SS men aboard, slowly rolled south. Out of fear of Allied planes, it halted several times along the short way and entered Hannover at dusk. The city lay in shambles. Almost every night over the past few months, Allied planes had buzzed high above Bergen-Belsen on their way to bombing different German cities. That night, as the Jews tried to catch a few hours of sleep in the car, Allied bombs again blasted the city. The train car shook and prisoners felt a mix of fear and revenge. The next morning, the train left Hannover in search of a route across the Elbe River. Over the coming days, it halted frequently, unable to find a bridge still safe to cross.[10]

On the evening of April 12, seven days after it left Bergen-Belsen and having advanced only 125 miles, the train came to a stop in a wooded ravine near Hillersleben. The next day, the prisoners woke to a hazy morning. They looked out the windows and didn't see even one German. During the night, all the SS guards had slipped away. Many Jews went outside to soak up the spring sun, while others, too weak to climb out of the car, lay amid the mingling odors of fresh grass, feces, morning dew, urine, and the decomposing bodies of the sixteen Jews who had died en route. They remained that way for a few hours, until at 1:00 p.m. the sound of armored vehicles rumbled from the surrounding woods. Some of the Jews spotted two tanks.

Major Clarence Benjamin of the 743rd Tank Battalion, 9th U.S. Army commanded a patrol composed of a Jeep and two light tanks. When they drove out of the woods, he and his soldiers saw that "on the banks of the tracks, as if to get some pitiful comfort from the thin April sun, a multitude of people in all shades of misery spread themselves in a sorry, despairing tableaux." As the Americans drew closer, they saw "shabby looking civilians by the side of the road. There was something immediately apparent about each one of these people, men and women, which arrested the attention. Each one of them was skeleton thin with starvation, a sickness in their faces and the way in which they stood—and there was something else. At the sight of the Americans they began laughing in joy—if it could be called laughing. It was an outpouring of pure, near-hysterical relief."[11]

Those still able to do so ran up the slope toward the tanks. Sergeant George Gross pulled out his camera and took a photograph of a woman holding a young girl's hand. In the background, another woman flung open her arms. The Jews hugged the soldiers, fell at

their feet, and spoke in a mix of Hungarian, Dutch, Greek, Slova-
kian, German, Polish, and Yiddish. Only a few knew English.

A moment after the photo was taken, the hollow-cheeked woman
with the outstretched arms noticed a bag abandoned by an SS man.
She seized it, combed through it, and pulled out a tin of canned
food. At the sight of the can in the woman's hands, the Jews turned
away from the Americans and rushed toward her, attempting to
scavenge the food, kicking and screeching. Sergeant Gross jumped
off his tank and rushed to pull the Jews away from one another.
The woman escaped into the woods to finish the meager meal.
Meanwhile, mothers proudly showed their children off to the soldiers, who handed out sweets.[12]

The American liberators ordered local German farmers to stay
up all night if necessary to provide meals for the starving Jews. They

soon feasted on foods they had not eaten in years: chicken, eggs, milk, fresh vegetables and fruits. Minutes later, this joyful moment turned to pain. Many experienced stomach cramps and vomiting, their bodies unused to food. The Americans delivered several of them to the local Wehrmacht hospital even as the German staff there was preparing to flee. One of the Jews taken to the hospital was Tsvi. His aunt Chana was able to convince a German doctor to operate on his appendicitis. Tsvi's life was saved, but eighty other Jews from the train died that night and were buried in Hillersleben.[13]

The surviving Jews moved in with farmers in Hillersleben and in the neighboring village of Farsleben. One family of survivors was that of Sophie Goetzel-Leviathan, her husband, David, and their young daughter, Micky. Sophie, who weighed seventy-seven pounds when liberated, ate and rested, hoping to regain her strength:

I eat heartily now, but I still have pain in my right side. My hands tremble to such a degree that I can hardly hold a cup of coffee or spread butter on bread. I cannot sleep. I hear the cries that reached us from the concentration camp near Belsen; they ring in my ears. If I close my eyes, I see corpses piled high and behind them I see the flames of the crematorium. I am tormented by the fear that the Germans will return to drive us out of the village. I know this is impossible, but fear remains within me, and no amount of reasoning can allay my anxiety.

Micky, meanwhile, befriended the twin German girls in whose house the Goetzel-Leviathans lived. For the first time in years she had toys to play with. "She strolls with a doll carriage and follows the geese into the fields. She communicates well with the children and has begun to speak a few words in German," Sophie wrote.[14] Like the Goetzel-Leviathans, the Nussbaums remained for weeks in the area of Hillersleben, slowly regaining their strength.

Allied forces advancing across Europe claimed more and more pieces of Stroop's territory of Rhein-Westmark. On March 23, 1945, American Sherman tanks rolled across a bridge constructed by U.S. military engineers over the Rhine at Mainz. In early April, the Americans neared Wiesbaden and Stroop hastily drove northeast with his family, their car navigating roads filled with convoys of escaping German refugees. Identifying it as likely containing a high Nazi official, Allied planes strafed the car; Stroop and his family were unharmed.[15]

On April 11, Stroop received a call from Himmler's office in Berlin. He was to report there the next day. Bidding farewell to Käthe and the children, Stroop drove off, hours later entering the smoldering streets of the Reich's capital. At Himmler's headquarters, Stroop received orders to travel seventy-five miles farther north to Prenzlau, the location of Himmler's concealed train.

He found the train on a side rail. Himmler, pale, weak, and sick, the man he had met more than twelve years earlier in Detmold, a man whose life was closely intertwined with his, greeted him. He asked Stroop if he would join his personal staff. Stroop, though deeply honored, refused. He had to establish a defensive line in Bavaria and the Austrian Alps and fight the foreign intruders to the last man. Himmler, who had already been secretly negotiating with the Allies, was shaken by Stroop's words. He embraced him. Then the two bid farewell, never to see each other again.[16]

Stroop traveled south to Bavaria. In local towns, he met with the leadership of the SS and Police and passed on Himmler's message that Germany could still overcome the intruders. In early May, Stroop retreated to Salzburg and from there on to Zell am See, where, on May 7, he conferred with other high-ranking officers in one of Himmler's private trains. For hours they sat around the train's conference table and deliberated their next move. To Stroop's horror, the officers concluded that the fate of the Third Reich had been sealed and that each man must fend for himself.[17]

The next day, after Alfred Jodl, chief of the Wehrmacht High Command Operational Staff, signed a document in France unconditionally surrendering all German forces, an American roadblock at the resort town of Rottau, Bavaria, stopped an officer dressed in a Wehrmacht uniform. The officer presented discharge papers with the name of Hauptmann der Reserve Josef Straup, and the Americans took him into custody. Two months after his arrest, in a Wiesbaden interrogation room, Stroop would confess to his real name and title, Jürgen Stroop, Höherer SS- und Polizeiführer of Rhein-Westmark.[18]

In the summer of 1945, an agent of the American CIC (Counter Intelligence Corps) received a hot tip from Josef Spacil, an SS officer from the Reich Security Head Office. At the end of the war, Spacil told the agent, Konrad had come to a mill near Taxenbach to collect 500,000 RM to pay his staff's salaries. At the time, Konrad pulled Spacil aside and told him the following secret: "I have seen the ex-

change of letters between Hitler and Eva Braun. I have the diaries of Hitler, and have buried them in zinc boxes. I have seen the suit of Hitler, which was torn on the right leg and on the breast. And I know that Hitler is dead."[19] The CIC became determined to find and arrest Konrad.

On August 22, Konrad paid a short visit to the home of his nephew, Rudolf Meier, in Kirchberg to see if the packages he had deposited with him were still intact. All his belongings were safe, Meier informed him. He asked Meier to travel to Schladming and make sure the Americans had not gotten hold of the items he had hidden there.[20] He was on his way to Innsbruck, Konrad told his nephew, to visit the home of his former mistress from Warsaw, Barbara Kalewska, who was attempting to help him obtain foreign papers. An hour after Konrad left, two CIC agents, Robert Gutierrez and William Conner, drove up to the Meiers' home.[21]

Later that day, a clean-shaven Konrad, dressed in army trousers and a civilian jacket, stepped off a train at the Kirchberg station and into the hands of American agents. Konrad was carrying 4,625 RM and a diamond brooch. From one of Konrad's pockets they pulled out a stack of photographs showing the destruction of the Warsaw ghetto.[22]

That night, Gutierrez and Conner faced Konrad in an interrogation room at the civilian internment camp, Camp Marcus Orr, near Salzburg. They started by questioning Konrad about his actions in the Warsaw ghetto. "Why did you flee arrest in Zell am See?" they asked. "Was your conscience really so bad?" Konrad flatly rejected the suggestion: "By no means; I've never done anything; I have no lives on my conscience." He repeated the last words, "I have no lives on my conscience." Gutierrez and Conner let the matter drop. For now, they were interested in other matters.[23]

"You probably know what we wish to learn from you," the CIC agents said. Konrad looked at them, expressionless. "Perhaps," he countered. Gutierrez and Conner got more specific: "What do you know about letters which might interest us?" In a half-statement, half-question tone, Konrad responded, "You mean the letters belonging to Eva Braun?" The letters, he went on unequivocally, were "burned in the main furnace in the central heating plant in Fischhorn." Ignoring the answer, Gutierrez and Conner pushed on to the key issue on their agenda. "Do you know about the diaries of Hitler?" they asked. There was a short silence. "I never saw any such diaries. There was one large chest or casket there [at Fischhorn], with a monogram, probably [with] the initials of Eva Braun," he answered.

Gutierrez and Conner pressed. "Do you know Spacil?" they asked. "Yes," responded Konrad, "I visited him in Taxenbach." The two interrogators then confronted Konrad with the information Spacil had related. Konrad did not miss a beat: "Yes, that's true, that I said to Spacil that I had seen the suit of Hitler." But, he went on, "I burned the suit; I burned everything. I didn't bury anything. . . . I'm sure I didn't mention anything to Spacil about diaries. The diaries of Hitler were never mentioned."

The investigation went on for hours. Konrad described tossing the correspondence of Braun and Hitler into the furnace at Fischhorn. Before burning them, he had skimmed some of Hitler's letters to Braun. In one such letter, he recalled, written after the July 20, 1944, attempt on his life, Hitler had written that "my hand is still trembling from the attempt on my life." But, the Führer continued, "I am full of hope for our coming victory." In the chest where the dozens of swastika-adorned letters lay, Konrad continued, was also Eva Braun's blue-covered diary, a notebook in which she outlined her letters to Hitler. "But," Konrad repeated, "I burned all of that. It took about an hour, to get it all burned."

Konrad said he had also burned Hitler's drawings, Braun's home-made movies, her photo albums, and other items that were sent from Hitler's Berghof to Fischhorn only days before capitulation. He had looked at the pictures before burning them, "photographs of the Berghof, of parties, of diplomatic receptions, and also personal pictures," he declared. "I burned up everything. . . . Believe me, I am very sorry that I didn't hold out at least one signature of the Führer as a souvenir. I burned every last scrap. I often have thought since that I should have kept the films. They should have been preserved for posterity."

Gutierrez and Conner ordered Konrad to repeat several times what he had burned. Finally, many hours into the questioning, Konrad revealed his secret. "What I am now about to tell you is the whole truth. I have the Führer's suit. I also have one letter from Hitler to Eva Braun, and one original signature. In addition, I saved one photo album. I burned everything else. I know nothing of the diaries of Hitler; I only know about the notebooks in which Eva Braun sketched the contents of her letters to Hitler. I burned these note-books too. . . . I took everything to my relatives in Schladming."

On August 24, Gutierrez traveled to Schladming to the homes of Konrad's relatives. In one of the houses, he entered the cramped cellar, where among old suitcases, storage boxes, and winter equipment, he found the carefully packed chests that had been delivered there months earlier. Gutierrez lifted the lid of one of the tin chests. Two sets of silverware glimmered in his flashlight's beam. On one set he identified the emblem of the Polish crown, and on the other the butterfly-shaped emblem of Eva Braun's initials, EB. Gutierrez uncovered another chest. It contained a jar with some of Eva Braun's jewelry and twenty-five to thirty photograph albums with personal photos of the Führer taken by her. From a suitcase, Gutierrez pulled out tattered black trousers and a jacket—Hitler's clothes from the assassination attempt. Later, in the interrogation room, Gutierrez asked Konrad why he kept Hitler's ragged pants and jacket. It was simple, Konrad replied. In a few decades "I might have been able to sell them in America for a large sum of money."[24]

In the winter of 1945, after Soviet forces liberated Warsaw, Rivkah walked to the city center in the hope of locating old kibbutz friends. She crossed the bridge over the Vistula and roamed the rubble, examining every passing face. None was familiar. Disappointed, she returned to her apartment. After a few more fruitless attempts to locate acquaintances in the shattered city, she stopped going.

One day Rivkah and her apartment mate walked along a sidewalk in Grochow. A wrinkle-faced woman passed by with a full shopping bag; in the park sat a couple of mothers watching their children in the sandbox; two men in worker's jackets, one short, the other tall, briskly walked toward a tram station. A few seconds later, Rivkah called out to her friend, "Hey, see who I am seeing!" "Your brother?" the friend cried back as Rivkah ran after the men. "Better than a brother," Rivkah responded. She pulled on the jacket of the tall man. He turned, yelped in surprise, and embraced her in his sturdy arms. It was Antek, one of the leaders of the Warsaw ghetto revolt and a kibbutz member. After she calmed down, Rivkah hesitantly asked Antek, "Where is Tsivyah?" An unverified rumor

had it that Tsivyah Lubetkin, Antek's companion, had been cap-
tured and killed by the Germans. It turned out to be a false rumor.
At that moment, Tsivyah approached and Rivkah heard her say,
"She looks so much like Rivkah, our girl . . ." Rivkah turned and
Tsivyah, shocked, asked, "How did you stay alive, with a face like
yours?" Rivkah answered simply, "I am alive, you see."[25]

In a nearby restaurant, Antek and Tsivyah listened to Rivkah's
detailed story. When Rivkah finished, they asked if she would join
the Berihah movement, a clandestine operation of Zionist youth
movements, to gather thousands of survivors and smuggle them
across European borders and over the Mediterranean to British-
controlled Palestine. Rivkah agreed. She traveled to Rzeszow, in
southeast Poland near the border with Czechoslovakia, where she
rented an apartment and worked as the representative of Dror
He-Halutz, all the while helping the secret operation. Every few
days, dozens of survivors with bundles arrived at her dwelling.
Rivkah arranged accommodations and handed them foreign currency before smuggling them on moonless nights along narrow
hilly paths while evading border patrols.

In the summer of 1945, Dror He-Halutz summoned Rivkah to
Budapest for a meeting of all its activists in Europe. There she ran
into Fischel Farber, whom she had last seen in the turbulent days
of September 1939 at the doorstep of 34 Dzielna. Fischel told
Rivkah he had later fled eastward in a stream of refugees and had
joined a Polish unit of the Red Army that battled the Nazis. In
turn, Fischel listened in awe to Rivkah's story, unable to connect
the determination of its heroine with the seemingly fragile woman
seated before him. They sat for hours talking. On their final day in
Budapest, when Fischel and Rivkah had to part ways, they promised
to keep in touch. For months they wrote each other long letters.

Months later, in the fall of 1945, after his return from a mission
to the Soviet Union, Fischel traveled to the town of Walbrzych, in
Poland, to where Rivkah had moved. There the two married. No

members of their families had survived, and only a few friends attended the ceremony and celebrated with them. Shortly thereafter, Rivkah fell ill. Doctors in Poland were unable to diagnose the disease, so the newly married couple traveled to Vienna. There doctors determined that Rivkah had a blood disease, probably a result of her experiences during the war, and operated to remove her spleen. It took her months to recuperate. When she left the hospital, the doctors warned her never to get pregnant. Were she to conceive and bear children, she would likely die.

In late October 1945, weeks after his arrest, Konrad was brought back into the interrogation room by the CIC agent Gutierrez and commanded to repeat his story. "You may do what you like with me," Konrad declared. "I have told you everything."

"Please tell me what you did with the films taken by Eva Braun," Gutierrez asked.

Konrad repeated the account he had given many times before. "I burned all of the films. I know that for sure. . . . Part of the films were lying loose, part were still wound on spools. There were perhaps twenty films. . . . I know for certain that I burned the films personally. I remember that clearly because I was able with the films to get a good fire going in the furnace."[26]

After Konrad retold his story, Gutierrez placed twenty-eight spools of film on the table. When Gutierrez had paid a second visit to Schladming, he had gone to Konrad's mother, who had handed him a small jewelry box and a suitcase with a name tag: Eva Braun. In the box, Gutierrez discovered a gold woman's watch set with fifty diamonds, four gold men's watches, two pairs of gold cuff links, as well as $1,000 and some other foreign currency. In the suitcase, he found films shot by Eva Braun of Hitler in his Alpine home on the Berghof. At the sight of the spools, Konrad, clearly confused, hesitantly responded, "I cannot explain that. I thought I had burned all of the films. Perhaps," he added, "I only burned the films which were not on spools. I'm not sure of that anymore." Noticing his confusion, Gutierrez repeated what Konrad's mother had told him: "Franz himself said that he had the letters [of Braun and Hitler]." But Konrad continued to refute the claim. The letters, he insisted, had been burned.[27]

In a report for their superiors, Gutierrez and Conner wrote that "these agents are convinced that Konrad not only had the exchange of letters between Hitler and Eva Braun in his possession, but that he also took measures to hide this correspondence, as well as the book bound in blue leather in which Eva Braun had sketched the contents of her letters to Hitler."[28]

Over the coming months, CIC agents continued to interrogate Konrad and search his relatives' homes in Schladming and Kirchberg, where they uncovered more jewelry, foreign currency, and 1,000,000 RM. A new CIC agent, "Walter," was brought into the investigation and offered Konrad a deal: if he surrendered Hitler's letters, he would be spared extradition to Warsaw. "I would accept this offer at any time if I could," Konrad responded. "I see my chance very well, which you offer me, however, I cannot take it although I would like to, because I do not own anymore or have owned anything except as you found." Shortly thereafter, the Americans ended the investigation and began the procedure to extradite Konrad to Poland.[29]

Weeks after the American forces had liberated them, Tsvi and his family traveled from Hillersleben via Brussels to Toulon. There, the Jewish Agency had arranged for some Hotel Polski Jews to join former Dachau and Buchenwald inmates, 186 orphaned Jewish children, and other survivors destined to travel to the Land of Israel. In early September 1945, the group boarded a twelve-ton vessel, the *Mataroa*, and sailed across the Mediterranean Sea—the same waters Tsvi had sailed six years earlier with his parents in the opposite direction.

Five days into the journey, on Saturday, September 8, a cry tore through the ship. Passengers rushed up onto the sunny upper deck. A few passengers had spotted Mount Carmel. There, at last, was the Promised Land. It was three o'clock on Rosh Hashanah, the Jewish New Year, when the *Mataroa* sailed into the calm waters of the port of Haifa. Some passengers put on their white-and-blue striped camp uniform jackets. Blue-and-white Star of David flags waved in the wind above the ship. At the pier, dozens of journalists, spectators, and Arab porters waited under a sign that read WEL-COME TO THE HOLY LAND. The chief rabbi of Haifa, Rabbi Yehoshua Kaniel, climbed up a wooden bridge to welcome the new immigrants.[30]

Tsvi, Shulim, and Chana took their bundles and joined the group walking down the wooden gangplank. On the pier, barbed wire enclosed a large disembarkation area. Rows of British policemen

dressed in khaki uniforms examined the new immigrants' papers. The passengers looked with trepidation at the men's uniforms, the wooden clubs in their hands, and the rifles resting on their shoulders.

After a few minutes in line, the Nussbaums reached the checkpoint. Shulim handed the officer their identification papers. The policeman examined their parcels and gestured for them to pass on. They walked between rows of armed men to the next checkpoint. A policeman asked for their names. He flipped through a long list of names on his table: "Markus," "Marton," "Nadel." Finally he found "Nussbaum" and pointed them to an opening in the barbed wire. They walked to a customs hall where food and drink awaited them.[31]

That night British policemen led the Jewish immigrants out of the customs hall. The group passed by warehouses, cranes, and ships until they neared a British freight train topped with guard posts. The soldiers placed the immigrants' bundles into the box-

cars and ordered them to board the open doors. At the sight of the
train, some of the survivors stopped in their tracks.

After all had finally boarded, the train traveled to the Atlit Detention Camp, less than an hour's journey south of Haifa. There
the doors opened and the Jewish survivors from Germany, Bel-
gium, France, and elsewhere stepped onto the sea-sand platform of
the train station. Nearby flashed the red lights of the ambulances.
The ambulances transported a pregnant woman and some weak-
ened passengers to a local hospital.[32]

The Nussbaums joined the rest walking on the sandy path to
the detention camp. At the sight of the camp—a compound of barracks surrounded by barbed-wire fences, lampposts, and guard
towers—some survivors held back. Soldiers led them to a tin shed
topped with a chimney from which white smoke rose. Men and
women were ordered to separate into two groups, undress, and
throw their clothes into a steam boiler for disinfection. The staff
sprayed the group with DDT. After getting their clothes back, the

survivors entered the separate men's and women's barracks and slept on bunk beds.[33]

In the morning, they woke up to a brilliant sun and views of the nearby Mount Carmel hills dotted with green trees. They ate breakfast in the camp dining room, and for many it was their first taste of an orange, a grapefruit, or a guava with its sour skin and sweet pulp. Later that day, visitors arrived from all over the country and searched across fences for relatives. Cries of happiness and hands reaching for each other across the barbed wire mixed with tears and cries for family members who had perished. Within days, the British permitted Tsvi and his aunt and uncle to leave the camp and join their relatives, the Brauners.[34]

Shortly thereafter, the three Nussbaums rented a small basement apartment in Ramat-Gan. Shulim and Chana sent eleven-year-old Tsvi to be educated in Negba, a kibbutz in the Negev. There he attempted to make friends with the local boys, working in the fields and sleeping in the communal dorms. But it was too rigid for Tsvi and he sent letters to Shulim and Chana describing how miserable and depressed he was. Shulim and Chana rushed to pull him

out of Negba and moved him to kibbutz Mishmar ha-Sharon, where, in the orchards and fields, he flourished.[35]

In late May 1947, an American military cargo plane carrying Stroop and Erich Mussfeld, the commander of the Majdanek crematorium, touched down at Tempelhof Airport in Berlin. A few months earlier, Stroop had been indicted for the murder of Allied pilots who had parachuted into Rhein-Westmark. Stroop pleaded not guilty. They had been shot attempting to escape, he claimed. The American military court at Dachau rejected Stroop's defense and sen-

tenced him to death by hanging. On boarding the plane to Berlin, an American major had told Stroop that the Americans wanted him to testify on Himmler's and Hitler's secret activities. In fact, the Americans were handing him over to the Polish authorities.[36]

In Warsaw, the Poles locked Stroop in the infamous Mokotow Prison and interrogated him extensively. In addition to these official interrogations, they permitted survivors of the Warsaw ghetto to ask Stroop questions. "Which times and sights of battles remained best etched in [your] memory?" was one question presented to Stroop in a written questionnaire. In response, Stroop wrote, "[In the ghetto] what left on me the deepest impression was the way people dedicated themselves so fanatically to something with no goal and no chance and [also] the degree to which one can instigate people; and also then the march of thousands to the train station. This impression, however, was obliterated [later] by the sights of great suffering and distress which I saw among the population of western Germany which were greater and blurred those [earlier sights]."[37]

Käthe Stroop was also one of those displaced at the end of the war and she now worked in the fields of Eicklingen, a hamlet ninety miles northeast of Detmold. Käthe, Renate, and Olaf, as well as Stroop's mother, sent him regular letters and packages containing cookies, chocolate, oranges, nuts, candles for Christmas night, and other items to ease his life in prison.[38] In his careful handwriting, Olaf described to his father his latest summer experiences:

Beloved father!

First let me sincerely congratulate you with many, many kisses and greetings for your 55th birthday. In the summer vacation which lasted from June 29th to August 2nd, I had on the last week traveled by bike to Detmold. There the celebrations of 75 years [of the Hermann Monument] exactly began. It was a commotion. All streets were attired with flags and other decorations. On each day was something else special. . . . All over [Detmold], I was greeted with friendship. When I left, I was again so much richer than before. From each one I was given a present. No one wanted to give less than the other. . . .

Well, remain healthy and jolly. Hopefully you received our package and you can celebrate your birthday with it. It is blessed with many, many kisses.

Yours, mommy

Yours, Renate

Yours, Olaf

And *all* Detmolders![39]

To the letter, fourteen-year-old Olaf attached a drawing he made especially for his father, a sketch of the Hermann Monument.

I n mid-May 1947, Fischel and Rivkah sailed from Marseille to the Land of Israel. There Rivkah reunited with her only remaining relative, her sister Dina, whom she hadn't seen in nine years. Fischel and Rivkah first moved to a kibbutz but found this life unsuitable;

the kibbutz made no allowance for Rivkah's sickness. They then moved in with friends in Kiryat Haim, a suburb of Haifa. Months later, Rivkah learned that she was pregnant. Despite the warnings of the doctors in Vienna, the gentle movements of the fetus in her womb felt to her like signals from a different world, announcing a better future.[40]

On March 3, 1948, Rivkah felt her first contractions and called on Fischel to take her to the hospital. Fischel, who was a member of the Jewish paramilitary organization Haganah, quickly arranged for a vehicle with an armed escort. To avoid Arab snipers who shot at Jewish cars in Haifa, they traveled not to the nearby hospital but east to the town of Afula. The car passed a refinery plant where just three months earlier forty-one Jewish workers had been killed by local Arab-Palestinians in retaliation for an attack by the Jewish Etzel underground that had killed six Arab workers. As they sped through Arab villages, Fischel and the escort scanned for possible ambushes.

An hour later they arrived at the hospital, where Rivkah gave birth to a baby boy. Rivkah and Fischel named him Haim in memory of Fischel's father, who had been murdered with the rest of the family by the Nazis. Haim, whose name means "life," symbolized for them their new life in the Land.

A few minutes before 10:00 a.m. on July 18, 1950, fifty observers sat on the long benches of Chamber IV in Warsaw's District Court. A side door to the courtroom opened and in was led the person accused of destroying a large section of the city. Wearing polished shoes, an ironed suit fastened with silver-colored buttons, and a black tie knotted around his neck, Stroop walked over to the prisoners' dock. He sat together with Franz Konrad, whom the Americans had extradited to Poland four and a half years earlier.

The clerk called the court to order, and the accused, attorneys, journalists, audience, and court staff all rose. In came Judge A. Puszkowski, chairman and vice president of the court, together with

judges Dr. Wl. Hanczakowski and M. Stepczynski, each taking a high-backed wooden chair. The audience sat down and, as silence was restored in the courtroom, the judges opened the case of *The People's Republic of Poland v. Franz Konrad and Jürgen Stroop.*

Within minutes, judge Puszkowski called Konrad to the stand. He walked up and stood directly across from the judges' bench.

"Name of the accused?" the voice of judge Puszkowski sounded in the courtroom.

"Franz Konrad . . ."

"Accused," the judge inquired, "do you have previous convictions?"

"No," Konrad declared.

Moments later the tribunal chair repeated the question: "Accused, do you have previous convictions?"

"Just during the war," Konrad responded.

The prosecutor, Leon Penner, rose to his feet. "Were you not imprisoned before you joined the Nazi party? Were you not convicted of stealing money?" He reminded Konrad of his 1932 conviction for stealing nine hundred schillings from his employer, a crime for which he had been sentenced to three months in prison.

Konrad, pointing at his attorney, Palatynski, replied, "My attorney had told me that that was time barred and that I should not declare it in court. I was penalized due to a conviction."[41]

Judge Puszkowski then moved on to verify that Konrad was aware of the content of the indictment now before him. Konrad was charged with having plundered Jewish property in the ghetto for the benefit of the German Reich and for his own personal gain. He was also being held accountable for taking part in the forced evacuation of two thousand of his workers to the Umschlagplatz and of the murder of Jews in the Lejzerowicz tannery in the ghetto.

The judge turned to Konrad. "Do you admit your guilt in the crimes that you are accused of in the indictment?"

"No," asserted Konrad emphatically. "I have been accused that a day before the [January 1943] resettlement, I asked to shoot the Jews in the tannery of Lejzerowicz. I know of no such thing. I did

not do such a thing. As someone who was in the administration, I had no executive power. . . . If I was this kind of person who killed people in the ghetto, then I would have killed myself. I would have not been able to be in the ghetto. I had to work day after day with these people. In this way, I would have issued my own death verdict."[42]

In fact, he countered, he had assisted the ghetto Jews. Just days before the final liquidation, one of his workers, in tears, told him that she was unable to smuggle her child across the ghetto walls. At the risk of his life, he smuggled the Jewish child out to Trzech Krzyzy Square on the Aryan side and into the shelter of a Polish family. He also had ordered a small opening be made in the brick ghetto wall by his office to enable Jews to escape. Rather than be tried, he ought more properly to be honored.[43]

The Jews had known he was their benefactor and cared for him. At the revolt's outset, Konrad testified, he had driven through the crossfire. Hours later, upon his safe return to his office, "the Jews rejoiced that nothing had happened to me."

Penner, the prosecutor, interrupted him. "As evidence for your appreciation of these Jews' happiness [at your safe return], you brought [two thousand of them] to the Umschlagplatz?" he asked in a cynical tone.[44]

"No." Konrad dismissed the accusation. He had taken "his" Jews to the Umschlagplatz only because he was fully confident that they would be sent to work in Lublin. He had never been told that they were to be sent to Treblinka like the masses. Although he had stood by Stroop throughout the liquidation and witnessed Stroop's criminal acts, he had never doubted that "his" productive Jews would be spared.[45]

What had he been doing standing beside Stroop in the liquidation? He had not, Konrad insisted, taken part in the horrible crimes of setting buildings on fire or mass executions. "I was not active," Konrad exclaimed. "I was photographing."[46]

When his turn to question Konrad came, Palatynski returned to what his client had done while standing by Stroop throughout the final liquidation. "Please say now, accused," he spoke slowly, "in which way your function of supervising Jewish property coincided with your presence at executions of Jews?"

At the outset of the uprising, Konrad explained, Stroop had commanded him to be nearby at all times. Consequently, he had ceased to function as head of the confiscation authority. "I was there as a neutral observer." As a witness to the crimes, he added, "I knew that in one way or another I must remember, and therefore I had taken photos and notes in my notebook." Konrad had also collected some photos from other security servicemen. He intended to use them as evidence against Stroop, "because of his liquidation of the Warsaw ghetto and his liquidation of people."[47]

He described how he had intended via his benefactor Fegelein to report Stroop's horrendous crimes to no less than the Führer himself. A few months after the *Aktion*, when in Vienna, Konrad had ordered his personal secretary to town so he could dictate to her his report of the uprising. When his secretary arrived in Vienna, Konrad recalled, he had to travel urgently to Hungary, and upon his return he was hospitalized for two months, due to the dreadful sights he had seen in the ghetto. These events had prevented him from writing his incriminating report. And after the July 20, 1944, assassination attempt on Hitler, it was impossible to gain access to the Führer and reveal Stroop's crimes.[48]

"Accused," asked Penner, "was it your opinion that Hitler was different from Stroop so that you could complain about Stroop to Hitler?"

Searching for words, Konrad answered, "I wanted to report." He fell silent for a moment. "I could not have reported to Himmler."

"Why could you not report to Himmler?" the prosecutor pressed.

He had bestowed the Iron Cross First Class on Stroop for this action in Warsaw, uttered Konrad.

"Accused, since when have you been a member of the party?"

"Since 1932."

"Had you heard the speeches of Hitler?. Did you know what Hitler had said about the Jews?"

Interrupting the prosecutor, Konrad said, "In any case not that one should execute them."

"And what do words such as 'the Jews must disappear' mean?" the prosecutor persisted.

"Despite that," Konrad concluded, "it would not have stopped me from reporting about it."[49]

The second day of the trial focused on Stroop. Judge Puszkowski called Stroop to the stand. The judge read out the indictment as it related to his actions in the ghetto. Stroop was accused of murdering at least 56,065 human beings; of burning thousands more alive in underground bunkers and buildings; of looting 10 million zloty, large amounts of currency, gold, and jewels; and of ordering the execution of one hundred Poles in retaliation for a July 1943 attack on a German column in Warsaw.

"I ask for the accused Jürgen Stroop: Do you plead guilty to the allegations set forth against you in the indictment?"

"I plead not guilty," Stroop stated.[50]

The judge asked for Stroop's version of events. Stroop described in detail his deployment to Warsaw and the first day of the *Aktion*. He had received an order from Himmler to destroy the ghetto with full force, he told the court. To fulfill Himmler's command, he had set ghetto houses on fire. He did so, he stressed, only after his men had called on the inhabitants to evacuate.

"It was after some time that we acted on the basis of a command from Himmler, who took the viewpoint of the Hague Convention that the terms franc-tireur, partisan, and bandit applied [to the rebels]. Bandits, which in accordance with the Hague Convention are not identifiable as combatants, must be shot on the spot."[51]

Judge Hanczakowski probed the logic of his argument: "When you received the command from Himmler to liquidate the Jews in accordance with the Hague Convention, did the thought not come upon you, that this kind of *Aktion*, which entails the liquidation of civilians and also the liquidation of a part of a defenseless city, cannot adhere to the Hague Convention?"

Stroop remained silent.

"Could you answer this question?" the judge demanded.

The command from Himmler came as a surprise, Stroop explained. "It was clear to me that I had to battle, that Germany found itself in a war. I had a command to clean up the ghetto. I faced an ongoing battle and I had to bring this battle to an end."[52]

The state prosecutor returned to Stroop's statement about the Hague Convention. Was Stroop aware, he asked, that according to international law "only a person who has clean hands can call upon international conventions? . . . A soldier who claims justice has to have clean hands. Your hands are dripping with blood."

"I am not aware of that," Stroop responded.

"Do you consider murdering children as a behavior agreeable with your conscience?"

"As far as I know children were not murdered. I am not responsible for that. I always in my entire life tried to behave like a knight. This is my greatest good that my children and my wife have from me. I always tried to apply this knightly behavior toward my wife and toward other women."[53]

The prosecutor then referred to Konrad's testimony of the previous day. "The accused Konrad was taking photographs which are in this album." He pointed at the leather-bound report placed on the court table, a document that minutes earlier Stroop had confirmed he had written.

"Did the accused see him [Konrad] taking the photographs?"

"I just learned about that yesterday," Stroop reluctantly responded. "I don't recall seeing him. I didn't like taking photographs."[54]

Konrad, the prosecutor pointed out, had testified on the previous day that Stroop ordered him to have a group of red-haired Jews executed in the ghetto.

"That is impossible," Stroop reacted.

"Do you admit that you yourself killed [people] and that in your presence people were killed?"

"I had only seen one execution."

"Where had this execution taken place?"

"That I can't remember," Stroop uttered.

"Did this execution possibly take place in the courtyard of the Judenrat?"

"I assume not."

Please describe this execution, the prosecutor demanded.

"It was of people who were still in possession of weapons. They were shot by the security police on the spot."

"After their weapons had been taken from them?" the prosecutor probed.

"In this moment when the people were arrested, a court hearing from the office of security police was held. The court determined that these people had revolted, that they were bandits and they were to be shot," Stroop resolved.

"In the ghetto? Did courts function there?" the prosecutor inquired.

"That could always be a possibility."

The prosecutor bellowed: "I am asking what was; do not lie. Our courts are accustomed to defendants who speak the truth." He restated the question: "Were all the executions carried out based on a court order?"

Stroop thought for a moment and then cautiously weighed his words. "If there were executions, these were not according to court order."

The prosecutor turned to the court translator. "Please show the accused the picture with the dead child. Was the shooting of this child based on a court order?"

Stroop examined the photo of four or five corpses lying on ghetto rubble. "You cannot determine from the photograph that this is a child," he challenged the prosecutor.

The prosecutor insisted. "Was this child killed based on a court order?"

The child, he said, died in battle. "It is written here on the photograph that 'the bandits were killed in a struggle.'" It was the fault of the child's parents, Stroop had explained in a pretrial declaration. They took their child into an active battlefield.

"Were children bandits?" The prosecutor was determined to get an answer from Stroop.

"Children were killed because they went into firefights with their parents," Stroop insisted.

The prosecutor again motioned the translator, who raised a photo of a little girl, her hands up, and a little boy, a cap on his head and his hands raised in the air. "Is this little girl in the photo or this little boy a partisan also?" the prosecutor asked.

Stroop took the photo in his hands. He read the title, "Pulled from the bunkers by force." "No, these are people pulled out from the ruins."

"Why were they shot?"

"They were not executed."

"They are no longer in Warsaw or in Poland."

"But they were not shot, Mr. Prosecutor."

"Do you remember the place where the executions always took place in the backyard of the Judenrat, there, where they burned the corpses, where the corpses were piled up on wood and were splashed with gasoline?"

Silence filled the courtroom.

"I didn't see that," Stroop answered.[55]

Over the following days, the judges heard more than twenty oral and written testimonies. Three days after that, they retired to their chambers. On Monday, July 23, 1951, in front of a packed courtroom, Judge Puszkowski read the almost thirty-page verdict. He first reread the long list of charges against the accused. Then he proclaimed, "The accused Jürgen Stroop and Franz Konrad are declared guilty."[56]

The judges refuted Konrad's claims that his aim had been to

assist the Jews or to document Stroop's crimes. "The court proceedings brought no evidence for any activities by the accused Konrad which he claimed to have undertaken to alleviate the suffering of the inhabitants of the ghetto. His defenses in this matter are empty words."[57] Stroop, the judges determined, acted "in full awareness, carried out the Hitlerite anti-Jewish policy and committed countless murders of the inhabitants of the ghetto, acts which expressed his own will and intentions."[58]

"The court," Judge Puszkowski asserted, "had at its disposal a vast amount of evidence. The most important document is the report by the accused Stroop dated Warsaw, May 16, 1943, under the title *The Jewish Quarter of Warsaw Is No More!*" The report "as well as photographs showing the operation of this action, all display a cynicism and barbarism unmatched by the human race before the rise of Hitlerism."[59] The court ruled unanimously, "on the basis of article 31, 33, and 34 of the penal law," to impose the punishment, "*for the accused Jürgen Stroop the death penalty . . . for the accused Franz Konrad the death penalty.*"[60]

On December 7, 1951, the Polish Supreme Court confirmed the death sentences. From his cell at Mokotow Prison in Warsaw, Stroop wrote a clemency request to the president of the Polish Republic.

Mr. President!

Hereby I present my request [that you], Mr. President, annul my pronounced verdict.

As the basis for my request I ask to mention the following: From my home I had been raised as a soldier. As a soldier I had carried out all the commands given to me, which were essential for my Fatherland. I know only unconditional obedience and I had to assume that the duty of my commanders was to examine the necessity of the given commands also in light of international rights. I was no politician and had not concerned myself with people's politics. . . . My entire life goal was to serve my Fatherland and ensure the well-being of my wife and children! Never in my life have I done or consciously undertaken something for which I could be punished. . . . Mr. President! With the thought of my family, and out of concern for them, allow me to repeat the request to annul the pronounced punishment.

Jürgen Stroop[61]

The Polish president turned down Stroop's clemency request.

Konrad likewise sent a clemency request to the Polish president. A day before the liquidation had begun, he wrote, he had been the one who had informed the ghetto residents about the upcoming *Aktion*. Without him, the rebels could not have launched their heroic revolt.

While working in the Ghetto, I behaved in an exemplary and humane way, which I was taught in my motherland, Austria. I was trying to fulfill my duties in the spirit of a true soldier avoiding any severe punishment. I didn't stain my hands with blood. . . . I am a family man sensitive and compassionate to human suffering. I felt empathy for the Jews, seeing their tragedy, as they were driven from their homes. . . . I can state with confidence that I didn't commit any injustice.

I had nothing to do with the liquidation of the rest of the Ghetto by SS General Stroop. I witnessed the methods with which the liquidation was conducted, and I was deeply outraged at the inhumane way it was implemented. I took photographs and wrote a journal to make an account of what was happening. It was supposed to be the basis for my protest against General Stroop.[62]

Just before sunset on March 6, 1952, almost nine years after the final liquidation of the ghetto, Stroop and Konrad walked out of their prison cells and to the execution chamber. No word was uttered about Hitler, Himmler, or Germany. Stroop followed the prison authorities' directions. He stood beneath the noose; he allowed it to be tied around his neck; he did not resist when it was tightened. At precisely 7:00 p.m., Stroop and Konrad swung by their necks.[63]

6

An Anguished End

In the backseat of a bus traveling to Urbach in Soviet-occupied Germany in the fall of 1947 sat a hideous-looking passenger, his face marked with scars, his jaw tilting sideways, his nose obscured, and his skin painfully stretched. In the small village, the bus stopped and the man got off. He asked for directions. When he found the address, he did not knock but simply opened the door and entered the living room. Blösche had returned home.

Blösche had spent the previous two years in captivity. After the Red Army captured him together with other Wehrmacht soldiers in May 1945, the POWs had been sent to a labor camp in the high altitudes of the Armenian plateau in the Soviet Republic of Azerbaijan. There, in the thin air, he labored in a quarry and shoveled asphalt to pave roads. In the winter, the Soviets transferred him back west to Czechoslovakia, where for a few months he worked in a factory and then was moved on to the Louis VII coal mine in Witowice near Ostrava.[1]

Two days into working at the mine, he boarded the mine shaft elevator and traveled down to the lowest level, where for the next seven hours he sweated chiseling coal. Two minutes past 11:00 p.m. on September 6, 1946, the shift over, he walked toward the elevator. Everything around him was unfamiliar. He peeked at the idle machinery. He looked down an abandoned tunnel. He watched crates full of coal travel away. He neared a group of black-faced mine workers waiting for the elevator. A cable squeaked. He poked his head through an opening in the shaft. The miners screamed, but it was too late. The elevator platform hit his head, dragged him down, his legs flailing in the air, his head caught between the mine floor and the pressing elevator platform. He lost consciousness.[2]

In the hospital, he underwent several painful surgeries to restore his crushed nose, cheek, and lower jaw. He lost sight in one eye. And he could hardly chew or swallow from pain. Four months later, he left the hospital, his face so deformed that it was hard to recognize him. He worked as a file clerk in the mine's office and

frequented the clinic. In the summer of 1947, a year after the accident, the doctor determined that Blösche was able to return to the tunnels. Blösche would not hear of it. He reported himself sick. A week later, the doctor again ordered him to the tunnels. Blösche decided to escape.[3]

He and a friend traveled by train west to the town of Znojmo. They stole across the border into Austria and arrived in Vienna, where they parted ways. Blösche crossed the border into Germany, traveling through the destroyed cities of Munich and Nuremberg and on to the border that separated the American and Soviet occupation zones. From correspondence with his sister Gertraud in Berlin, he had learned that his parents now lived in Urbach, to which they had fled from Frydlant at the war's end. He crossed the border near the town of Sonneberg and on September 9, 1947, was reunited with his parents.[4]

In Urbach, Hanna Schönstedt was awaiting the return from the eastern front of her husband, a Wehrmacht soldier and the father of her two-and-a-half-year-old daughter, Ulla. More than two years had passed since the war had ended, and her hopes for his safe return had dwindled. Shortly after the thirty-five-year-old Blösche arrived in Urbach, the two became acquainted. Hanna, nine years younger, saw beyond Blösche's deformed face to a caring man. He worried anytime Ulla got sick, and he and Ulla seemed to grow fond of each other. When Hanna informed her parents that she and Blösche planned to marry, they refused to approve the marriage. They saw nothing wrong in Blösche, but their daughter should not marry without official confirmation that her husband had indeed fallen in battle. Months later, Hanna told her parents that she was carrying Blösche's child.

That summer, a knock came at the couple's door. Hanna, deep into her pregnancy, answered it. An unfamiliar woman stood there. She introduced herself: Suzanne Held. During the war, Held told Hanna, she was Blösche's fiancée. In July 1944, just before the Polish revolt in Warsaw began, Held was evacuated. In the chaos of war their paths separated. All this was news to Hanna.[5]

Later that day, Blösche returned home from work to find Held sitting on a couch in his living room. Held urged him to return with her to her home in Cuxhaven near Hamburg. Blösche pointed at Hanna's belly, and at Ulla, who had grown to see him as her father. No, he would not leave them, he told Held. Hanna was relieved. Held stayed with the Blösches for a few days, befriended Hanna, and in years to come kept in touch with them via mail. In early September 1948, Hanna gave birth to a baby boy, Klaus, and fifteen months later, in December 1949, to a baby girl, Birgitt.[6]

After the birth of the two children, the couple married. Blösche was a diligent breadwinner. Not only did he work shifts at the local potash mine in Volkenroda, where he inspected the potash to assure the grain size did not exceed four millimeters, but he also supplemented the family's income toiling in local fields. In addition, he was a dedicated employee. He almost never took sick leave, even when a full mine cart struck him. When coworkers asked Blösche to fill in for them, he readily agreed, even on weekends.[7]

At home after a hard day's work, when the children finally were asleep, Blösche and Hanna would relax on the living room sofa and watch a sports broadcast or catch the news on the East German state-controlled television station. Each time a war story came on, Hanna noticed, Blösche would rush to turn off the television, and then run to their bedroom or out the front door. He would return a few minutes later, still carrying about him some of his earlier nervousness. Also, in the first years of their marriage, he occasionally woke up sweating in the middle of the night. He would get up and walk around to calm down. Hanna asked him if it was the memory of the accident that caused his unrest. He told her no. Was it bad memories from the war? she asked. He never responded. Only once did he tell her that he had served in the SS, and Hanna immediately suggested they attempt to escape to West Germany. Blösche ruled that option out: he had nothing to hide, he had done nothing wrong.[8]

On December 9, 1965, the phone rang in a Stasi office in East Berlin. Heinż Schenk, the head of the Jewish community there, informed the Stasi that he had just received a letter from Heinz Galinski, the head of the Jewish community in West Berlin. The letter contained information about a Nazi criminal living in East Germany. It identified him as Josef Blösche, living in Urbach in Thüringen. Blösche, the letter pointed out, was suspected of murdering sixteen Jews in the Warsaw ghetto. There were also two cropped photographs of Blösche, blown up to show his face. At the bottom left-hand corner of one of these photos was a small raised white palm.[9]

The Stasi collected the letter and photos and ordered Schenk to remain silent. A preliminary investigation was launched. Agents dug up documents from archives, combed scholarly books as well as witness accounts, and collected reports from informants in both Urbach and the potash mine in Volkenroda. Special assistance requests were sent out to the Czechoslovakian and Polish security services, and after receiving their responses Stasi representatives traveled to these countries to collect firsthand testimonies.

Months later, as the Stasi continued its investigation, the chief prosecutor of the Hamburg District Court requested that the East German authorities extradite Blösche to West Germany. Witnesses in the Hamburg trial of Dr. Hahn—the former SIPO and SD commander in Warsaw—had repeatedly given incriminating testimony against Blösche. In addition, Blösche's name had come up again and again in the 1965 trial of Klaustermeyer, his Gestapo comrade who stood to Blösche's right in the photo of the little boy. The Bielefeld District Court convicted Klaustermeyer of singlehandedly shooting nine Jewish men, women, and children in Warsaw and sentenced him to nine consecutive life imprisonments.[10] The East Germans, who never seriously considered complying with the West German request to extradite Blösche, still saw an opportunity to bolster their own investigation. They requested that the West Germans hand over copies of the incriminating testimonies against Blösche so they could consider the request. The West Germans complied. Now the East Germans had at their disposal more incriminating evidence against Blösche, material to be used in case of a future trial in East Germany.

A year after its launch, piles of documents bearing the name "Blösche" were stacked in the file cabinets of the Stasi's headquarters. The minister of state security, Erich Mielke, received regular updates on the investigation's progress. Arresting Blösche, wrote Hauptmann Schulz from Stasi department XX/2, would not only prevent West Germany from bringing to trial an East German citizen, but in addition would make plain to the world that "in the DDR only one person resides who took part in the so-called crimes, whereas in West Germany lives one of the key accountables and several partakers."[11]

On January 11, 1967, Stasi agents Fehse, Pascher, and Krentz, accompanied by the state prosecutor Friedrich, drove into the parking lot of the mine in Volkenroda. It was 6:35. The night shift had ended, and the miners streamed out of the gate into an ice-cold morning. One of the miners, wrapped in a warm leather jacket and carrying his lunch box, walked across the parking lot to his Trabant 600 to drive home after a long night. The rear door of a black car with a Berlin license plate opened. The three agents climbed out. Approaching the miner, one of them called: Blösche? The miner nodded. The Stasi agents grabbed him by his arms, handcuffed him, searched him, and pushed him into the back of the car. Almost twenty-two years after the end of the war, Friedrich informed Blösche that he was under arrest.[12]

It was still dark outside when loud calls and fierce bangs came at the front door of the Blösches' home. Hanna turned on the outside light and saw a group of men standing on her doorstep. She pulled the door open and the men swarmed in. Friedrich presented Hanna with a search warrant issued the previous day by a court in Berlin. Her husband was under arrest, he informed her, "for strong suspicions of committing grave crimes against humanity during the Fascistic period."[13]

The Stasi agents emptied every drawer and kitchen cupboard, examined every paper. Three hours later, after they had also searched Blösche's mother's home, the Stasi departed with several documents, which included Blösche's birth certificate, his curriculum vitae, his East German Sports Association membership booklet, and twenty photos, including a composite of Hanna and Blösche—Blösche's photo taken before the accident that disfigured his face—they had made for their wedding.[14]

Hanna was dazed by what had just happened. She could make no sense of it. Her husband of seventeen years, the man she loved, had been arrested by the Stasi—the notorious security service whose name alone terrified any East German citizen. It was impossible that her caring husband, who worried over the slightest ailment suffered by any of their three children, had taken part in any crime, let alone crimes against humanity. She was certain that a grave mistake had been made.[15]

At this time, Blösche sat pressed between Stasi agents in a speeding car. A sack over his head, he had no idea where the car was going. After a long ride, it finally came to a halt. Blösche heard the window open and a voice asking for identification papers. The driver exchanged short sentences with the person outside. He heard a latch unlock and a gate drag open, and the car drove ahead and halted. Again Blösche heard the rattling of papers. Another gate squeaked open. The car rolled ahead, took a few sharp turns, and stopped. Large doors shut behind. The car door opened and someone pulled the sack off. They were in a dark garage. The agents led Blösche into a building. They passed through two locked gates equipped with surveillance cameras and entered a room.[16]

A prison guard registered Blösche's personal details. He ordered him to place all his possessions on the counter. Blösche emptied his pockets: a comb, six keys, a wallet with 2.07 DM, a box with three cigars, a health insurance card, and a driver's license. The guard then ordered him to undress. Blösche handed the guard his leather jacket, brown pants, an undershirt, long underpants, socks, and brown shoes. Another guard stuck a flashlight in his mouth, using it to raise Blösche's tongue and look underneath it. He pulled a glove over his hand and ordered Blösche to kneel. Blösche complied. The guard shoved his hand up Blösche's rectum. No findings, he reported. Blösche was handed a document listing all his possessions. He signed it, confirming that he had "the following objects removed and handed over to the prison administration for safe keeping."[17]

Dressed in prison clothes, with his hands and legs cuffed, Blösche was taken to another room, where he was fingerprinted and photographed. From there the guards walked him down a fluorescent-lit corridor lined with heavy gray steel doors. At every corner, the guards stopped him and waited until a red light was replaced by a green one—a traffic light system used throughout the prison to ensure that no prisoner ran into any other. All corridors were monitored by closed-circuit television. Then the guards stopped in front of a locked prison gate. They unlocked the gate and led Blösche out of the cell wing and into the facility's investigation wing.

They walked along another corridor with identical gray wooden doors on both sides. The guards knocked on one. A low voice ordered them in. One bulb lit the spare office. The window curtains were shut. A guard seated Blösche on a stool in a corner and ordered him to sit with his hands under his thighs. Blösche struggled to sit upright on the backless stool. Two yards away, behind a table, under a portrait of a party leader, sat Stasi officer Harry Hesche in a gray-brown uniform. In the dim light, Blösche could hardly see Hesche's face.[18]

Without preamble, Hesche ordered Blösche to detail his personal history. His father, Blösche said, had an inn and a farm in Frydlant. Until the age of fourteen he attended school and also worked for his father. Hesche interrupted him repeatedly to correct or add a detail. He already seemed to know everything about him. Hesche pulled a page from a pile of documents on his desk, rose, crossed the room, and stood above Blösche. He handed him the page, which contained a list of names. Number 1 was his friend Hans Adler, with whom Blösche had attended the border police school in Pretzsch. He also knew number 7, Karl Beer, number 13, Johannes Fleck, and number 67, Karly Mally from the same police school. Number 10 was Josef Blösche.[19]

From Pretzsch, he reported, he had traveled to Platerow, where he served as a guard on the border. Later, when the war with the Soviet Union broke out, he had been transferred east with an Einsatzgruppe to the area of Baranovichi. His one and only duty there had been to guard the barracks. Next he had been stationed in the ghetto in Warsaw, where he had patrolled the streets. No, he had at no time experienced any special events in the ghetto, he informed Hesche.[20]

Hesche demanded for the third or fourth time that Blösche describe his actions while serving in the ghetto. He repeated his account, and over and over the officer kept pressing him. Through the window curtains he made out the sky turning dark. Hours had passed since he had completed his night shift and since he had last slept. Blösche felt his eyelids close. The interrogation seemed nowhere near an end. Hesche indicated he would let Blösche go to his cell after he described his actions in the ghetto in greater detail. The officer seemed to know everything already, and Blösche badly needed sleep. He decided to surrender one story.

It was Brandt, Blösche said, who had once commanded him to shoot a Jew. Where? Hesche asked. It was in the courtyard entry of a neighboring building to the Gestapo outpost in the ghetto, which was headed by Brandt. Describe the details of the shooting, Hesche demanded. Blösche described how he had held the Jew by his shoulder, pushed him out of the courtyard, drew his 7.65-mm Walther pistol, and released one shot into the Jew's neck. It was done, he insisted, on the command of Brandt. Hesche demanded he repeat the story.[21]

Blösche retold the story, then told another, one he hoped would mitigate the previous. One day, he and his Gestapo associate Rührenschopf had escorted Stroop around the Umschlagplatz. There, Stroop spotted a nineteen- or twenty-year-old Jewish girl, ordered her to undress, and questioned her. Then, Stroop ordered Blösche to shoot her, an order, Blösche insisted, he was reluctant to follow. He took her out of the Umschlagplatz, but he did not shoot her. In fact, he thought of letting her go after Stroop had humiliated her, but then a different SS man, whose name he could not recall, had jumped from behind him and shot her.[22]

The first day of investigation ended at nine-thirty, more than seven hours of questioning with only a short break. The guards chained Blösche's hands and legs and took him down the long corridors, past prison gates, and into the cell wing. They stopped in front of one of the steel doors, with a small shut window and a peephole above. One of the guards opened the door's two locks.

The cell had one window, a bed, a toilet, and a sink. On the wooden bed lay a blue-and-white striped mattress and one blanket.

The steel door closed behind him. The light went off. Blösche lay down on the thin mattress, searching for a comfortable position. He finally rested on his side, his hands under the blanket to protect him from the cold in the unheated cell. He fell asleep. The next thing he knew, the cell was filled with bright light, so strong he thought that a new day had begun. But it was a powerful bulb pushed through a small glass opening above the steel door. The peephole cover moved and a rattle sounded. Sleep on your back, the voice barked, your hands above the blanket. The light went out. Blösche lay on his back, his hands outside the blanket. Minutes later the bright light again filled the cell. Every few minutes for the rest of the night, the room was lit as bright as day.[23]

At five o'clock, roll call awakened Blösche. The door's small window opened and a roll with margarine was slipped in. Blösche heard the rain tapping on the cell's window, but he could see nothing through it. It was made of glass bricks and admitted meager light. He could not recognize where he was, nor could he see a bird or a cloud.

Soon the guards escorted the sleep-deprived Blösche through the long gray corridors back to the investigation room. Hesche—whose name Blösche did not know and would never come to know—gestured the guard to seat him not on the corner stool but on a chair near a table. On it lay seven densely typed pages. Read them, Hesche commanded.

> The shooting took place in the gateway of the building next to that of the Gestapo office. I myself had shot with my own hands one Jewish citizen. I had led this Jew out of the Gestapo office to the gateway. I held on to him by the shoulder and pushed him out, that is, I had pushed him along. In the gateway, with my service pistol, a Walther 7.65 mm, I killed the Jewish citizen with a

shot to the neck. With my left hand I held on to his arm and with my right hand I placed the pistol against his neck and pressed. After I shot, the Jewish citizen was immediately dead.

On it went, an edited account of his testimony from the previous day. He had never said "Jewish citizen" or the "fascistic Waffen-SS." Brandt's name appeared, but rarely. The investigator never spoke to him in the third person as it appeared in the text but instead had repeatedly threatened him. On the final page, a line read, "The content corresponds in all parts to my testimony. My words are rendered here correctly." At the bottom of the page was typed his name and above it a blank line. Hesche handed him a pen and motioned for him to sign. Blösche took the pen and signed as ordered at the bottom of each page.[24]

A new day of investigation began. Hesche pulled from his stacks a photograph of a column of Jews marching through the burning streets of the Warsaw ghetto. He put it on the table. Tell me about this, he ordered Blösche. The photo showed an *Aktion*, Blösche explained, in which Gestapo men led Jews along the ghetto streets to the Umschlagplatz. "On such *Aktionen*," he added, "as one can see in the photo, I did not take part."[25]

Hesche waited a moment and then chose another photo. He flipped it over and showed Blösche a little boy with his hands up and a helmeted SS soldier with a rifle standing behind him. Blösche's deformed face startled. Turn the photo over, Hesche ordered, and write on the back side: "The person pictured on the opposite side of the photograph in SS uniform, with submachine gun in assault position and riding glasses on the steel helmet, is me. This picture shows me as a member of the Gestapo in the Warsaw ghetto, with a group of SS members in a deportation *Aktion*."[26]

That afternoon, in a windowless truck, the Stasi delivered Blösche to the courtroom of Judge K. Krautter. Based on Blösche's admission the previous day that he had murdered a Jew, an admission that he had certified with his signature, the prosecutor formally requested Blösche's arrest. The judge, using almost word-for-word the prosecutor's request, approved the arrest. Blösche, who had no attorney representing him, had only one request: "I ask to inform my wife of my arrest and imprisonment."[27]

Three weeks into her husband's arrest, on January 31, 1967, Hanna sat at her kitchen table and wrote a letter to the state prosecutor Friedrich. "Due to my husband's arrest and as mother of our children," she wrote, "I am deeply concerned. You will surely understand, dear honorable state prosecutor," she wrote in her small cursive script, "that I ask you to please inform me what stands against my husband and in which direction are the accusations. I am convinced that on the basis of our constitution you will communicate to me the information to which I am entitled and [I] thank you in advance for that. Regarding myself, I should assure you, that after 17 years of marriage to my husband, I have now, as before, confidence and trust in him." She mailed the letter together with a birthday card for

Blösche, who would turn fifty-five in five days, to the Stasi office in Berlin.[28]

Friedrich's typewritten response, together with a letter from Blösche, arrived three weeks later.

> Dear Frau Blösche,
>
>   I ask you to assure that your letter [to the internee] should not exceed the size of two DIN A4 pages. References or comments on the actions which are subject for investigation should not be noted. . . . As for your letter of January 31, 1967, I inform you that your contention that you have no knowledge about the cause of your husband's arrest is not clear to me. I personally informed you on January 11, 1967, that your husband had to be taken into custody due to strong suspicions of his having committed grave crimes against humanity in the time of fascism. You were at the time informed that at present and in the foreseeable future a more detailed account cannot be communicated. . . .
>
> Friedrich, State Prosecutor [29]

Ten months passed, during which Hanna wrote more letters to Friedrich asking for details on the specific accusations against her husband and information on the date of his trial. During this time she was permitted two one-hour-long visits with Blösche. On October 19, 1967, Hanna journeyed from Urbach to the Lichtenberg jail in Berlin for her third visit. There, between the hours of 2:00 and 3:00 p.m. precisely, Hanna and Blösche sat in the presence of a Stasi agent. Hanna told stories about their teenage children and Blösche's ailing mother. At the end of the sixty-minute reunion, she bid her husband farewell and went to meet State Prosecutor Friedrich.

The prosecutor reiterated that Blösche was suspected of committing grave crimes against humanity. He still refused, however, to provide further details. Hanna assured Friedrich that if her husband had indeed killed someone, he had done so only because he had had no other choice. After her many years of marriage to Blösche, she was certain that he was not a bad person. From her bag Hanna produced a postcard she had received from a bereaved parent who had contacted her after Blösche's arrest. My "greatest misfortune," the parent wrote, is "that my son was shot, because he could not follow a command to shoot a Jewess and her child."[30] Surely, she indicated, Blösche too had faced a similar life-or-death decision. Before Hanna departed, Friedrich said he would shortly communicate to her the date of the trial.

In January, Blösche's second birthday in prison neared and Hanna sent to Friedrich in her name and that of her children a letter with a special request.

> Dear Herr State Prosecutor,
>
> My wish is not big. If you want you can fulfill it for me. I attach 10 DM and ask you to buy one packet of F6 [cigarettes], a box of mocha beans, and one packet of grape-sugar . . . as a birthday present from us to my husband. When for 19 long years one enjoys repeatedly another person's love, so one should like to bring him also a small delight. . . . A humble request shall not remain unfulfilled.
>
> Respectfully,
> Hanna Blösche[31]

Friedrich never responded.

In the prison, Blösche received Hanna's birthday card, as well as cards from friends.[32] A new Stasi officer appointed to his case, Reiner Stenzel, handed him the envelopes previously opened and censored by Stasi agents.[33] Blösche read the good wishes and the letter, into which Hanna fit as much information as the two permitted pages allowed. His mother's health was deteriorating. A family in the village was going on vacation. The marriage of Gertraud was nearing.

Blösche read it all eagerly. When he was done, the officer handed Blösche a pen. At the bottom of the letter, just beside Hanna's farewell words, Blösche wrote "brought to attention" and signed. Stenzel took away the mail and filed it in a Stasi folder.[34]

Once a month, the Stasi investigators handed Blösche a piece of graph paper on which he could write a letter home. In his large cursive handwriting, which unlike Hanna's never filled the two permitted pages, Blösche thanked Hanna in his poorly written German for providing him with money and asked her to send him an additional 15 or 20 DM so he could purchase more tobacco. In her last visit to him, he pointed out, she had forgotten to show him a photo of their granddaughter. Does she visit you on her own? he asked. He hoped not. The traffic along the narrow streets of Urbach was very dangerous. He asked Hanna to make sure that the children wrote him. Also, she should send him a photo of his son, Klaus, who had been drafted into the East German army. To see his son dressed in uniform would give him great pleasure, he wrote.[35]

The months passed, and in November of 1968, Hanna wrote again to Friedrich.

> Dear honorable Herr State Prosecutor,
>
> You know my question without me presenting it. When will the trial take place and should we expect a good ending? You had promised me that it will take place this year. . . . You should please believe me that my husband is not such a terrible man, only the war is to blame, and I pray daily that no war should occur again, as we have a young son who is a soldier, who also concerns me. He assures me time and again, Mommy, you shouldn't worry, I am only fighting for peace.
>
> I hope for a fast, calming response, as it is almost two years that this miserable uncertainty yanks on my nerves. Should we again have a sad Christmas night? . . .
>
> Respectfully,
> Hanna Blösche[36]

Hanna and the children indeed experienced another sad Christmas night. An additional four months passed until finally, in March 1969, "Mr. Josef Blösche, at present in investigation facility, Berlin," was summoned to appear in the District Court of Erfurt, which had jurisdiction over Urbach. His trial was to begin on April 21, at 9:00 a.m.[37] A week before the trial, Hanna visited the Erfurt office of Joachim Müller, the attorney who would represent her husband. When Müller read to her excerpts from her husband's confessions, Hanna broke down. "I do not know how I can tell my children, I do not know how I should break the news to them that the trust that they had up until now in their father, was in the past so terribly abused by him."[38] Hanna, whose sixth and last visit to her husband had been a few weeks earlier, would not attend his trial.[39]

On Mount Carmel, Rivkah, now a mother of two boys, worked as a housewife in her home. As she cut vegetables for dinner, or swept the living room floor, she took pleasure in the chatter of her boys, Haim and Jacob, playing with the neighbors' children in the garden or in the stairwell. She also enjoyed it when on weekends her sister Dina with her husband and children came for a meal or, in turn, when she, Fischel, and the boys traveled down to their relatives' kibbutz in southern Israel.

On Friday nights, the family sat around the kitchen table, covered with a white tablecloth, and Rivkah and Fischel told the boys stories about their life in Europe. Unlike many other survivors, who refused to tell their children such stories, Rivkah and Fischel repeatedly discussed what they had experienced. The boys learned about their mother's life in the ghetto and her clandestine life among Poles, and time and again they asked her to retell the story of how she had jumped off the train. They listened attentively as she recalled smuggling Jewish survivors through thick forests, over snowy mountains, and across borders en route to the Land of Israel. Sometimes, Rivkah showed the boys the shabby envelope in which she

kept a few black-and-white photos of her parents. "This is all I have left of them," she would tell them.[40]

At an early age, Haim and Jacob joined the youth movement of Mahanot ha'Olim, which was linked to the Dror He-Halutz youth movement in which Rivkah and Fischel had been members. In 1965, the teenagers in the local Haifa branch elected seventeen-year-old Haim to represent them at the movement's national gathering. The key topic on the agenda was the sensational decision of Israel's prime minister, Levi Eshkol, to establish diplomatic relations with West Germany.

Haim strongly opposed the decision. "Can we rely," he forcefully argued, "on a murderer?" Speaking of the reparation agreements between Israel and West Germany signed in 1952 (the benefits of which Rivkah refused to sign up for), he stated that "the reparation agreement is a satanic idea that only a German mind, which planned for years how to annihilate a nation, is able to invent." He concluded, "One must act before the nation's moral deterioration arrives."

Fiercely proud of their sons, Rivkah and Fischel saw them as following in their path.[41]

Almost twenty-six years to the day from the start of the Nazis' final liquidation of the Warsaw ghetto, on April 21, 1969, the Stasi had completed all preparations for the Blösche trial. The investigators in charge of the case had arrived in Erfurt a few days earlier to examine the courtroom, the witness waiting room, the phone connections, and the recording devices. They also arranged for undercover agents to shadow and closely monitor the seven witnesses arriving from Poland and especially the three witnesses invited from West Germany. Sixty to seventy people handpicked by the Stasi—party members, Stasi workers, reporters for state-controlled media, members of the Polish secret service and prosecution, representatives from the Volkenroda mine and from Urbach—as well as Blösche's son-in-law sat that morning in the courtroom of the monumental nineteenth-century building of the District Court in Erfurt as the trial began.[42]

The chief justice of the court, Walter Kubasch, and Assistant Judge Schmidt managed the trial. On their table lay a 147-page indictment, which the state prosecutor Geyer had copied almost word-for-word from the final Stasi report of Blösche's investigation. The indictment accused Blösche of dozens of individual murders and participation in almost twenty mass executions.[43]

At the opening of the trial, Geyer handed the judges three mounted photos of Blösche. Two of the pictures predated the war; in one he was roughly twenty years old, in another in his early twenties. These were compared to a postwar photograph of the deformed face of Josef Blösche. Geyer presented a report by the Stasi's technical department analyzing and comparing the images, to determine if they were of the same person. Based on the shape of the head, the wavy hair and hairline, the broad forehead, the slender mouth, the oval shape and the length of the ears, the distance between eyes and mouth edge, the report determined that these were all photographs of "one and the same person."[44]

The report's findings accepted, the trial proceeded.

The court turned to Blösche and asked him about an event in August 1942, when he shot a young man in a window while patrolling the ghetto streets.

"... [I] can't remember....."

"March of 1943, [you] shot several inhabitants in Muranowski Square...?"

"... [I] can't remember...."

"Summer of 1942 on the ghetto fence, [you] shot two small children?"

"I dispute that... because then I was in the Einsatzkommando... I wasn't then in Warsaw."[45]

A West German witness, Nathan Rosenberg, took the stand. He stood directly across from the dock in which Blösche, old and

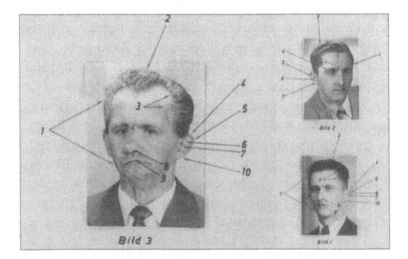

Bild 3

fragile looking, sat. During the ghetto liquidation, Rosenberg described to the court, Blösche shot at women running atop blazing buildings.

The prosecutor challenged the witness: Blösche says he simply shot in the air.

That is a complete lie, Rosenberg responded. He pointed to Blösche: "When he and Klaustermeyer entered the ghetto they did not travel out without leaving behind ten or twenty dead. As a pious man would say, 'I am going to the church,' so they went into the ghetto in order to shoot."

"I do not know of that anymore today," Blösche responded.

The judge voiced his opinion: "I believe you have done so much that you can't recall anything anymore."[46]

On the third day of the trial, April 23, the chief prosecutor of East Germany, Dr. Josef Streit, came from Berlin to sit in on the court proceedings. During a recess, Streit spoke with the West German witnesses about the advantages of the East German justice system over that of the West. The case of Blösche, he told them, demonstrates the forceful pursuit of Nazi criminals in East Germany, which stands "in contrast to the West German statute of limitations and rehabilitation politics." Unlike in West Germany, Streit declared to his captive audience, where Dr. Hahn, Blösche's superior, lived freely for many years while awaiting a prolonged set of trials, in East Germany, Blösche had to rot in jail for more than two years awaiting his trial, a trial that would be done and over in fewer than ten days.[47]

The trial resumed. Did you ever resist a command to kill anyone, the judges asked. Blösche, standing in the dock, holding one of his hands behind his back, spoke into the microphone.

> I had at that time refused to shoot a girl that Stroop had ordered to undress . . . in front of the entire escort. She had to dress up again and he said: 'We can't let her run away now. You, shoot her. . . .'

Then I was left with the girl. I was so angered, he had acted so unconscionably . . . and she was so young, I couldn't do it and because he had heard no shot, he sent Klaustermeyer after me and he came rushing and shot her.[48]

The judge presented Blösche with the photograph of the little boy.

"You [stand] with a machine gun . . . a small child, whom you had pulled out of a house, [stands] with raised hands. . . . How did the people behave at this moment?"

"They were terrified."

". . . That, most notably, one sees in the little boy. . . . What thought went through your head?"

"At the time of the complete liquidation, a person did not come to think at all."

"Your daily bread . . . no regret in your face . . ."

"A man saw this every day during the liquidation."[49]

On Saturday, April 26, the fifth day of the trial, the prosecutor, Geyer, rose to give his closing statement. "Honorable Court!" he began. The presentation of evidence was now closed. The accusations against Blösche, he went on, were also accusations against

> the still existing imperialistic system, which had and still does organize such crimes. . . . We have portrayed how numerous men, women, children, sick, elderly, pregnant women, had been rounded up in the ghetto and shot—hundreds [of them]—and how the accused and his SS accomplices had organized a true battue. No person's life was safe anymore on the ghetto streets. Fear, great mental torment, at every step prepared to land in the hands of an SS beast, these were the constants of Jews found in the claws of the barbaric German imperialists, embodied in the SS hangmen. . . .
>
> All people today are aware that German imperialism, from the turn of the century to the present younger West Germany, has never given up on its aspiration to control Europe, believing this will serve as a precondition for a new world order.[50]

After completing his critique of West German imperialism, Geyer detailed the accusations leveled against Blösche. For hours he described shootings inside and outside the ghetto. Ending his speech, Geyer declared that "Blösche had through his terrible crimes excluded himself from human society."[51]

Two days later, Blösche's attorney, Müller, gave his closing statement. He opened by asserting that in his entire career he had never witnessed such a gruesome set of charges. He would not dispute any of the facts, he declared, only urge the court to take into account that Blösche had not acted on his own initiative. Müller pleaded that Blösche be sentenced only to life in prison.[52]

At 2:00 p.m. on Wednesday, April, 30, on the eve of the International Workers' May Day celebration, this year with a special focus on the twentieth anniversary of the German Democratic Republic, Justice Kubasch read the verdict:

The accused was a member of the SS and had taken an active part as a staff member of the SD in the liquidation of the Jewish people in a beastly and inhuman manner. He was the horror of the ghetto. When they saw him, the Jewish people fled from him. No one's life was safe.

The accused was a fanatic champion of the fascistic ideology. He unconditionally obeyed all instructions and commands of his superiors. About that, the hearing brought clear evidence. He had no scruple when it came to liquidating masses of people.[53]

Blösche was sentenced to death.

Back in his cell in the secret East Berlin prison, Blösche was deeply shocked by the verdict. Writing to Hanna, he declared that they could "only hope that in the appeal proceedings in Berlin this frightful verdict should not be validated, but [replaced by] a reduced sentence." He saw, he wrote, their son-in-law, Ulla's husband, in the courtroom. "I hope," he concluded, "you did not communicate the verdict to my mother?"[54]

Blösche's attorney, Müller, appealed his case to the East German Supreme Court. Shortly thereafter the attorney mailed Hanna a letter on the results of the appeal:

Dear Frau Blösche:

The appeal hearing in the criminal case against your husband took place in front of the East German Supreme Court on 13.6.69.

In this proceeding the appeal I handed in was rejected as baseless.

The verdict of the district court of Erfurt from 30.4.69 is therefore effective.

We are left only with a clemency request directed at Mr. Chairman of the State Council of East Germany. I ask you to visit me immediately after you make an appointment by telephone.

Sincerely,

Joachim Müller[55]

A few weeks later Hanna learned that the chairman of the State Council had turned down the request.

On the eve of July 29, Hanna sat at her kitchen table, exhausted after a day's work, and wrote a letter to her husband:

Beloved father!

Today we received your lovely letter and so I will try to answer you immediately. All that has assailed us and that we have had to learn about the horrible crimes that you had to take part in was to us very shocking. Why had you not somehow done something? But what use is it now, the facts can't be changed.

Birgitt does not go to her studies and Klaus was not accepted at the mine and he will have to worry about it somehow over the next vacation. . . .

We have picked our cherries. There were not as many as in the previous year. . . .

It is now again the time to go to sleep. I am not as I used to be. I need a lot of quiet, so as to manage to do something during the day. I need to make a big effort if I wish to earn M400. . . .

> Best wishes and kisses,
> Hanna and the children[56]

Blösche never received this letter. That morning he had been transferred to the correctional facility in Leipzig. At 10:40, a firing squad executed him. His body and possessions were cremated that day. His remains were buried in an unknown location. Weeks later, Hanna was informed of his execution.[57]

In the late 1960s, Haim was drafted into the army and volunteered for the paratroopers, a unit that four years later Jacob joined. On October 6, 1973, on Yom Kippur, the Day of Atonement, emergency sirens wailed all over Israel. In their apartment atop Mount

Carmel in Haifa, Rivkah and Fischel heard the sirens and learned
that Egyptian and Syrian forces had launched a surprise attack on
Israel. The Egyptian forces had crossed the Suez Canal into the Si-
nai Desert and Syrian troops neared the Jordan Valley. Both Haim
and Jacob, who had completed their compulsory service, were
drafted into the reserve forces. They fought against the Egyptians
on the southern front. Back in Haifa, Fischel and Rivkah awaited
word from them. A week after the war broke out, Haim had his first
opportunity to reassure his parents that he was safe. He sent them a
note, saying, "You should know you have nothing to worry about
and that I am fine. At nights I am wearing a sweater so I won't catch
a cold. Meanwhile, we did not do anything serious and let's hope the
whole business will be over soon."[58]

A few days later, an army officer knocked on Rivkah and
Fischel's apartment door. They feared the worst. Haim, the officer
informed them, was missing in action. There was a possibility that
he was a prisoner of the Egyptian army. As the first television foot-
age of Israeli prisoners of war was broadcast from Cairo, Fischel
and Rivkah stared at the TV screen, searching for their son. They
would point at the image of one prisoner after another, arguing
over which resembled Haim.

On November 11, 1973, the news that Fischel and Rivkah
dreaded arrived. Haim, their eldest son, had been killed in battle.
They journeyed with Jacob to the sands of Be'eri, where the bodies
of soldiers killed in action had been buried in makeshift graves.
There they drifted between lines of small wooden signs posted in
the sand, marking the graves of dozens of fallen soldiers whose
identities remained unknown. "In Be'eri I called out to you, Haim,"
Fischel wrote later. "You did not answer me; just the echo of my
lonely and hurting voice came back to me. How is it that you are not
answering me? Why? Here we are still waiting for an answer."[59]

On a cold November day, Fischel, Rivkah, and Jacob followed
an olive-colored army truck on which lay a casket containing the

remains of Haim. A long procession of cars, their headlights on, drove behind them down Mount Carmel to the military cemetery by the sea, where Haim was put to final rest. Rivkah and Fischel sat shivah for the requisite seven days over their son, killed in an Egyptian ambush. Many friends visited to pay their condolences. Friends of Haim from the kibbutz, school, and the youth movement gathered in the small second-floor apartment. A friend brought a note and a portrait of Haim she had received only two months before he was killed. "I do not know," Haim had written, "if the photo is as good as the original, but when I will cease to be, I believe that from time to time you will glance at the photo and ask your soul: Is this the lad?!"[60]

God does not want me anymore, Rivkah repeatedly told Fischel. "Each person has a ration of suffering. . . . Did I not suffer enough?" Rivkah lost interest in life. Feeble and weak, she went in and out of hospitals. In June 1977, she was diagnosed with abdominal cancer. She was operated on and went through chemotherapy and radia-

tion. Jacob, who had been planning to move to Japan as part of his work for Israel's defense ministry, stayed by his mother and tried to persuade her to fight on. She refused.

Fischel, whom Rivkah had nursed a few years earlier when he had suffered a stroke, couldn't bring himself to transfer her to a hospital. Every two or three hours, Fischel injected Rivkah with painkillers. In mid-February 1980, three years into her sickness, Fischel conceded to Rivkah's repeated requests that she not remain such a burden on him; she was transferred to a hospital. Four days later, she lost consciousness. "Slowly slowly, I caressed her face," Fischel wrote. "I leaned forward and kissed her on her forehead. All her life was so quiet and noble and so too was her departure."[61] On February 23, Rivkah died. She was buried in a cemetery that overlooked the cemetery in which Haim had been laid to rest.

In April 1982, Dr. Tsvi Nussbaum rushed from surgery in a New York hospital to visit his patients in the ear, nose, and throat unit. Tsvi, who now lived with his wife and their four daughters in New City—an hour's drive north of New York City—had emigrated from Israel to the United States thirty years earlier with his aunt and uncle and their two young daughters. Thanks to a generous scholarship, Tsvi attended Yeshiva University High School and later the City University of New York, from which he graduated in 1958. Tsvi chose medicine and otolaryngology to help cure his uncle, who had lost his voice as a result of conditions in the concentration camp. He graduated from the Albert Einstein College of Medicine and later specialized in surgery.

Walking down a hospital corridor, Tsvi saw one of his patients, Mark Berkowitz, a Holocaust survivor. He stopped and briefly chatted. Tsvi remembered something that had been on his mind. "Mark, do me a favor, I don't have the time. Would you be kind enough to get me this picture of the little boy?"[62] Earlier, Tsvi had written the Simon Wiesenthal Center in Los Angeles asking for an enlarged copy of the photo, but he had not heard back. Every time he saw this iconic picture on television, in a newspaper, or in a book, Tsvi told Mark, he was reminded of his own experience at the Hotel Polski on July 13, 1943, a day when he, like the boy in the picture, had had to raise his arms at the motion of a Nazi's gun, a day when he too was torn apart from his family, a day when he too had stood alone in the world.[63]

Standing in the chaotic hospital corridor, Mark popped a question that Tsvi had never considered: "How do you know it is not you?" Tsvi rebutted the thought. "Mark, I was never in the Warsaw ghetto. I remember some place, some hotel, I know the date and what happened to me." Unconvinced, Mark repeated, "How do you know that it is not you?" Tsvi remained silent. Then he said, "I don't know." "Give me the pictures you have when you were young," Mark requested, "and let me do an investigation."[64]

Mark returned a few days later to Tsvi's clinic and spread an enlarged copy of the famous photograph on his desk. Pointing at the little boy in the photo, he announced to Tsvi's amazement, "This is you." Mark placed a photo of Tsvi as a toddler in Tel Aviv before the war and a photo of ten-year-old Tsvi taken in Brussels after liberation alongside the photo of the boy. He pointed out the striking similarities. The upper lips of both the little boy and Tsvi were thin and their lower lips were thick, their nostrils had the same shape, their noses and cheeks matched. Both boys' eyes—full of deep pain and sadness—were identical. Tsvi looked at the picture of the little boy, and the memory of that one fateful day of July 13, 1943, flashed back at him. He remained silent. Days later he pasted the two photos of him taken in Tel Aviv and Brussels beside the image of the little boy. He hung the collage on his office wall.[65]

Mark informed the Israel Bond Organization of the discovery of the little boy. The organization immediately contacted Tsvi and enlisted him as a speaker. He gave speeches at special dinners in

Winnipeg, Detroit, Miami, and Long Island to raise money for Israel, the land to which he felt he owed his life.[66]

Jewish Week, a local New York newspaper, soon learned that the boy had survived. On its front page, the newspaper splashed the headline "Frightened Little Boy Whose Photo Symbolized Nazi Terror Is Alive and Well; A Physician, He Works Hard for Israel, His Future Home." The caption under the photo of the adult Tsvi standing beside the photograph of the little boy read, "*Then and Now:* Dr. Nussbaum looks at the famous picture of himself as a young, frightened boy, has [*sic*] arms aloft as Nazi troops herded him and other Jews to a train that took them to Bergen-Belsen."[67]

The publication of Tsvi's story caused some controversy. A few Jewish organizations and individuals adopted the story; others casted doubt. *The New York Times*, which described the photo as "one of the indelible images of history . . . perhaps the most enduring exhibit of the epoch," ran a story on the dispute. The reporter, David Margolick, who met Tsvi, pointed out that Tsvi made the claim "almost reluctantly." The historian Lucjan Dobroszycki, from the YIVO Institute for Jewish research, he went on to report,

> said that several elements in the picture cast doubt on the latest claim. The scene, he noted, is on a street, not in the courtyard in which the Hotel Polski roundup took place. Some of the Jews are wearing armbands that they surely would have shed while in the "Aryan" quarter of Warsaw. The German soldiers would not have needed combat uniforms at the hotel. The heavy clothing worn by most of the Jews suggests that the photograph was taken in May— the date General Stroop put on the report—rather than July. Moreover, every other photograph in the Stroop report was taken in the Warsaw ghetto.

In conclusion, the *Times* reporter stressed that Tsvi "is not, however, dogmatic about it. 'I'm not claiming anything—there's no reward,' he said. 'I didn't ask for this honor. I think it's me, but I can't honestly swear to it. A million and a half Jewish children were told to raise their hands.' "[68]

Responding to the critics, Tsvi gave a possible rationale for why he might indeed be the boy in the photo. He explained that many of the photos in *The Stroop Report*

> have, in my mind, no connection with the Warsaw ghetto. . . . What interested me in the reports of Jürgen Stroop was that at the time of the revolt from April 20 to May 16, he [Stroop] . . . did not have the time to collect important information. . . . So this is the way I see it: Stroop was asked at first just to prepare a report and if he could to also add to it pictures. The pictures were added with no connection to the [written] report and some of them even do not have captions. Since Stroop was asked to submit the report after the destruction of the ghetto, the only thing he could have done was to attach pictures which partly were from the ghetto and partly—I am sure of this—were not from the ghetto. . . . If Himmler received the album between May and July, it is not my photo. . . . But if the album was sent in August or September, it is possible that it is me. . . . In my mind, the album was prepared not before the end of 1943 and possibly in early 1944.[69]

Ever since the story that the boy in the photograph was Tsvi broke in 1982, world media, from Israel to Germany, from the United States to Britain, from Australia to Italy, repeated it.[70] In numerous interviews, Tsvi rarely discussed his past besides his experience on that one day of July 13, 1943. "It's very hard," he told the *Jerusalem Post* reporter Sue Fishkoff in 1993. "Some guys can talk about it in the third person, as if they weren't really there, but I can't do that." The reporter ended her article by pointing out that no absolute identification had been made between Tsvi and the boy. Still, she wrote, "Tsvi's story is real and as harrowing as whatever it was that drew the lines of worry and anguish on that famous little boy's face."[71]

Epilogue

On November 20, 1945, in courtroom 600 of the bomb-damaged Palace of Justice at Nuremberg, the trial of twenty-two leaders of the Nazi regime accused of crimes against humanity began. Despite the harmless look of the group of "miserable men" and "broken men" in the prison docket, pointed out the chief U.S. prosecutor, Chief Justice Robert Jackson, "these prisoners represent sinister influences that will lurk in the world long after their bodies have returned to dust. They are living symbols of racial hatreds, of terrorism and violence, and of the arrogance and cruelty of power."[1]

Some time into his speech Chief Justice Jackson also made a short reference to the Nazi regime's crimes against the Jews. Taking into his hands a black volume from the prosecution table, Jackson stated:

> I hold a report with Teutonic devotion to detail, illustrated with photographs to authenticate its almost incredible text, and beautifully bound in leather with the loving care bestowed on a proud work. It is the original report of the SS Brigadier General Stroop in

charge of the destruction of the Warsaw Ghetto, and its title page carries the inscription "The Jewish Ghetto in Warsaw no longer exists." It is characteristic that one of the captions explains that the photograph concerned shows the driving out of Jewish "bandits"; those whom the photograph shows being driven out are almost entirely women and little children.[2]

Major William Walsh of the U.S. prosecution returned to the report on December 14, introducing it as "this finest example of ornate German craftsmanship, leather bound, profusely illustrated." He asked the court's permission to read portions of "the boastful but nonetheless vivid account of some of this ruthless action within the Warsaw ghetto." Permission granted, he read out loud excerpts from one of Stroop's daily communiqués:

"One building after the other was systematically evacuated and subsequently destroyed by fire. . . . Not infrequently the Jews stayed in the burning building until, because of the heat and the fear of being burned alive, they preferred to jump down from the upper stories after having thrown mattresses and other upholstered articles into the street from the burning buildings. With their bones broken they still tried to crawl across the street into blocks of buildings which had not yet been set on fire or were only partially in flames. . . .

"The longer the resistance lasted, the tougher the men of the Waffen-SS, Police, and Wehrmacht became. They fulfilled their duty indefatigably in faithful comradeship and stood together as models and examples of soldiers. . . . High credit should be given to the pluck, courage, and devotion to duty which they showed. . . . Officers and men of the Police . . . again excelled by their dashing spirit."[3]

Listening to Walsh in the courtroom dock, Alfred Jodl, the chief of the Wehrmacht High Command Operational Staff, was inflamed by these excerpts. During the recess he shouted, "The dirty arrogant SS swine! Imagine writing a 75-page boastful report on a little murder expedition, when a major campaign fought by soldiers against a well-armed enemy takes only a few pages!"[4]

The recess over, the prosecution screened five of Stroop's photos.[5] As the black-and-white images from *The Stroop Report* flashed in the darkened courtroom, Viktor von der Lippe, a German jurist, was overwhelmed. "No words can express the brutality, cynicism, and madness (in the original sense of the word) of these ideas of Hitler, Himmler, and their agents and helpers!" he wrote. 'Outrageous' is too weak; 'devilish' and 'satanic' are more like it. It is contemptible that Stroop should call his operation a 'battle'—the SS suffered 16 'casualties,' while 65,000 [*sic*] Jews were 'destroyed.' . . . Now we must acknowledge that even such bestialities actually occurred. It drives me to despair! How the German name has been sullied!"[6]

Unlike von der Lippe, the New York–based Yiddish poet Aron Glanz-Leyeles did not see in this picture "madness," nor "devilish" or "satanic" forces. Rather he saw there something very different: pure human evil. In a poem published in 1947, he writes about the little boy, "chased to the oven, to smoke and fire / Driven with rifles—this is reality!" He then turns to the gentile world that had inflicted upon the boy "tortures," "fear," and "woes," assuring them that they can find in the photo the reality they sought, the image they desired:

> *Calm yourselves; the Warsaw boy is dead,*
> *the Jewish dream is melted in the fire.*
> *The world remains as you have made it—*
> *just corpses piled tall as towers.*

Glanz-Leyeles, however, could not calm himself as he peered into the boy's face. He spotted in the picture his *own* "shame," his

own "guilt," remorse shared by "whoever has a grown man's hand."
In the poem's last stanza, he addresses the boy:

> And you, Jewish boy, in guilt I kiss your face,
> Your pure and kosher Jewish eyes.
> Through a million years, 'til the end of days,
> They demand an answer, your child's cries.[7]

On Photographs, History, and
Narrative Style

This book, my inquiry, was possible only thanks to the efforts and insights of previous scholars. Few subjects have received as much rigorous scholarly attention as the Holocaust. We now know in extraordinary detail the how of the Holocaust: the chronology of events, the chain of decisions and command, and the mechanics and bureaucracy of the Jewish genocide. A line of historical research that begins at least with Christopher Browning has also explored with sophistication and methodological nuance the more troubling questions about why ordinary Germans turned into mass killers. Indeed, a vast academic literature has wrestled without certain resolution with the reasons for man's repeated inhumanity to man. While deeply indebted to this vast and ongoing scholarly effort, this book does not pretend to give a definitive answer. Indeed, the choices I made in the writing of this book—most important, my style of writing, which employs imagination—reflect a desire to approach anew this recurring question at the center of Holocaust historiography, the question of how one set of people could come to see a man, a woman, or a child as the dregs of humanity. It is my belief that only repeat and creative engagement with it can shed more light for more readers.[1]

Looking critically at the photo of the little boy gives us an additional opportunity to approach this question anew. Common knowledge has it that in observing historical photos one sees the reality of the past. Yet, as several scholars have argued, photos frequently advance not a realistic view of the past but rather a mythical sense of knowing. Looking at a photograph, the viewer sees the surface facts and comes to believe he or she has grasped the inner truth of the event depicted, can feel the pain, can see the evil while in fact knowing nothing of the protagonists, circumstances, or context associated with those events. In this way, photographs can not only hinder the understanding of an event but also advance a perception of knowing where only surface knowledge exists. Adding captions to pictures hardly solves this problem, but rather extends this superficial knowing by titling photos from a specific vantage point or by providing the photographs with empty and meaningless titles that give the impression of knowledge.[2]

The proliferation of myth increases when it comes to iconic images such as that of the little boy. As Cornelia Brink points out, one may think that iconic Holocaust photographs, like religious icons, convey some transcendent truth. The icon of Christ positioned in front of the altar is seen as an external expression of an inner transcendental truth; so, too, iconic Holocaust photographs seem to indicate that there is a larger, deeper truth to the piles of corpses. But Brink is quick to dispel this analogy.

> What photographs represent, however, is purely from this world—even though the depicted object seems to suggest otherwise. There

is no absolute "evil" equivalent to the "inner sanctum" which the icon wall represents and hides. . . .

The deeds in the camps confront the viewer with a reality that cannot be grasped spontaneously. . . . In fact, looking at these pictures paralyzes us and makes us fall silent. The result is often a remarkable "inviolability" which seems to preclude a detailed pictorial analysis and only seldom leads to questions concerning the origins and use of photographs. A picture, so the saying goes, is worth a thousand words. But this kind of alleged immediacy—of reality's photographic representation as well as of the emotions it creates—soon turns out to be a myth.[3]

The little boy photograph is a case in point of the kind of myth-making perpetuated by photographs. One of the most repeated, as the guide at the Yad Vashem Holocaust Museum declared, is that it represents a Holocaust story with a "happy ending." A different sort of myth is advanced when this picture is published under the title "The Holocaust," as it is frequently, but without any historical context, explanation of its origins, or account of events preceding or following the moment photographed. Not only have iconic photographs such as that of the little boy not promoted remembrance of the Holocaust or helped prevent other genocides, points out Barbie Zelizer, but "it may be, then, that at times we have begun to remember so as to forget."[4]

To dispel the myth built around and caused by photographs, it is necessary to study the photographs, to analyze them, to articulate their meaning. To overcome their mythmaking, points out Susan Sontag, one needs to come to understanding.

Photography implies that we know about the world if we accept it as the camera records it. But this is the opposite of understanding, which starts from *not* accepting the world as it looks. All possibility of understanding is rooted in the ability to say no. Strictly speaking, one never understands anything from a photograph. Of course, photographs fill in blanks in our mental pictures of the present and the past. . . . Nevertheless, the camera's rendering of reality must always hide more than it discloses. . . . In contrast to the amorous relation, which is based on how something looks, understanding is based on how it functions. And functioning takes place in time, and must be explained in time. Only that which narrates can make us understand.[5]

In short, to understand a historical event as presented in a photograph, narration is essential.

But narrate how? Twelve-year-old Susan Sontag saw the photos from concentration camps and more than thirty years later wrote that "nothing I have seen—in photographs or in real life—ever cut me as sharply, deeply, instantaneously. . . . When I looked at those photographs, something broke. Some limit had been reached, and not only that of horror; I felt irrevocably grieved, wounded, but a part of my feelings started to tighten; something went dead. Something is still crying."[6] In pursuit of understanding, how should one narratively evoke the photograph's immediacy, preserve the image's effects on the viewer?

The expression "a picture is worth a thousand words," while justifiably criticized as advancing the myth of the photograph as reality, still has a certain truth to it. Photographs do stir the emotions in a manner that words rarely do. And it is this element of feeling and emotion that one should try to preserve in a narrative focused on photographs. In a history aimed to undermine the myth of photographs as knowledge and at the same time promote public understanding of the event depicted, imagery and narration must be integrated. The picture should not be simply an annotation to the words, the words not an abstraction of the photograph. Rather, they should work in tandem to preserve people's sentiment and advance their knowledge.[7]

That was the goal I set myself in writing *The Boy*, a goal that shaped my narrative tone. As a result, in a number of instances in my telling of this history, I have gone beyond the bare facts accounted for in the photos and the documents. For example, when I describe someone's journey through a forest or over the sea, I draw on related relevant sources, experiences, and imagination. In a few cases, I fill in gaps in a story. In doing so, I have attempted to "think—or rather feel, intuit—what is beyond it, what the reality must be like if it looks this way."[8]

Filling in gaps and imagining scenes are not uncommon in the profession of history. My use of imagination is disciplined, the exercise of what R. G. Collingwood called the historian's "*a priori* imagination," which he points out is inherent in the profession of history. "The historian's picture of the past is thus in every detail an imaginary picture, and its necessity is at every point the necessity of the *a priori* imagination. Whatever goes into it, goes into it not because his imagination passively accepts it, but because it actively demands it."[9]

Yet, in those sections in which I draw on my a priori imagination, I do not speculate in the way a writer of historical fiction might. Quite the contrary. It is a controlled usage, aided by analytical tools and clearly circumscribed. I was restricted by the known historical evidence and matched the existing historical context with probabilities suggested by multiple sources and research.[10] *The Boy*, then, is decidedly not a work of historical fiction. In full appreciation of the attending difficulties, it is the responsibility of a historian to narrate photographs with analytic rigor, even while retaining, and indeed deepening, their immediacy and meaning.

Although I wrote this book as a story, I verified the facts as much as possible and based my account on the sources. The sources, however, often are problematic—as they are in almost any historical study. The authors of many of the primary sources I used had hidden, and sometimes not-so-hidden, agendas. For example, Stroop saw *The Stroop Report* as an opportunity to promote himself among his superiors. In the same spirit he probably overstated the number of Jewish casualties in the ghetto. Other sources came from postwar criminal investigations in which the perpetrators, for obvious reasons, attempted to conceal, lie, and mislead investigators. Furthermore, in some instances, as I imply in the case of Blösche, the interrogators did not record the investigations verbatim but rather in a manner consistent with their ideology. This of course does not mean that the basic outline of facts is distorted, but it does require the researcher to treat these sources and testimonies with caution. For very different reasons, survivors' testimonies also require a critical distance, due to the problematic nature of memories of trauma given decades after their occurrence.

Consequently, I attempted wherever possible to corroborate accounts with other sources. Yet, because of the specific sources this narrative depends on, it was in many instances impossible to corroborate all testimonies. As occurs with any history, finally I was left to judge events on the basis of consistency, historical contextualization, and my familiarity with the protagonists and the wider historical context, as well as on the basis of my own judgment as a historian.

Notes

ABBREVIATIONS

BStU   Bundesbeauftragte für die Unterlagen des
Staatssicherheitsdienstes der ehemaligen Deutschen
Demokratischen Republik [Ministry for State Security (Stasi)
Archives], Berlin

IPN   Instytut Pamiece Narodowej [Institute of National
Remembrance], Warsaw

NARA   National Archives and Record Administration, Washington, DC

StA DT   Stadtarchiv Detmold, Germany

USHMM   United States Holocaust Memorial Museum archives,
Washington, DC

YVA   Yad Vashem Archives, Jerusalem

PROLOGUE

1. Jürgen Stroop, *The Stroop Report—The Jewish Quarter of Warsaw Is No More!* trans. Sybil Milton (New York: Pantheon Books, 1979). Yosef Kermish, *Mered geto Varshah be-'ene ha-oyev; ha-dohot shel ha-General Yur-*

gen Shtrop [The Warsaw Ghetto Revolt as Seen by the Enemy: General Jürgen Stroop's Reports] (Jerusalem: Yad Vashem, 1966), 107. Adolf Eichmann had also studied the photos in this album: "I transported them . . . to the butcher," *Life* magazine, November 28, 1960, p. 106.

2. The bald man behind the girl is identified on the USHMM photo archive website as Abraham Neyer, a Bund activist in Poland; the woman to his right as his mother; and the woman on the left side of the photo as his wife, Yehudit. The young girl is reported to be Abraham and Yehudit's daughter. Only Abraham Neyer survived the Holocaust; the other family members perished. I was unable to verify this identification.

3. Kermish, *Mered geto Varshah be-'ene ha-oyev*, 107; Eichmann, "I transported them . . . to the butcher," 106.

1 RISING TO POWER

1. On the significance of the Hermann Monument for Stroop, see NARA, M-1095, RG 549, p. 1976.

2. There is no historical basis for the myth that German nationalism was built around the image of Hermann der Cherusker, yet it served as a powerful location for the German nationalist movement.

3. StA DT, L101A Pers. Nr. 245, Akten des Joseph Stroop [Files of Joseph Stroop].

4. Kazimierz Moczarski, *Conversations with an Executioner*, ed. Mariana Fitzpatrick (Englewood Cliffs, NJ: Prentice-Hall, 1981), 14. Many researchers consider Moczarski's book, which contains few references, as problematic. I have therefore relied on it mostly for tangential facts and, wherever possible, corroborated it with other sources.

5. Wolfgang Müller, "Jürgen (Joseph) Stroop, der Mann aus Detmold" [Jürgen (Joseph) Stroop, the man from Detmold], in *Nationalsozialismus in Detmold—Dokumentation eines stadtgeschichtlichen Projekts* [National Socialism in Detmold—Documentation of a Local History Project], ed. von Hermann Niebuhr and Andreas Ruppert (Bielefeld: Aisthesis, 1998), 81–82.

6. StA DT, L101A Pers. Nr. 245, Akten des Joseph Stroop; NARA, M-1095, RG 549, p. 1947.

7. NARA, M-1095, RG 549, p. 1947.

8. YVA, O.68/839, "Stroop—curriculum vitae."

9. Moczarski, *Conversations*, 24, 29.

10. StA DT, L101A Pers. Nr. 245, Akten des Joseph Stroop; NARA, RG 165, entry 179, box 736—26 July 1945.

11. StA DT, L 101A Pers. Nr. 245, Akten des Joseph Stroop.

12. Joachim Jahns, *Der Warschauer Ghettokönig* [The Warsaw Ghetto King] (Leipzig: Dingsda, 2009), 201. Konrad gave different accounts of his life,

which contrast at times: YVA, O.68/243, "Konrad—curriculum vitae"; NARA, RG 319, box 645–46, "Konrad's report," January 2, 1946; also e-mail between author and Steiermärkisches Landesarchiv, July 25, 2007, and with Stadtamt Liezen, July 26, 2007. See also Josef Wulf, *Das Dritte Reich und seine Vollstrecker* [The Third Reich and Its Executors] (Berlin: Arani, 1983), 254–60.

13. Jahns, *Der Warschauer Ghettokönig*, 202–203.

14. NARA, M-1095, RG 549, p. 1976; Moczarski, *Conversations*, 33.

15. Müller, "Jürgen (Joseph) Stroop," 84.

16. Moczarski, *Conversations*, 29; Kermish, *Mered geto Varshah*, 235; the Examus family lived very close to Stroop's home on Mühlen Street. Two members of this family, David and Emmy, were shipped to the Warsaw ghetto and then on to their deaths in Treblinka; see Gudrun Mitschke-Buchholz, *Gedenkbuch für die Opfer der nationalsozialistischen Gewaltherrschaft in Detmold* [Memorial Book for the Victims of National Socialistic Tyranny in Detmold] (Bielefeld: Verlag für Regionalgeschichte, 2001), 55–57.

17. *Nachrichtenblatt des Bundes ehem. 256er (Ref. Inf. Regt. 256)*, July 1927.

18. "Gedächtnisfeiern am Totensonntag" [Sunday in Commemoration of the Dead], *Lippische Landeszeitung*, November 22, 1927.

19. Kurt Bauer, *Elementar—Ereignis. Die österreichischen Nationalsozialisten und der Juliputsch 1934* [Elementary—Event. The Austrian National Socialists and the July 1934 Putsch] (Vienna: Czernin, 2003), 215–16.

20. A month after the successful March 1938 annexation of Austria by the Third Reich, Konrad returned triumphant to the Liezen district, where he served as an SS administrative officer in Bruck an der Mur.

21. NARA, M-1095, RG 549, p. 1976; Müller, "Jürgen (Joseph) Stroop," 92; YVA, O.68/839, "Stroop—SS Personnel File."

22. For the account of one Jew who lived in town at this time, see Ruth Michaelis-Jena, *Heritage of the Kaiser's Children: An Autobiography* (Edinburgh: Canongate, 1983), 94–101. Michaelis-Jena does not mention Stroop by name.

23. *Lippishe Landeszeitung*, January 5, 1933; *Lippisher Kurier*, January 5, 1933; Moczarski, *Conversations*, 48–51.

24. Joseph Goebbels, *Die Tagebücher von Joseph Goebbels* [The Diaries of Joseph Goebbels] (Munich: K. G. Saur, 2006), part 1, vol. 2/III, 106. Martin Broszat, *Hitler and the Collapse of Weimar Germany*, trans. V. R. Berghah (New York: St. Martin's Press, 1987), 129.

25. Müller, "Jürgen (Joseph) Stroop," 87.

26. Ibid.; Bericht Brands, StA DT D 70 Nr. 66, pp. 23–25.

27. Andreas Ruppert, "Felix Fechenbach, Lecture," trans. Katrin von Keitz, Detmold, August 6, 2003 (unpublished).

28. Felix Fechenbach, *Mein Herz schlägt weiter* [My Heart Beats On] (Passau: Andreas Haller, 1987), 47–48, 56–58.

29. Müller, "Jürgen (Joseph) Stroop," 88–89. Some of the men who murdered Fechenbach were put on trial after the war: Trial of Paul Wiese and Dr. Karl Segler, State Archives in North Rhine–Westphalia, LAV NRW OWL D 21 C 188/93; Trial of Friedrich Grüttemeyer, D 21 C 24/84. One suspect, Josef Focke, escaped, and his case was closed.

30. Blösche speaks about his prewar life in his investigation, BStU, MfS, HA IX/11 ZUV 15, vol. 1, p. 123, vol. 3, pp. 245–51. See also "Testimony of Rudolf Hauptig," BStU, MfS, ZUV 15, HA IX/11, vol. 4, pp. 21–22; BStU, MfS, HA IV, 13897, pp. 13–17; Wulf, *Das Dritte Reich*, 309–10.

31. Heribert Schwan and Helgard Heindrichs, *Der SS-Mann: Leben und Sterben eines Mörders* [The SS Man—Life and Death of a Murderer] (Munich: Knaur Taschenbuch, 2005), 32–37; BStU, MfS, HA IX/11 ZUV 15, vol. 1, pp. 123, 267–68.

32. "Testimony of Rudolf Hauptig," BStU, MfS, ZUV 15, HA IX/11, vol. 4, pp. 21–22.

33. BStU, MfS, HA IX/11 ZUV 15, "Investigation about Gustav Blösche," vol. 13, pp. 227–34.

34. Josef Korbel, *Twentieth-Century Czechoslovakia: The Meanings of Its History* (New York: Columbia University Press, 1977), 113–16.

35. BStU, MfS, HA IX/11 ZUV 15, vol. 1, pp. 267–68, vol. 3, pp. 389–92.

36. Schwan and Heindrichs, *Der SS-Mann*, 282; Laurenz Demps et al., *DDR-Justiz und NS-Verbrechen* [GDR Justice and Nazi Crime] (Amsterdam: Amsterdam University Press, 2002), vol. II, case 1049, p. 399; BStU, MfS, HA IX/11 ZUV 15, vol. 1, pp. 267–68, vol. 2, p. 67.

37. All information related to this incident comes from State Archives in North Rhine–Westphalia, LAV NRW OWL L113 Nr. 43.

38. Moczarski, *Conversations*, 31, 55; YVA, TR10/794, "Stroop-Konrad trial protocol—second day," 7–8.

39. NARA, M-1095, RG 549, p. 1984; Müller, "Jürgen (Joseph) Stroop," 92; YVA, O.68/839, "Stroop—SS Personnel File."

40. YVA, O.68/839, "Stroop—exam, Dachau, February 2, 1938"; NARA, M-1095, RG 549, p. 1977.

41. Moczarski, *Conversations*, 66–68.

2 THE ROAD TO WARSAW

1. The account of Rivkah Trapkovits'-Farber is based on her autobiography, *Le-Maydanek lo higa'ti: 'edutah shel Rivkah Trapkovits'-Farber* [In Majdanek I Did Not Arrive: The Testimony of Rivkah Trapkovits'-Farber] (Lohame ha-geta'ot: Bet lohame ha-geta'ot, Israel, 198?); and a transcript of tape-recorded testimony she gave at the Ghetto Fighters' Museum Archive: Trapkovits'-Farber, "Testimony," December 19, 1979, file 14423.

Trapkovits'-Farber also gave a short account of her Holocaust experience, "Be-ma'avak la-hayim" [In a Struggle for Life], in *Be-shadmot Grokhov: Kibuts-ha-hakhsharah Grokhov u-felugotav: me'asef* [In the Fields of Grochow: Kibbutz Hakhsharah Gorochow and Its Groups: A Collection] eds. Sarah Segal and Aryeh Pyalkov (Tel Aviv: ha-Kibuts ha-me'uhad, 1976), 395–98.

2. Dina Trapkovits', "Yaldut u-ne'urim be-bet abba" [Childhood and Youth in Father's Home], in Trapkovits'-Farber, *Le-Maydanek lo higa'ti*, 3–4; author interview with Jacob Farber, June 28, 2007.

3. On life in the Borochov Kibbutz in Lodz, see the collection of testimonies in *Sipuro shel Kibuts-hakhsharah: ha-Kibuts 'al shem B. Borokhov be-Lodz u-venoteha: me'asef* [The Story of Kibbutz-Hakhsharah: The Kibbutz Named after B. Borokhov in Lodz and Its Extensions: a Collection], ed. Fischel Even-Shoshan (Tel Aviv: ha-Kibuts ha-me'uhad, 1970).

4. Photo of dormitory, in ibid., facing p. 73.

5. Photo of the sewing shop, in Trapkovits'-Farber, *Le-Maydanek lo higa'ti*, facing p. 12.

6. Hanan Pundik, in *Sipuro shel Kibuts-hakhsharah*, 142; Tuvyah Ga'ash, in ibid., 190–92.

7. A copy of the original handwritten text is at http://urila.tripod.com/ Rokdim.htm.

8. Josef Kornianski, *Bi-shelihut halutsim* [In the Mission of Pioneers] (Lohame ha-geta'ot: Bet lohame ha-geta'ot, 1979), 12; Tsivyah Lubetkin, *Bi-yeme kilayon va-mered* [In the Days of Destruction and Revolt] (Lohame ha-geta'ot: Bet lohame ha-geta'ot, 1979), 18; Rivkah Perlis, *Tenu'ot ha-no'ar ha-halutsiyot be-Polin ha-kevushah* [The Pioneering Zionist Youth Movements in Nazi-Occupied Poland] (Lohame ha-geta'ot: Bet lohame ha-geta'ot, 1987), 12–17, 34–41.

9. One report states that 270 departed from Lodz en route to Warsaw, while another gives the number as 400. See Mordechai Halter, in *Sipuro shel Kibuts-hakhsharah*, 309; Yosef Kornianski, in ibid., 326.

10. Trapkovits'-Farber, "Testimony," 1–2.

11. Halter, in *Sipuro shel Kibuts-hakhsharah*, 309.

12. Trapkovits'-Farber, *Le-Maydanek lo higa'ti*, 6; Trapkovits'-Farber, "Bema'avak," 395; Yisra'el Eshcoli, in *Sipuro shel Kibuts-hakhsharah*, 318.

13. Trapkovits'-Farber, "Testimony," 1; Trapkovits'-Farber, *Le-Maydanek lo higa'ti*, 6.

14. YVA, Testimony, p. 644072.

15. Trapkovits'-Farber, *Le-Maydanek lo higa'ti*, 6; Trapkovits'-Farber, "Testimony," 2.

16. Trapkovits'-Farber, *Le-Maydanek lo higa'ti*, 6.

17. Halter, in *Sipuro shel Kibuts-hakhsharah*, 309; Eshcoli, in ibid., 318; Kornianski, in ibid., 326–27.

18. Fischel Farber, "Hayai im Rivkah'leh" [My Life with Rivkah'leh], in Trapkovits'-Farber, Le-Maydanek lo higa'ti, 61–69.

19. Trapkovits'-Farber, Le-Maydanek lo higa'ti, 8.

20. Eshcoli, in Sipuro shel Kibuts-hakhsharah, 318–19; Trapkovits'-Farber, Le-Maydanek lo higa'ti, 7–8; Trapkovits'-Farber, "Be-ma'avak," 395.

21. Ben-Sasson (Dreifuss) Havi, "Warsaw Ghetto," in Guy Miron, ed., The Yad Vashem Encyclopedia of the Ghettos During the Holocaust (Jerusalem: Yad Vashem, 2010), 897–921.

22. Yisrael Gutman, The Jews of Warsaw, 1939–1943: Ghetto, Underground, Revolt, trans. Ina Friedman (Bloomington: Indiana University Press, 1982), 48–50; Barbara Engelking and Jacek Leociak, The Warsaw Ghetto: A Guide to the Perished City (New Haven: Yale University Press, 2009), 36–47; Chaim A. Kaplan, Megilat yisurin: yoman geto varshah 1 be-September–4 be-Ogust 1942 [Scroll of Agony: The Warsaw Ghetto Diary, September 1–August 4, 1942] (Tel Aviv: 'Am 'oved, 1966), 70, 78–79; Ben-Sasson (Dreifuss), "Warsaw Ghetto."

23. Trapkovits'-Farber, "Testimony," 4–5; Lubetkin, in Bi-yeme kilayon, 24.

24. Trapkovits'-Farber, "Testimony," 6; Trapkovits'-Farber, Le-Maydanek lo higa'ti, 12.

25. Trapkovits'-Farber, "Testimony," 3; Trapkovits'-Farber, Le-Maydanek lo higa'ti, 7.

26. Trapkovits'-Farber, "Testimony," 5; Trapkovits'-Farber, Le-Maydanek lo higa'ti, 12.

27. Trapkovits'-Farber, Le-Maydanek lo higa'ti, 9–10; Trapkovits'-Farber, "Testimony," 19–20.

28. The account of Blösche's experience in Pretzsch in the next passages is based on BStU, MfS, HA IX/11 ZUV 15, vol. 1, pp. 123–25, 282–83, vol. 3, pp. 19–23, 386–87; Schwan and Heindrichs, Der SS-Mann, 49–51, 282–83; Demps, DDR-Justiz, 399–400.

29. BStU, MfS, HA IX/11 ZUV 15, vol. 3, p. 248.

30. Ibid., pp. 25–28.

31. For more on Grochow, see the collection of testimonies and documents in Be-shadmot Grokhov.

32. Kornianski, Bi-shelihut halutsim, 48.

33. Trapkovits'-Farber, "Be-ma'avak," 395.

34. Blumah Lichtenberg and Uziel Lichtenberg, "Shikumah shel Grokhov" [The Restoration of Grochow], in Be-shadmot Grokhov, 389–90.

35. Hannah Gelbard, Mi-ben homot Varshah, mi-yomane halutsim ba-mahteret [From Between the Walls of Warsaw, from the Diaries of Pioneers in the Underground] (Ein Harod: ha-Kibuts ha-me'uhad, 1943), 26–27; Hannah Gelbard, "Mi-ben homot Varshah," in Be-shadmot Grokhov, 386 and many other references to the evacuation in this book.

36. Trapkovits'-Farber, Le-Maydanek lo higa'ti, 15; Itzhak Zuckerman and

Tsivyah Lubetkin, "Be-yeme ha-kibush ha-nazi," in *Be-shadmot Gro-khov*, 354.

37. Trapkovits'-Farber, *Le-Maydanek lo higa'ti*, 15; Trapkovits'-Farber, "Be-ma'avak," 396; Trapkovits'-Farber, "Testimony," 8–9.

38. Kornianski, *Bi-shelihut halutsim*, 81–83; Itzhak (Antek) Zuckerman, *Sheva' ha-shanim ha-hen: 1939–1946* [Those Seven Years: 1939–1946] (Lohame ha-geta'ot: Bet lohame ha-geta'ot, 1990), 91, 117; Gelbard, *Mi-ben homot Varshah*, 36–39.

39. BStU, MfS, HA IX/11 ZUV 15, vol. 1, pp. 273–74.

40. Schwan and Heindrichs, *Der SS-Mann*, 61–62.

41. BStU, MfS, HA IX/11 ZUV 15, vol. 1, pp. 277–78.

42. Ibid.

43. Demps, *DDR-Justiz*, 400; BStU, MfS, HA IX/11 ZUV 15, vol. 1, pp. 134–36, 277–81, vol. 3, pp. 252–56. Blösche remembered these first shootings, the forest, the path, the ditches, the mercy shot. He did not, however, describe his emotions and thoughts, which I added based on the accounts of other perpetrators who describe their first shootings as traumatic. The fact that Blösche remembered his first shootings, while not being able to recall the many other shootings in which he took part, is to my mind telling.

44. Kaplan, *Megilat yisurin*, 514. For a comprehensive account of the situation in the Warsaw ghetto at this time, see Engelking and Leociak, *The Warsaw Ghetto*. The testimony of Rivkah on her time in the ghetto in 1942 remains unclear. She states that she returned to the ghetto in the fall of 1942, yet she testifies that she saw the murder of a child in the ghetto in April 1942 and that she experienced the large *Aktion* that took place in the summer.

45. Gelbard, *Mi-ben homot Varshah*, 29, 32.

46. Emmanuel Ringelblum, *Notes from the Warsaw Ghetto: Journal of Em-manuel Ringelblum* (New York: Schocken Books, 1974), 233.

47. Ibid., 205–06.

48. Kaplan, *Megilat yisurin*, 492.

49. BStU, MfS, HA IX/11 ZUV 15, vol. 1, p. 284, vol. 3, pp. 141–44; Schwan and Heindrichs, *Der SS-Mann*, 74–75.

50. BStU, MfS, HA IX/11 ZUV 15, vol. 16, "Testimony of Helena Kusmier-czyk," pp. 105–108, vol. 4/1, pp. 55–58. I was unable to determine if Helena's mother, Leokadia, survived the war.

51. Trapkovits'-Farber, *Le-Maydanek lo higa'ti*, 11; Zuckerman, *Sheva' ha-shanim ha-hen*, 154–55. In Engelking and Leociak, *The Warsaw Ghetto*, 696, the age of the boy and the location of the murder differ slightly.

52. BStU, MfS, HA IX/11 ZUV 15, vol. 16, "Testimony of Marek Edelman," p. 25; BStU, MfS, HA IV, 13897, p. 6. For the names of the remaining fifty Jews murdered on what is called "the bloody night," "Black Friday," or "Bartholomew's Night," see YVA, M10.AR1/293. This was the first mass execution in the ghetto. Small units of the Gestapo penetrated the ghetto

and, supplied with a list of names, dragged fifty-two Jews out of their homes and executed them, substituting others for those Jews on the list who couldn't be located. See Gutman, *The Jews of Warsaw*, 176–80; Engelking and Leociak, *The Warsaw Ghetto*, 683–85.

53. Tsvi Nussbaum, in *'Et Ezkerah: sefer kehilat Tsoizmir (Sandomiyez')* [A Time of Memory: Community Book of Tzoyzmir (Sandomierz)], ed. Eva Feldenkreiz-Grinbal, Levi Dror, and Joseph Rav (Tel-Aviv: Irgun yots'e Tsoizmir be-Yisra'el, 1993), 296–301; *Tsvi Nussbaum Video Recording: A Boy from Warsaw* (Teaneck, NJ: Ergo Media, 1990); Richard Raskin, *A Child at Gunpoint—A Case Study in the Life of a Photo* (Aarhus, Denmark: Aarhus University Press, 2004), 87–92; *Jerusalem Post*, April 18, 1993; *New York Post*, February 20, 1990; *New York Times*, May 28, 1982. On the Jewish community in Sandomierz, see *Pinkas Hakehillot—Polin*, vol. 7 (Jerusalem: Yad Vashem, 1999), 363–68.

54. Itzhak Gorzychanski, in *'Et Ezkerah*, 130–33.

55. Ibid., 161–63, 296.

56. BStU, MfS, HA IX/11 ZUV 15, vol. 1, pp. 165–66, vol. 2, pp. 14–16, vol. 3, pp. 386–88.

57. Ibid., vol. 2, p. 16.

58. Ibid., vol. 3, pp. 9–10.

59. Ibid., vol. 2, pp. 35–37, vol. 3, p. 44.

60. Ibid., vol. 2, p. 35, vol. 3, pp. 44, 50. For the account of Jewish witnesses of Blösche's actions, see ibid., vol. 16. During the trial of Klaustermeyer in West Germany in the first half of the 1960s, the issue of shooting bikes comes up several times. See Irene Sagel-Grande, H. H. Fuchs, and C. F. Rüter, eds., *Justiz und NS-Verbrechen—Sammlung deutscher Strafurteile wegen nationalsozialistischer Tötungverbrechen 1945–1966* [Justice and Nazi Crimes—A Collection of Penal Sentences Concerning National Socialistic Murder Crimes 1945–1966] (Amsterdam: University Press of Amsterdam), vol. 20, case 586.

61. Marek Edelman, *The Ghetto Fights* (London: Bookmarks, 1990), 55–62.

62. BStU, MfS, HA IX/11 ZUV 15, vol. 1, pp. 166–69; BStU, MfS, HA IV, 13897, p. 5.

63. BStU, MfS, HA IX/11 ZUV 15, vol. 1, pp. 166–69.

64. This section is based on a detailed account by Konrad in NARA, RG 319, box 645–46, "Konrad's report," and other documents there as referenced in note 12, page 225.

65. YVA, O.68/243, "Konrad—SS Personnel File"; NARA, RG 319, box 645–46, "translation, transcript of interrogation of Hauptsturmführer Franz Konrad—August 1945," pp. 21–26.

66. For a Jew's account of the Werterfassung, see Aharon Karmi, *Min ha-delekah ha-hi: mi-pi havre ha-irgun ha-Yehudi ha-lohem be-geto Varshah* [From That Fire: Testimony of Members of the Jewish Fighting Organization in the Warsaw Ghetto] (Tel Aviv: ha-Kibuts ha-me'uhad, 1961), 82–83.

67. Kermish, *Mered geto Varshah*, 30.
68. NARA, RG 319, box 645–646 "Konrad's report," January 2, 1946.
69. BStU, MfS, HA IX/11 ZUV 15, vol. 5, "Stroop-Konrad trial protocol," 252.
70. NARA, RG 319, box 645–646, "Konrad's report," January 2, 1946.
71. YVA, M-49E/2046. For the German translation of the verdict, see YVA, TR10/794, p. 24, and BStU, MfS, HA IX/11 ZUV 15, vol. 5, "Stroop-Konrad trial protocol," 387. For an English translation, see Towiah Friedman, *The Trial Against SS-General Jürgen Stroop in Warsaw Poland* (Haifa: Institute of Documentation in Israel, 1986), 24.

3 INSIDE THE GHETTO

1. NARA, RG 319, box 645–46, "Konrad's report," January 2, 1946, pp. 52–53. A large part of this report, including the reference to the meeting in the office of Von Sammern-Frankenegg, was reprinted in Nachman Blumental and Yosef Kermish, *ha-Mery veha-mered be-geto Varsha* [Resistance and Revolt in the Warsaw Ghetto] (Jerusalem: Yad Vashem, 1965), 370.
2. BStU, HA IX/11 ZUV 15, vol. 1, p. 166, vol. 2, pp. 205–206.
3. Ibid., vol. 5, p. 377; YVA, TR10/794, "Stroop-Konrad trial protocol—second day," 18; Moczarski, *Conversations*, 88–89, 101, 114, 126.
4. Trapkovits'-Farber, *Le-Maydanek lo higa'ti*, 17–20; Trapkovits'-Farber, "Testimony," 10–12; Ya'akov Putermilkh, *Ba-esh uva-sheleg: zikhronot shel lohem* [In Fire and Snow: Memories of a Fighter] (Lohame ha-geta'ot: ha-Kibuts ha-me'uhad, 1981), 67–68; Karmi, *Min ha-delekah ha-hi*, 82.
5. Trapkovits'-Farber, *Le-Maydanek lo higa'ti*, 18–20; Trapkovits'-Farber, "Testimony," 10–12.
6. Lubetkin, *Bi-yeme kilayon va-mered*, 106–10.
7. Ibid., 108; Gutman, *The Jews of Warsaw*, 314–15; Engelking and Leociak, *The Warsaw Ghetto*, 765–66.
8. Lubetkin, *Bi-yeme kilayon va-mered*, 107; Itzhak Zuckerman, *Surplus of Memory: Chronicle of the Warsaw Ghetto Uprising* (Berkeley: University of California Press, 1993), 283–84.
9. Toviyah Boz'ikovski, *Ben kirot noflim* [Between Falling Walls] (Tel Aviv: ha-Kibuts ha-me'uhad, 1964), 34.
10. Karmi, *Min ha-delekah ha-hi*, 99.
11. Wolfgang Scheffler and Helge Grabitz, *Ghetto-Aufstand Warschau 1943: Aus der Sicht der Täter und Opfer in Aussagen vor deutschen Gerichten* [The Ghetto Revolt, Warsaw 1943: Testimonies of Murderers and Victims in Front of German Courts] (Munich: W. Goldmann, 1993), 183–84; see also French L. MacLean, *The Ghetto Men: The SS Destruction of the Jewish Warsaw Ghetto—April–May 1943* (Atglen, PA: Schiffer Publishing, 2001), 54.
12. MacLean, *The Ghetto Men*, 54.

13. Scheffler and Grabitz, *Ghetto-Aufstand*, 184.

14. Kermish, *Mered geto Varshah*, 212–13.

15. NARA, RG 319, box 645–46, "Konrad's report," January 2, 1946, pp. 56–57; IPN, SWMW, sygn. 874, t. viii, Konrad Statement for Protocol, 1205; YVA, TR10/794, "Stroop-Konrad trial protocol—second day," 23–24; Kermish, *Mered geto Varshah*, 213; Stroop, *The Stroop Report*, teletype of April 20, 1943.

16. Stroop, *The Stroop Report*, 4.

17. Trapkovits'-Farber, "Testimony," 11. For a slightly different account of hers, see Trapkovits'-Farber, *Le-Maydanek lo higa'ti*, 19.

18. Havi Dreifuss (Ben-Sasson), "Hell Has Risen to the Surface of the Earth," *Yad Vashem Studies* 36, no 2. (2008): 21–22.

19. YVA, TR10/794, "Stroop-Konrad trial protocol—second day," 26.

20. NARA, RG 319, box 645–46, "Konrad's report," January 2, 1946, pp. 55–56; Blumental and Kermish, *ha-Mery veha-mered*, 371–72; Aryeh Nyberg, *Ha-ahronim* [The Last Ones] (Merhavyah: Sifriyat po'alim, 1958), 54.

21. BStU, 13897, 58–59; Schwan and Heindrichs, *Der SS-Mann*, 155–56. For testimony of Pawel Golabeck on Stroop standing and watching people burn to death, see USHMM, DS. 894/417. Himmler had ordered Stroop "to clear the Warsaw ghetto and raze it to the ground" (*Trial of the Major War Criminals before the International Military Tribunal*, Nuremberg Trials, Blue series (Nuremberg, 1949), vol. xxxiii, 3841-PS, pp. 201–02). See also BStU, HA IX/11 ZUV 15, vol. 2, pp. 177–81.

22. NARA, RG 319, box 645–646, "Konrad's report," January 2, 1946, pp. 65–66, 72–73; Blumental and Kermish, *ha-Mery veha-mered*, 374–75, 378–79. Blösche is questioned about the shooting throughout his investigation, for example, BStU, HA IX/11 ZUV 15, vol. 1, pp. 171–76, 230–35, 286–91, vol. 5, pp. 62–63.

23. NARA, RG 319, box 645–46, "Konrad's report," January 2, 1946, pp. 72–73; Blumental and Kermish, *ha-Mery veha-mered*, 378–79. See also BStU, HA IX/11 ZUV 15, vol. 5, "Stroop-Konrad trial protocol," 234–35; NARA, RG 319, box 645–46, "Translation and transcript of interrogation of Hauptsturmführer Franz Konrad," August 21–26, 1945.

24. NARA, RG 319, box 645–46, "Translation and transcript of interrogation of Hauptsturmführer Franz Konrad," August 21–26, 1945.

25. Kermish, *Mered geto Varshah*, 25; Moczarski, *Conversations*, 115–16, 126; Stroop, *The Stroop Report*, 6; Blumental and Kermish, *ha-Mery veha-mered*, 317–20.

26. Blumental and Kermish, *ha-Mery veha-mered*, 317–20.

27. Ibid., 320.

28. *The Stroop Report*, April 24. On the people who transcribed and sent the teletypes, see Scheffler and Grabitz, *Der Ghetto-Aufstand*, 181–82.

29. Stroop, *The Stroop Report*, April 24.

30. Rivkah does not describe her time in the bunker except to say it was terrible. I base her experiences on common experiences of other Jews who hid in ghetto bunkers during this period: Hella Rufeisen-Schüpper, *Peridah mi-Mila 18: sipurah shel kasharit* [Farewell from Mila 18: The Story of a Liaison Woman] (Tel Aviv: ha-Kibuts ha-me'uhad and Bet lohame ha-geta'ot, 1990), 104–108 (Rufeisen-Schüpper also hid in a Muranowska hideout and bunker); Dreifuss (Ben-Sasson), "Hell Has Risen," 21–43; Halina Birenbaum, *Hope Is the Last to Die: A Personal Documentation of Nazi Terror*, trans. David Welsh (New York: Twayne Publishers, 1971), 52–56; Thaddeus Stabholz, *Seven Hells*, trans. Jacques Grunblatt and Hilda R. Grunblatt (New York: Holocaust Library, 1990), 2–8; Nyberg, *Ha-ahronim*, 76–133; Gutman, *The Jews of Warsaw*, 387–91.

31. BStU, HA IX/11 ZUV 15, vol. 2, pp. 90, 174–75, 193–94, vol. 3, p. 380; Moczarski, *Conversations*, 148–51.

32. Stroop, *The Stroop Report*, 8, teletype report of April 21, 1943; Moczarski, *Conversations*, 131–32.

33. Nyberg, *Ha-ahronim*, 112. The story of the three women in the photo appears in *Ba-mahaneh*, April 9, 1968, p. 18; *Yedi'ot Yad va-shem* 39, no. 3 (1968): 29; YVA, O3/3108.

34. Dreifuss (Ben-Sasson), "Hell Has Risen," 42–43. Dreifuss points out the possibility that the pages of the diary were salvaged from the rubble by engineer-architect B. Goldman and passed on to the archives of the National Jewish Committee (18n24).

35. Trapkovits'-Farber, *Le-Maydanek lo higa'ti*, 20.

36. Rivkah mentions only that the Germans photographed her and the other Jews coming out of the bunker. She does not describe this scene.

37. Nyberg, *Ha-ahronim*, 97.

38. Stabholz, *Seven Hells*, 8–9.

39. The photo of the suicide here was taken at 25 Niska Street, while Stabholz reports an event at 11 Nalewki. In Stroop, *The Stroop Report*, two similar photographs were titled "Bandits jump to escape arrest" and "Bandits who jumped."

40. Stabholz, *Seven Hells*, 9; Nyberg, *Ha-ahronim*, 150.

41. BStU, HA IX/11 ZUV 15, vol. 1, pp. 127–28, vol. 2, pp. 58–59, vol. 5, p. 72; Schwan and Heindrichs, *Der SS-Mann*, 287.

42. Stabholz, *Seven Hells*, 16.

43. Birenbaum, *Hope Is the Last to Die*, 78–81.

44. Trapkovits'-Farber, *Le-Maydanek lo higa'ti*, 21.

4 THE ROAD FROM WARSAW

1. NARA, RG 165, entry 179, box 704—CI—IIR/25—18 October 1945, p. 7.

2. Stroop, *The Stroop Report*, introduction.

3. Scheffler and Grabitz, *Ghetto-Aufstand*, 223–25 and n70; BStU, HA IX/11 ZUV 15, vol. 5, "Stroop-Konrad trial protocol," 260–61.

4. YVA, M9/752, pp. 7–9; Stroop, *The Stroop Report*, teletype of May 13; Andrzej Wirth, "Introduction," *Es gibt keinen jüdischen Wohnbezirk in Warschau mehr!* [The Jewish Quarter in Warsaw Is No More!] (Neuwied: H. Luchterhand, 1960).

5. The description of Stroop's selection of photos is based on my comparison of the entire available set of photos taken in the Warsaw ghetto during the revolt with those included in *The Stroop Report*.

6. IPN, SWMW, sygn. 874, t. viii, Konrad Statement for Protocol, 1207; BStU, HA IX/11 ZUV 15, vol. 5, "Stroop-Konrad trial protocol," 233–34.

7. BStU, HA IX/11 ZUV 15, vol. 2, p. 206.

8. YVA, TR.2, no-2573; Wulf, *Das Dritte Reich*, 71; Kermish, *Mered geto Varshah*, 75.

9. Moczarski, *Conversations*, 171–72.

10. YVA, O68/839, "Letter from Stroop to von Herff," June 26, 1943.

11. Trapkovits'-Farber, *Le-Maydanek lo higa'ti*, 23; Trapkovits'-Farber, *Beshadmot Grokhov*, 397–98.

12. Trapkovits'-Farber, *Le-Maydanek lo higa'ti*, 25.

13. Ibid., 27.

14. Ibid., 29.

15. Ibid., 29–30.

16. Ibid., 33.

17. For more on the Czerniakow farm and about Zatwarnicki, see Zuckerman, *Surplus of Memory*, 75–77.

18. Trapkovits'-Farber, *Le-Maydanek lo higa'ti*, 34.

19. In Nussbaum, *'Et Ezkerah*, 298, her name appears as Frumcia, whereas on the website of the Ghetto Fighters' House Archives it appears as Freda. Several accounts of the Hotel Polski are collected in Abraham Shulman, *The Case of Hotel Polski* (New York: Holocaust Library, 1982); Engelking and Leociak, *The Warsaw Ghetto*, 745–48. Nussbaum tells of his experiences in the Hotel Polski in *Tsvi Nussbaum Video Recording*; Nussbaum, *'Et Ezkerah*, 297–99; and many newspaper publications referenced in chapter 6, note 70.

20. For an account of an arrival at the Hotel Polski, see YVA, O3/11742, "Testimony of Ilana Ilotovich," 37–38. On the hotel viewed as a Nazi trap, see Zuckerman, *Surplus of Memory*, 438–45; Wladka Meed, *On Both Sides of the Wall*, trans. Steven Meed (New York: Holocaust Library, 1979), 219–26. Tsvi does not speak in detail about the stay in the hotel. I used the following sources to reconstruct the experiences at the hotel and after: Shulman, *The Case*, 39–112, 140–80; YVA, M49 E/2, M49 E/3271, M49 E/4659, M49 E/460, M49 E/1534, O3/5927.

21. Shulman, *The Case*, 44.

22. Ibid., 93, 192–94.

23. YVA, O3/862, "Testimony of Ella Sendowska and family letters"; see also Shulman, *The Case*, 85–88.

24. Shulman, *The Case*, 88–90.

25. BStU, HA IX/11 ZUV 15, vol. 1, pp. 132–33, vol. 2, pp. 229–33.

26. Ibid., vol. 2, pp. 229–33, vol. 5, p. 78.

27. Shulman, *The Case*, 63.

28. Nussbaum, '*Et Ezkerah*, 298–99. While Nussbaum states that his aunt Regina and Marek and Aron boarded the trucks, a published list of names contains only that of Aron. See Agnieszka Haska, *Jestem Zydem, Chce Wejsc: Hotel Polski W Warszawie, 1943* [I Am a Jew, Let Me In: Hotel Polski, Warsaw, 1943] (Warsaw: Wydawn, IFIS PAN, 2006), 172. However, as Engelking and Leociak point out in *The Warsaw Ghetto*, 745–48, it is impossible to compile an accurate list, as many traveled on false identities.

29. Nussbaum, '*Et Ezkerah*, 299, and many other sources (see chapter 6, note 70) in which Nussbaum repeats this traumatic moment in his life.

30. Shulman, *The Case*, 63.

31. YVA, O3/862; Shulman, *The Case*, 90.

32. YVA, O3/862.

33. One of the Hotel Polski Jews, Simcha Korngold, points out that the group was photographed at the train station. He does not, however, specify by whom, although it seems from the context that he is referring not to the Nazis but rather to the Swiss diplomats, the Red Cross representatives, or the journalists (Shulman, *The Case*, 63). Nussbaum's account mentions being photographed at the Gdansk train station by Brandt and Hendke and states that "possibly they were also at Hotel Polski and took photos of us in the courtyard" ('*Et Ezkerah*, 299). See also Sophie Goetzel-Leviathan, *The War from Within*, ed. Rebecca Fromer, trans. Geoffrey A. M. Block (Berkeley, CA: Judah L. Magnes Museum, 1987), 59.

   In my effort to locate these photos, I contacted both the International Committee of the Red Cross in Geneva and the Polish Red Cross in Warsaw. The photos from the Gdansk station were not found. The archive of the Polish Red Cross, whose members were most likely to be present at the station, was set on fire in August 1944 and therefore no photograph of the assembling of Jews remains (author correspondence, May 6, 2008). No photos were located in the Swiss National Archives either (author correspondence, August 20, 2008).

34. Shulman, *The Case*, 143.

35. Ibid., 143; YVA, O3/11742, "Testimony of Ilana Ilotovich," 41.

36. Goetzel-Leviathan, *The War from Within*, 60.

37. Shulman, *The Case*, 90, 143–44.

38. YVA, O3/11742, "Testimony of Ilana Ilotovich," pp. 42–43; Goetzel-Leviathan, *The War from Within*, 60–62; Shulman, *The Case*.

39. Trapkovits'-Farber, *Le-Maydanek lo higa'ti*, 38.

40. Ibid., 39.

41. Ibid.

42. Wulf, *Das Dritte Reich*, 310.

43. BStU, HA IX/11 ZUV 15, vol. 1, pp. 185–86, vol. 3, pp. 36–38, 351–52; Schwan and Heindrichs, *Der SS-Mann*, 196.

44. Schwan and Heindrichs, *Der SS-Mann*, 197.

45. BStU, HA IX/11 ZUV 15, vol. 3, pp. 273–74.

46. Trapkovits'-Farber, *Le-Maydanek lo higa'ti*, 23–41. In addition to Rivkah's autobiography, I used accounts of other Jews who lived in hiding in the area of Warsaw to describe the life and experiences of Rivkah from her jump off the train until her liberation. Michael Zylberberg, *The Warsaw Diary, 1939–1945* (London: Vallentine Mitchell, 1969); Irit Kuper, *El otam ha-kefarim* [To Those Same Villages] (Tel Aviv: Yedi'ot aharonot, 1997); Helena Szereszewska, *Perek ha-aharon: zikhronot mi-Varshah ha-kevushah* [The Last Chapter: Memories from Occupied Warsaw] (Lohame ha-geta'ot: Bet lohame ha-geta'ot, 740, 1980); Bathia Temkin-Berman, *Yoman ba-mahteret* [An underground diary], trans. H. S. Ben-Avram (Tel Aviv: ha-Kibuts ha-me'uhad, Bet lohame ha-geta'ot, 1956).

47. Trapkovits'-Farber, *Le-Maydanek lo higa'ti*, 40.

48. Ibid., 41.

49. NARA, RG 165, entry 179, box 704—CI—IIR/25—18 October 1945, p. 9; Michael Molho and Yosef Nehamah, *Sho'at Yehude Yavan: 1941–1944* [The Holocaust of Greek Jewry: 1941–1944] (Jerusalem: Yad Vashem, 1965), 138–39; Moczarski, *Conversations*, 190–94.

50. NARA, RG 165, entry 179, box 704—CI—IIR/25—18 October 1945, p. 10, dates his appointment as October 23, 1943; Mark Mazower, *Inside Hitler's Greece: The Experience of Occupation, 1941–44* (New Haven: Yale University Press, 1993), 222–23.

51. NARA, M-1095, RG 549, p. 1948; NARA, RG 165, entry 179, box 704—CI—IIR/25—18 October 1945, pp. 9–11. For slightly different numbers, see Moczarski, *Conversations*, 199–202.

52. Aktives Museum Spiegelgasse, *Rundgänge in Wiesbaden, Spurensuche II* [Tours of Wiesbaden: Searching for Remains] (Wiesbaden, 2003), 66–69. For Stroop's admiration of Wagner, see Moczarski, *Conversations*, 201–202, 262. One of the copies of *The Stroop Report* was located at war's end in Wiesbaden by the American 3rd Army.

53. NARA, M-1095, pp. 1961–62, 1971–72.

54. National Archives microfilm publications pamphlet describing M-1095, United States Army Investigation and Trial Records of War Criminals, *United States of America v. Jürgen Stroop et al.*, 3–5.

55. NARA, M-1095, p. 1972; YVA, O.18/226 CI—IIR, no. 24—10 October 1945, p. 2.

56. Trapkovits'-Farber, *Le-Maydanek lo higa'ti*, 42.
57. Ibid., 43.
58. Schwan and Heindrichs, *Der SS-Mann*, 199; BStU, HA IX/11 ZUV 15, vol. 1, pp. 186-87, vol. 3, pp. 76-77.
59. BStU, HA IX/11 ZUV 15, vol. 1, pp. 186-92, vol. 3, pp. 200, 209-10, 304; Schwan and Heindrichs, *Der SS-Mann*, 201-203.
60. BStU, HA IX/11 ZUV 15, vol. 1, pp. 188-92, vol. 3, pp. 209-10.

5 FACING JUSTICE, ENCOUNTERING LIFE

1. NARA, RG 319, box 645-46, "Interrogation of Unterscharführer Johannes Haferkamp," November 8, 1945.
2. Ibid.; "Interrogation of Willy Pichler," November 1, 1945; "Interrogation of Fritz Konrad," October 31, 1945.
3. NARA, RG 319, box 645-46, "Konrad report," January 2, 1946.
4. Ibid., "Interrogation of Franz Konrad," August 25, 1945.
5. Ibid., October 29, 1945, and "Interrogation of Unterscharführer Johannes Haferkamp," November 8, 1945.
6. Ibid., "Memorandum," July 18, 1949.
7. Ibid., "Memorandum," August 26, 1945, October 29, 1945.
8. Ibid., "Interrogation of Franz Konrad," October 17, 1945.
9. For information on the Hotel Polski Jews deported to Auschwitz, see Shulman, *The Case*, 120, 140; Rufeisen-Schüpper, *Peridah mi-Mila 18*, 133-35; *Tsvi Nussbaum Video Recording*.
10. Shulman, *The Case*, 166-67, 173-75; Rufeisen-Schüpper, *Peridah mi-Mila 18*, 144-46. The train from Bergen-Belsen was probably destined for Theresienstadt.
11. Wayne Robinson, *Move Out, Verify: The Combat Story of the 743rd Tank Battalion* (Germany: no publisher, 1945), 162-63. See the testimony of Sergeant George Gross, Hudson Falls High School, World War II Living History Project, www.hfcsd.org/ww2/. See also *Tsvi Nussbaum Video Recording*; Goetzel-Leviathan, *The War from Within*, 75; Rufeisen-Schüpper, *Peridah mi-Mila 18*, 145-46.
12. George Gross's testimony; Goetzel-Leviathan, *The War from Within*, 75.
13. Nussbaum, *'Et Ezkerah*, 299; *Tsvi Nussbaum Video Recording*; Goetzel-Leviathan, *The War from Within*, 72-76; YVA, O3/11742, "Testimony of Ilana Ilotovich," 57-58.
14. Goetzel-Leviathan, *The War from Within*, 77-78.
15. Barry W. Fowle, "The Rhine River Crossings," in Barry W. Fowle, ed., *Builders and Fighters: U.S. Army Engineers in World War II* (Fort Belvoir, VA: Office of History, U.S. Army Corps of Engineers, 1992), 471-72; NARA, M-1095, RG 549, p. 1961.

16. Moczarski, *Conversations*, 238.
17. NARA, RG 165, entry 179, box 704—CI—IIR/25—18 October 1945, pp. 2–3; Moczarski, *Conversations*, 237–44.
18. NARA, RG 165, entry 179, box 736, July 26, 1945.
19. NARA, RG 319, box 645–46, "Memorandum," August 26, 1945.
20. NARA, RG 319, box 645–46, "Interrogation of Rudolf Meier," October 25, 1945.
21. Ibid., "Memorandum," August 26, 1945.
22. Ibid., RSHA Funds, June 5, 1945; "Memorandum," January 1946 (the exact date is indecipherable).
23. Ibid., "Interrogation of Franz Konrad," n.d.
24. Ibid., "Interrogation of Franz Konrad," October 29, 1945.
25. Trapkovits'-Farber, *Le-Maydanek lo higa'ti*, 47.
26. NARA, RG 319, box 645–46, "Comments on Persons interrogated regarding Konrad," n.d.
27. Ibid., "Interrogation of Franz Konrad," October 17, 1945.
28. Ibid., "Memorandum," November 22, 1945.
29. Ibid., "Walter," July 4, 1946.
30. The arrival of the *Mataroa* at Haifa and the trip to Atlit were reported in various newspapers, including the *Palestine Post, Haaretz, Davar,* and *Al-ha-Mishmar,* all September 10, 1945. For other Hotel Polski Jews who traveled on the *Mataroa,* see YVA, O3/11742, "Testimony of Ilana Ilotovich," 60–61. See also Naftali Lau-Lavi, *'Am ke-lavi* [Nation as a Lion] (Tel-Aviv: Sifriyat Ma'ariv, 1993), 165–69. He arrived on the *Mataroa* a few months earlier and also was held in the detention camp in Atlit.
31. The list of Jews who arrived on the *Mataroa* is available in the archives of the Atlit Detention Camp Museum.
32. *Palestine Post*, September 10, 1945.
33. For life in the camp, see Lau-Lavi, *'Am ke-lavi,* 165–69; Zvi Yanai, *Shelkha, Sandro* [Yours, Sandro] (Jerusalem: Keter, 2006), 295–96. Lau-Lavi and Yanai both arrived on the previous trip of the *Mataroa* in July 1945.
34. E-mail correspondence of author with the Atlit Detention Camp Museum Archive, July 17, 2008.
35. *Tsvi Nussbaum Video Recording.*
36. NARA, M-1095, RG 549, p. 1960. See also M-1095, RG 338 and RG 153, *United States of America* v. *Jürgen Stroop et al.,* March 29, 1945–August 21, 1957; M-1019, RG 338, p. 309; Moczarski, *Conversations*, 258.
37. Wulf, *Das Dritte Reich,* 181, 187–88; Kermish, *Mered geto Varshah,* 196, 203.
38. IPN, PG 346, p. 340.
39. Ibid., pp. 254–57.
40. No author, *Haim Farber,* 7. Published by and obtained from the Farber family.

41. BStU, MfS, HA IX/11 ZUV 15, vol. 5, pp. 207–209. The protocol of the trial can also be found in YVA, TR10/794.

42. BStU, MfS, HA IX/11 ZUV 15, vol. 5, pp. 219, 224.

43. Ibid., pp. 225, 230.

44. Ibid., p. 261.

45. Ibid., pp. 261–62.

46. Ibid., p. 261.

47. Ibid., pp. 282–83.

48. Ibid., p. 232. See also NARA, RG 319, box 645–46," Konrad report," January 2, 1946, Zell am See. Konrad ended up writing his report in the American prison, and it is laden with lies and half-truths and aimed to prevent his extradition to Poland. For a different view of this report and of Konrad's actions, see Jahns, *Der Warschauer Ghettokönig.*

49. BStU, MfS, HA IX/11 ZUV 15, vol. 5, pp. 253–54.

50. YVA, TR10/794, "Stroop-Konrad trial protocol—second day," 21. For the Yiddish version of this protocol, see the entire issue of *Bleter far geshikhte* 3, nos. 1–2 (1953).

51. YVA, TR10/794, "Stroop-Konrad trial protocol—second day," 27.

52. Ibid., 30.

53. Ibid., 37.

54. Ibid., 33–34.

55. USHMM Archives, 1998.A 0255 reel 2, Stroop pretrial declaration, 1021–22. YVA, TR10/794, "Stroop-Konrad trial protocol—second day," 52–54. There are some differences between the Polish and German texts. For example, in the Polish version, Stroop rejects the possibility that a photo showed a child lying dead on the rubble; in the German version, he says, "One can assume that this is a child." I chose to integrate the Polish version, as it matches Stroop's insistent denial of the accusations against him throughout the trial.

56. This translation is from an English version of the verdict; see Friedman, *The Trial Against Stroop,* 3. See also YVA, TR10/794, Stroop-Konrad Verdict, July 23, 1951.

57. Friedman, *The Trial Against Stroop,* 24.

58. Ibid., 16.

59. Ibid., 10–11.

60. Ibid., 5.

61. For the decision of the Supreme Court of Poland, see BStU, HA IX/11 ZUV 15, vol. 5, pp. 376–423. The original clemency letter is located in IPN, SWMW, 874, t. II; a large section of the request is also quoted in Müller, "Jürgen (Joseph) Stroop," 80–81.

62. IPN, SWMW, 874, t. II.

63. Moczarski, *Conversations,* 265–66. Konrad's death was confirmed in e-mail correspondence between the author and Stadtamt Liezen, July 26, 2007.

6 AN ANGUISHED END

1. BStU, MfS, 2862/70, vol. 1, p. 74.

2. Ibid., 8616/72, vol. 2, pp. 17–22, report of the accident in the mine.

3. Ibid., HA IX/11 ZUV 15, vol. 1, pp. 268–71, vol. 4, p. 277, report of Zentrales Haftkrankenhaus für Psychiatrie Waldheim [The Central Prison Hospital for Psychiatry, Waldheim], March 28, 1967.

4. Schwan and Heindrichs, Der SS-Mann, 214–15.

5. Ibid., 77, 199, 225–27; BStU, HA IX/11 ZUV 15, vol. 1, pp. 215–16.

6. Schwan and Heindrichs, Der SS-Mann, 225–27; BStU, MfS, HA IX/11 ZUV 15, vol. 1, pp. 215–16.

7. BStU, MfS, HA IX/11 ZUV 15, vol. 17, Report of VEB Kaliwerk Volkenroda, June 13, 1967, pp. 208–10, vol. 3, pp. 322–23.

8. Ibid., vol. 7, p. 81.

9. BStU, MfS, 2682/70, vol. 1, pp. 7, 14.

10. Ibid., pp. 83–87. For the verdict in the Klaustermeyer case, see Sagel-Grade et al., Justiz und NS-Verbrechen, vol. 20, case 586. Klaustermeyer died in prison a few years later.

11. This claim, of course, had no basis in fact. BStU, MfS, 2682/70, vol. 1, p. 86; Schwan and Heindrichs, Der SS-Mann, 260.

12. BStU, MfS, HA VII/RF/1776/12, pp. 5–7; HA IX/11 ZUV 15, vol. 1, p. 41. I base my account on the experiences of others arrested and investigated by the Stasi in general and in Hohenschönhausen Prison specifically. See Sandra Pingel-Schliemann, Zersetzen—Strategie einer Diktatur [Breaking Up: A Strategy of a Dictatorship] (Berlin: Robert-Havemann-Gesellschaft, 2002); Jürgen Fuchs, Vernehmungsprotokolle: November '76–September '77 [Investigation Protocol: November 1976–September 1977] (Reinbek bei Hamburg: Rowohlt, 1978); Hubertus Knabe, ed., Gefangen in Hohenschönhausen: Stasi-Häftlinge berichten [Captive in Hohenschönhausen: Stasi Prisoners Report] (Berlin: List, 2007).

13. BStU, MfS, HA IX/11 ZUV 15, vol. 1, pp. 62–63, vol. 27, pp. 26–27; HA VII/RF/1776/12, pp. 5–7.

14. BStU, MfS, HA VII/RF/1776/12, pp. 5–7.

15. Schwan and Heindrichs, Der SS-Mann, 249; BStU, MfS, HA IX/11 ZUV 15, vol. 4, Investigation of Hanna Blösche, September 9, 1968, pp. 4–6.

16. For more on the Hohenschönhausen Prison, where Blösche was taken, see Peter Erler and Hubertus Knabe, The Prohibited District—The Stasi Restricted Area Berlin-Hohenschönhausen (Berlin: Jaron, 2004). For obvious reasons, the Stasi left no account of their tactics in Blösche's incarceration or interrogation. I have based my account on the testimony of other Stasi prisoners, scholarly studies of Stasi methods, and personal visits to the Hohenschönhausen Prison (see note 12 above).

17. BStU, MfS, HA IX/11 ZUV 15, vol. 1, pp. 54–55, 58.

18. The officers who took part in the investigation of Blösche were from the Stasi department IX/10. The head of the investigation team was Horst Bauer. Harry Hesche fell ill during the investigation and died from cancer shortly thereafter (Schwan and Heindrichs, *Der SS-Mann*, 265).

19. BStU, MfS, HA IX/11 ZUV 15, vol. 1, pp. 122–24.

20. Ibid., pp. 125–26.

21. Ibid., p. 127.

22. Ibid.

23. For the sleeping conditions at Hohenschönhausen Prison, see Erler and Knabe, *The Prohibited District*, 46.

24. BStU, MfS, HA IX/11 ZUV 15, vol. 1, p. 128.

25. Ibid., p. 131.

26. For a slightly different version of this admission, see ibid.

27. Ibid., Akt 1, pp. 39–40, 44.

28. Schwan and Heindrichs, *Der SS-Mann*, 248–49.

29. BStU, MfS, HA IX/11 ZUV 15, vol. 27, pp. 26–27. This letter, and many others, is cited in Schwan and Heindrichs, *Der SS-Mann*, 330ff.

30. BStU, MfS, HA IX/11 ZUV 15, vol. 27, p. 167. See also letter of Hanna to Friedrich, March 20, 1968, p. 160, and other letters on pp. 167–68.

31. BStU, MfS, HA IX/11 ZUV 15, vol. 27, p. 151.

32. Ibid., vol. 11, pp. 781–91.

33. Schwan and Heindrichs, *Der SS-Mann*, 265.

34. The collection of letters is located in BStU, MfS, HA IX/11 ZUV 15, vol. 11.

35. Ibid., p. 603.

36. Schwan and Heindrichs, *Der SS-Mann*, 336.

37. BStU, MfS, HA IX/11 ZUV 15, vol. 7, p. 4.

38. Schwan and Heindrichs, *Der SS-Mann*, 303.

39. BStU, MfS, HA IX/11 ZUV 15, vol. 27, p. 300. Hanna's not attending the trial, as well as her expressions of discomfort with Blösche's actions, may have resulted from pressures placed on her by the Stasi, or from fear of the Stasi, more than from her own choice.

40. Author interview with Jacob Farber, June 28, 2007.

41. *Haim Farber*, 22–23.

42. BStU, MfS, HA XX, 3316, pp. 4ff; HA IX/11 ZUV 15, vol. 7, pp. 237–41.

43. Andreas Mix, "Das Ghetto vor Gericht. Zwei Strafprozesse gegen Exzesstäter aus dem Warschauer Ghetto vor bundesdeutschen und DDR-Gerichten im Vergleich" [The Ghetto in Court: A Comparison Between Two Criminal Proceedings Against Extreme Perpetrators from the Warsaw Ghetto in West Germany and East Germany], in Stephan Alexander Glienke, ed., *Erfolgsgeschichte Bundesrepublik? Die Nachkriegsgesellschaft im langen Schatten des Nationalsozialismus* [The Success Story of the

Federal Republic? The Postwar Society in the Long Shadow of National Socialism] (Göttingen: Wallstein, 2008), 331. Compare the Stasi final report prepared by Unterleutnant Stenzel (BStU, 13897) and the indictment in BStU, MfS, HA IX/11 ZUV 15, vol. 23, pp. 1–147.

44. BStU, MfS, HA IX/11 ZUV 15, vol. 4, pp. 263–67.
45. Schwan and Heindrichs, *Der SS-Mann*, 289.
46. Ibid., 296–97.
47. BStU, MfS, HA IX/11 ZUV 15, vol. 7, p. 239.
48. Schwan and Heindrichs, *Der SS-Mann*, 287.
49. Ibid., 285.
50. BStU, MfS, HA IX/11 ZUV 15, vol. 38, pp. 74–76. The use of the case of Blösche as a propaganda tool is stated explicitly in several Stasi documents, for example, BStU, 2682/70 vol. 1, pp. 86–87; BStU, MfS, HA IX/11 ZUV 15, vol. 7, p. 133. See also Mix, "Das Ghetto vor Gericht," 332–33.
51. BStU, MfS, HA IX/11 ZUV 15, vol. 38, p. 187.
52. Schwan and Heindrichs, *Der SS-Mann*, 299–301.
53. The verdict appears in Demps, *DDR-Justiz*, 398–99.
54. BStU, MfS, HA IX/11 ZUV 15, vol. 11, May 13, 1969.
55. Ibid., vol. 7, p. 67.
56. Schwan and Heindrichs, *Der SS-Mann*, 342–44.
57. Ibid., 344–45.
58. *Haim Farber*, 10.
59. Ibid.
60. Ibid., back flip cover.
61. Farber, "Hayai im Rivkah'leh," in Trapkovits'-Farber, *Le-Maydanek lo higa'ti*, p. 69.
62. *Tsvi Nussbaum Video Recording*. See also Nussbaum, *'Et Ezkerah*, 300.
63. Nussbaum, *'Et Ezkerah*, 300.
64. *Tsvi Nussbaum Video Recording*.
65. Ibid. For other identifications of the boy, all of which I find unconvincing, see Raskin, *A Child*, 81–94.
66. *Jewish Week*, May 9, 1982.
67. Ibid.
68. *New York Times*, May 28, 1982.
69. Nussbaum, *'Et Ezkerah*, 300–301. See also *Tsvi Nussbaum Video Recording*.
70. For other reports on Tsvi Nussbaum as the little boy, see *New York Post*, February 20, 1990; *Jerusalem Post*, April 18, 1993; *Courier Mail* (Australia), September 19, 1995; *Stern*, September 2, 1999; *St. Petersburg Times* (Florida), April 17, 2001; *Palm Beach Post*, June 25, 2001; *Focus*, September 24, 2001; *Der Spiegel*, May 5, 2003; *Sunday Times* (London), August 15, 2004; *la Repubblica*, July 16, 2004; *Frankfurter Rundschau*, July 14, 2005; André Groenewoud, "Ich habe überlebt" [I Survived], *Cicero*, June 2005, pp. 22–23.

Holocaust deniers maliciously adopted the identification of Tsvi as the little boy, hinting that since Tsvi survived, that casts doubt on the entirety of the Holocaust as a historical event. Mark Weber, "The 'Warsaw Ghetto Boy,'" *Journal of Historical Review* 14, no. 2 (March–April 1994): 6–7.

71. *Jerusalem Post*, April 18, 1993.

EPILOGUE

1. Robert H. Jackson, *The Nürnberg Case as Presented by Robert H. Jackson, Chief of Counsel for the United States, Together with Other Documents* (New York: Alfred A. Knopf, 1947), 31.
2. *Trial of the Major War Criminals*, vol. II, p. 126. For Jackson's account of the murder of the Jews, see Robert H. Jackson, *The Nürnberg Case as Presented by Robert H. Jackson—Chief Counsel for the United States* (New York: Alfred A. Knopf, 1947), 52ff.
3. *Trial of the Major War Criminals*, vol. III, pp. 554–55, cited in Michael R. Marrus, *The Nuremberg War Crimes Trial, 1945–46: A Documentary History* (Boston: Bedford Books, 1997), 195.
4. *Trial of the Major War Criminals*, vol. III, December 14, 1945, pp. 553–58; G. M. Gilbert, *Nuremberg Diary* (New York: Farrar, Straus and Company, 1947), 69.
5. *Trial of the Major War Criminals*, vol. III, December 14, 1945, p. 558. A partial copy of the report was reproduced as document 1061-PS, *Trial of the Major War Criminals*, vol. XXVI, pp. 628–94. The photos presented at the trial did not include the photo of the little boy. *The Stroop Report* was referenced in other instances in the trial, on December 20, 1945; April 23, July 11, July 27, 1946; and in the judgment.
6. Viktor von der Lippe, *Nürnberger Tagebuchnotizen—November 1945 bis Oktober 1946* [Nuremberg Diary Notes—November 1945 to October 1946] (Frankfurt a.M.: Fritz Knapp, 1951), 65; Telford Taylor, *The Anatomy of the Nuremberg Trials: A Personal Memoir* (New York: Alfred A. Knopf, 1992), 202.
7. Aron Glanz-Leyeles, *A Yid oyfn yam: lider un poemen* [A Jew at Sea: Collected Poems] (New York: Cyco Bicher, 1947), 66–67. I thank Ken Moss for his translation of this poem.

ON PHOTOGRAPHS, HISTORY, AND NARRATIVE STYLE

1. This book is indebted to many previous historical studies, most particularly Christopher Browning's *Ordinary Men: Reserve Police Battalion 101 and the Final Solution in Poland* (New York: Harper Perennial, 1993). Browning's study drew on social-psychological literature to examine Ger-

244 Note to page 218

man reservists who murdered scores of Jews. The elderly reservists of the battalion, Browning concluded, took part in the mass execution of Jews not out of "putative duress," battlefield brutalization, or bloodlust, but rather out of social conformity shaped within the context of war, racist ideology, and propaganda. Browning ends his book with the poignant question: "If the men of Reserve Police Battalion 101 could become killers under such circumstances, what group of men cannot?" (189).

Whereas Browning offered a multifaceted answer, a few years later Daniel Goldhagen, who had studied the same unit, offered in *Hitler's Willing Executioners: Ordinary Germans and the Holocaust* (New York: Alfred A. Knopf, 1996) a different point of view. Goldhagen's work focuses on one central explanatory factor for the Holocaust, which he dubbed "eliminationist antisemitism." Unlike the more functionalist approach of Browning, Goldhagen stresses ideology, pointing to a long tradition of lethal anti-Semitism within German culture. This anti-Semitic ideology, Goldhagen argues, resulted in ordinary Germans' "willing" participation in the execution of Jews. Many scholars had serious reservations about Goldhagen's one-dimensional explanation (for one collection of responses to Goldhagen's book, see Robert R. Shandley, ed., *Unwilling Germans? The Goldhagen Debate* [Minneapolis: University of Minnesota Press, 1998]).

In his extensive work *Nazi Germany and the Jews*, Saul Friedländer pointed to "redemptive anti-Semitism" as being central to the "Final Solution." This lethal strand of anti-Semitism, which was at first limited to an elite group within German society (at first that of the "Bayreuth circle" and then by the Nazi Party's hard core), drew on an earlier belief in religious redemption to view the Jews as a menace to German society and their expulsion or possible elimination a way to redeem Germany. In Hitler's worldview ("*Weltanschauung*"), the Jews invented liberalism, communism, and other ideologies to facilitate taking control of nations and the Aryan race specifically, thus threatening the very existence of German society. Within the context of Nazi Germany and a world war, this worldview served Hitler, who was obsessed with the so-called Jewish menace, as a means to mobilize German society. "The anti-Jewish drive became ever more extreme along with the radicalization of the regime's goals and then with the extension of the war." It is within this context, writes Friedländer, that one can "locate the emergence of the 'Final Solution'" (*Nazi Germany and the Jews, 1939–1945: The Years of Extermination* [Harper Perennial, 2008], xix).

The German historian Götz Aly offers yet another explanation, this one centered on the financial benefits that German society and its military reaped from the plunder of Jews. Aly suggests that such "structural factors" motivated German soldiers to kill Jews. "Field officers," he writes, had an "interest in extracting the largest possible contributions from occupied countries toward the costs of occupation." The economic and social benefits that resulted from the murder of the Jews, he claims, were key structural motivations for the perpetrators (*Hitler's Beneficiaries: Plunder, Racial War and the Nazi Welfare State*, trans. Jefferson Chase [New York: Metropolitan Books, 2007], 280–81).

While I drew on these scholarly works, a study such as *The Boy*, which is focused on a specific group of individuals within a specific context, must necessarily differ. This book draws selectively from those previous studies and at times—based on the available evidence and interpretation—even stands in tension with them.

In addition, this book also brings together the viewpoints of Germans and Jews. In this, I have adopted a position long held by Israeli and Jewish historians, such as Yisrael Gutman, Yehudah Bauer, and (demonstrated most powerfully, albeit in a very different way) Saul Friedländer. In studying the Holocaust, one should focus not on the perspective of the perpetrators alone but also on that of the victims, and even bystanders. Victims should be seen neither as passive actors nor as reacting in one voice.

In examining the viewpoint of the victims, especially valuable were studies focused on the Warsaw ghetto, particularly Yisrael Gutman's *The Jews of Warsaw 1939–1943*, trans. Ina Friedman (Sussex: Harvester Press, 1982), as well as the important work of Barbara Engelking and Jacek Leociak, *The Warsaw Ghetto: A Guide to the Perished City* (New Haven: Yale University Press, 2009). These works provided crucial details to help explain the Jews' day-to-day reactions to German decrees and actions.

Finally, I owe a tremendous debt to the rich body of research on Holocaust photographs. Sybil Milton, "The Camera as Weapon: Documentary Photography and the Holocaust," *Simon Wiesenthal Center Annual* 1, (1984): 45–88, and Judith Levin and Daniel Uziel, "Ordinary Men, Extraordinary Photos," *Yad Vashem Studies* 29 (1998): 265–93, helped illuminate the anti-Semitic perspective embedded in many Holocaust-era photos, pictures mostly taken from the gaze of Nazi soldiers.

2. Susan Sontag, *On Photography* (New York: Farrar, Straus and Giroux, 1977), 20; Barbie Zelizer, *Remembering to Forget: Holocaust Memory Through the Camera's Eye* (Chicago: University of Chicago Press, 1998), 1–6; Caroline Brothers, *War and Photography: A Cultural History* (New York: Routledge, 1997), 18–19.

3. Cornelia Brink, "Secular Icons: Looking at Photographs from Nazi Concentration Camps," *History and Memory* 12 (2000): 144–45.

4. Zelizer, *Remembering to Forget*, 6, 202.

5. Sontag, *On Photography*, 23; see also Susan Sontag, *Regarding the Pain of Others* (New York: Farrar, Straus and Giroux, 2003), 89.

6. Sontag, *On Photography*, 19–20.

7. Simon Schama, "Visualizing History," *Culturefront* 7 (Winter 1998): 8–9.

8. Sontag, *On Photography*, 23.

9. R. G. Collingwood, *The Idea of History* (New York: Galaxy Books, 1956), 245. On this issue, see also the introduction to Niall Ferguson, *Virtual History: Alternatives and Counterfactuals* (New York: Basic Books, 1999).

10. Ferguson, *Virtual History*, 89.

Acknowledgments

A book like *The Boy* is never the project of an individual. While only I carry responsibility for the words inscribed on these pages, I benefited from the knowledge, wisdom, and generosity of several people. To all my deepest gratitude. These include Chaya Alhassid, Emanuel Altbauer, David Bankier, Lothar Bembenek, Ulrich Berzbach, Florian Biermann, Kimmy Caplan, Smadar Chaouat, Alon Confino, Chana Dar Starowicz, Miri Elfassi, Sue Fendrick, Avraham Frank, Ilana Friedman, Yaron Girsh, Jenny Gohr, Gaby Goldberg, John Gross, Tim Gross, Elissa Hecker, Detlev Hellfaier, Michael Hess, Elisabeth Hollender, Elisabeth Katznelson, Izzy Katznelson, Sylvia Klingberg, Irit Koren, Judy Marcus, Ralph Marcus, Grace McMillan, Martin Meyer-Hamme, Yehudah Mirsky, Andreas Mix, Kenneth Moss, David Myers, Dena Ordan, Eryk Piasecki, Fern Reiss, Matt Rozell, Elisabeth Schaub, Yossi Shavit, Naama Shilo, Shaul Stampfer, Chava Turniansky, Brigitte Wolf, Johann-Jakob Wulf, and Steve Zipperstein.

In libraries and archives around the world, eager staff members helped me locate books, documents, and photos, all indispensable to the fulfillment of this project. I am grateful to all these institutions for permitting me access: Yad Vashem Library and Archive; the Ghetto Fighters' House Archives; the archive and library of the United States Holocaust Memorial Museum in Washington, D.C. (and especially the head of the photo archive, Judith Cohen); the Library of Congress; the National Archives at College Park; the Institute of National Remembrance in Warsaw; the BStU archive in Berlin (Die Bundesbeauftragte für die Stasi-Unterlagen); the Detmold City Archive; the Lippische Landesbibliothek Detmold; the Landesarchiv Nordrhein-Westfalen in Detmold; the Nuremberg City Archive; the Hessische Landesbibliothek Wiesbaden; Aktives Museum Spiegelgasse, Wiesbaden; and the Government Press Office in Jerusalem. It is a special pleasure to thank the outstanding staff of the Judaica Reading Room at the National Library in Jerusalem, where I have been working for the past twenty years: Aliza Alon, Elona Avinezer, Zipporah Ben-Abu, Ruth Flint, and the other staff members who are always helpful, efficient, and cheerful.

On a visit to Washington, D.C., in the winter of 2005 I met Anita Andreasians, who became my trusted assistant for the next five years. In her diligence and professionalism she assisted me in locating documents in the USHMM archive, read the manuscript of this book, and took it upon herself to find material that I had already given up on. I am deeply thankful to her.

Tsvi Nussbaum opened the door to his home to me and spoke to me about his painful experiences during the war. Jacob Farber hosted me at his home and spoke with me over the phone about his late mother and brother. I am sure these moments of recalling a traumatic past were not easy for them, and I appreciate their efforts.

Robert Johnston has always been there when needed to lend a good word and a sound piece of advice. Sandy Johnston was one of my first assistants on this project, and at the age of seventeen surely the youngest assistant I have ever had. His abilities in the field of history are truly outstanding.

In a Tel Aviv coffee shop in December 2006, Omer Bartov helped me see what I had under my hand and prompted me to reconceptualize my entire project. That meeting was decisive in shaping this book. I thank him for this and for his continuous willingness to help out.

Gershom Gorenberg, Tom Gumpel, David Silberklang, and Heidmarie Uhl read the entire manuscript, gave me insightful comments, and corrected mistakes. I appreciate their friendship and collegiality.

My students and academic colleagues at the Hebrew University School of Education, as well as the administrative staff, have been supportive and enriched my outlook with their multidisciplinary perspectives. I am grateful for the opportunity to work in such a nourishing environment.

Lee Shulman and Sam Wineburg shaped my professional upbringing, leaving on me a long-lasting mark, one most strongly expressed in this book. I take this opportunity to thank them for these many years of mentoring. My friends Mark Brilliant and Simone Schweber helped me in my first steps of writing in English. It has been a long journey since they worked with me on the Stanford campus, but without their initial encouragement and teaching I would never have come to this point.

Yael Shapira was a confidante on this project, sharing my enthusiasm and encouraging me in moments of dejection.

Working with Thomas LeBien as my editor was a real honor. His initial rejection letter was so eloquent that upon reading it I knew I must try my best to work with him. Luckily I was successful. He was committed to the topic no less than I was, and his comments were always eye-opening and intelligent. My deepest gratitude to him. The staff members at FSG, including June Kim, Elizabeth Maples, Brian Gittis, and especially Dan Crissman, were always accessible, helpful, and efficient.

I have never before experienced a level of academic generosity such as that offered by Havi Dreifuss (Ben-Sasson), who shared with me her sources and her incredible knowledge. Her reading of drafts helped me see things in a more complex and nuanced manner. While from the outset we had our disagreements about this book, especially when it came to the narrative style, I believe we continue to share a mutual respect and friendship.

Andreas Ruppert, the chief archivist of Detmold, went out of his way to dig up documents about Stroop, and on my visit to Detmold he took me on a memorable tour through the Jewish sites of the town.

My mother-in-law, Menucha Nuriel, shared the enthusiasm and excitement about this project. My father served as my first critic on each and every draft, always full of wisdom and encouragement. Vered shared my moments of pleasure and failure. The idea of writing this book would never have come to my mind without her showing me, from our first years of marriage, what creative thinking is all about. And always our three children, Ma'ayan, Roey, and Naveh, remain our joint source of pride.

Finally, my heart fills with pain at the thought that my mother did not live to see this book. Her love of history is embedded in each and every word. I believe she would have been proud to see this book. I dedicate it to her memory.

Index

Illustration Credits